An Anthropologist Among the Marxists and Other Essays

An Anthropologist Among the Marxists and Other Essays

RAMACHANDRA GUHA

permanent black

Published by

PERMANENT BLACK
D-28 Oxford Apartments, 11, I.P. Extension,
Delhi 110092

Distributed by

ORIENT LONGMAN LTD
Bangalore Bhubaneshwar Calcutta Chennai
Ernakulam Guwahati Hyderabad Lucknow
Mumbai New Delhi Patna

ISBN 978 81 7824 001 5

First published 2001

Typeset in Adobe Garamond
by Guru Typographics, Palam, New Delhi 110045
Printed and bound by Manipal Technologies Limited, Manipal

MIX
Paper | Supporting responsible forestry
FSC™ C043100

for Akka

'He was always quick to love and quick to fight . . .'

—Syed Mushtaq Ali, speaking of Lala Amarnath

Contents

PATRIOTS

PLAYERS

Preface and Acknowledgements

PREVIOUSLY published essays have been revised, expanded and updated for this book. Earlier versions appeared in *Civil Lines, Economic and Political Weekly, Himal, India Today, Indian Express, Indian Review of Books, London Magazine, Outlook,* and *The Pioneer.* Over half of these essays, however, were first printed in one or the other of those estimable newspapers, *The Hindu* and *The Telegraph.* I am deeply grateful to Nirmala Lakshman of *The Hindu* and Rudrangshu Mukherjee of *The Telegraph* for giving me licence to roam and open space besides.

My understanding of the people and ideas discussed in these pages owes much to conversations over the years with Basudev 'Robi' Chatterji, Keshav Desiraju, Bernard D'Mello, Gopal Gandhi, Anjan Ghosh, Sujata Guha, Mukul Kesavan, Sunil Khilnani and Sujit Mukherjee. Vasudha Dhagamwar and Shekhar Pathak, sterling Indians and true public intellectuals, have provided both friendship and inspiration. I wish also to thank my friends '5', '6' and '7'—Chandan Mitra, Swapan Dasgupta and Paranjoy Guha Thakurta—who first encouraged me to write for other-than-an-academic audience.

This book is dedicated to my brilliant and courageous cousin Dharma Kumar. I hope its tributes to men and women older than myself are in keeping with the generosity she has always shown towards the young.

Introduction

INSIDE every thinking Indian there is a Gandhian and a Marxist struggling for supremacy. The battle was joined in 1917, the year of the Bolshevik Revolution, also the year of the first satyagraha on Indian soil. In their aftermath, some young Indians quickly made up their minds. In Bombay, S.A. Dange wrote a tract exalting Lenin at the expense of Gandhi; across the subcontinent, in Calcutta, Nirmal Kumar Bose declared a preference for the philosopher of non-violence. Dange went on to become the most notable and controversial of Communist agitators; Bose achieved distinction as an anthropologist and authority on Gandhian thought.

Within other Indians, however, the struggle continued. Jayaprakash Narayan came to Gandhi early, but then went to America to study, his visit coinciding with the Great Depression. Picking oranges in California and meeting trade unionists in Wisconsin made him a militant socialist. On returning home he would still touch the Mahatma's feet, yet out of earshot was prone to refer to him dismissively as 'the old man'. His faith in non-violence was uncertain and he considered Gandhi's Congress to be beholden to the propertied class. He was not so far gone, however, as to join the Communist Party of India. The inward fight of competing ideologies resulted, for JP and his Gandhian-Marxist comrades, in the formation in 1936 of a formal socialist faction within the Congress. Twelve years later Narayan left the parent party altogether to help found the Socialist Party of India. This too proved a temporary home. In 1952 he abruptly turned his back on politics to become a *sevak* of the most prominent living Gandhian, Vinoba Bhave. *Ahimsa* and *brahmacharya* were to be joined to constructive work within his Sarvodaya movement. After this, for two decades and more the fiery former socialist preached peace and reconciliation, using Gandhi's methods to bring together the landed and the landless, the dacoits and the police, the Naga rebels and the Indian state.

Then in 1973 his wife Prabhavati, who was always a more steadfast Gandhian, died, and at the same time Indira Gandhi took her first certain steps to a personal dictatorship. Narayan left Sarvodaya as dramatically as he had joined it. The erstwhile underground hero of the 'Quit India' movement had become the visible public face of the 'Indira, Quit' movement. The language he now used was confrontational; the social change he worked for was no longer incremental. He spoke of 'Total Revolution', a term that resonated with Leon Trotsky's 'Permanent Revolution' and the 'Cultural Revolution' of Mao Zedong.

Numerous other Indians have followed JP in this oscillation between Gandhi and Marx. Of course, for them the shifts were (or are) not as dramatic as his; nor will their words or actions have a comparable impact on the course of history. A critic once rudely remarked of JP that his own shifts could be traced to his native village, Sitabidiara. This lies in the flood plain of that turbulent river, the Kosi, and depending on the river's moods the village might be in Uttar Pradesh one year, in Bihar the next. Narayan's twists and turns were, it seems, geographically coded at birth. A nice story, but how does that explain the rest of us?

In truth, there are solid sociological reasons for the twin appeal of what at first sight seem to be incompatible ideologies. The Marxist theory of modes of production provides a neat, logical explanation of why some Indians are rich and so many others poor, while the Marxist practice of class struggle suggests how one might move towards a less deeply divided society. The appeal of Marxism was enhanced by the fact that Indian scholars and activists have been overwhelmingly from the middle class. The guilt they felt about their own relative privilege could be best assuaged by adherence to a philosophy which assured them they were on the right side, and that soon they would not be so privileged anyway.

And so, between 1917 and 1989, some of the best and brightest among India's young joined the Communists. Not all, however, were prepared to make this decisive move. These others were more convinced than the party faithful of the stories of the Gulag, of the mass killing of class enemies in Russia and China, and of the imprisonment and torture of political dissidents. They saw too that classical Marxism had no answer to questions such as caste discrimination and religious disharmony. These questions had been raised—and at least partly answered—by a home-grown philosopher, Gandhi. The Mahatma's appeal was enhanced by the transparency of his personal life and his decency towards political opponents. Moreover, he lived more actively and more intensively with the poor of India than admirers of the Communist Manifesto.

Thinking Indians were attracted to Gandhi, but not to all sides of him. They rejected his idiosyncratic views on sex and diet. They respected his religious tolerance but wondered why he made such a show of his own personal Hindu faith. And they sensed that his economics was largely irrelevant to the contemporary world. These limitations made them turn away from Gandhi—back, perhaps, to Marx.

Even among Indians who made their choice public, the competing belief system retained more than a shadow of influence. During the Cold War, anti-Communist Gandhians such as J.C. Kumarappa instinctively preferred the Russians and the Chinese to the Americans. And where Western Marxists are always hedonistic and sometimes duplicitous, Indian Marxists have tended to follow the Mahatma in the austerity of their personal lives and the integrity of their financial dealings. This was true of that old Stalinist E.M.S. Namboodiripad, and it was true of that young Maoist C.V. Subbarao—two of the most heroic of the many heroes honoured in the pages of this book. Fortunately, the question that most categorically separates Gandhi from Marx, the question of violence, did not much trouble the characters in this book. None, not even the CPM General Secretary or the Naxalite sympathiser, ever had a gun placed in their hands—not that they would have known what to do with it.

II

A good part of this book is taken up with Gandhians and pseudo-Gandhians, Marxists and anti-Marxists. I have written here of individuals I have known or studied, admired or disliked. Through their lives and works one might, of course, come to know something about their ideologies. But this remains principally a personal work of appreciation and depreciation, not an impersonal work of 'scholarship'.

The writing of sketches and portraits, long or short, does not come easily to Indians. Does this, I wonder, have something to do with our dominant religion? The historian David Cannadine has written that biography is 'the only certain form of life after death'. Perhaps in Britain; but hardly so in a land where minutes after the heart stops beating the soul transmigrates to another life form. Why pay tribute to a dead man if he has already been reborn?

In the cosmic order of things the individual is insignificant anyway, a belief the Hindu shares with the professional historian and social scientist. For, to write a book or even an extended essay on a single person is to succumb to what E.H. Carr once dismissed as 'the Good Queen Bess or Bad King Jack theory of history', that is, the belief that an individual can have a determining impact on society. The academy teaches that 'objective forces', such as social classes and technologies of production, influence history far more than merely 'subjective' ones such as ideas and personalities.

That, at any rate, is what the academy taught me. I trained as a sociologist and social historian, and was for many years more comfortable writing about and analysing aggregates such as 'peasants' and the 'state'. Two things helped unburden me—an incurable orientation towards hero-worship, and an invitation by my then editor (and present publisher) to write a personal history of Indian cricket. Now, cricket is the most intensely individualistic of all team sports, its matches remembered in terms of the technique and statistics of this or that player. To recall the rise of Karnataka cricket was to remember the late-cut of G.R. Viswanath and the looping off-break of Erapalli Prasanna; to narrate the story of cricket in Delhi was to speak of how a Sardar from Amritsar, Bishan Bedi, took the Amarnath brothers and Madan Lal and Chetan Chauhan and made of them all the finest team in the land.

Cricket writing liberated me. The sociologist who traced the evolution through time of abstract aggregates had now to speak directly of persons and personal achievement. In time, I learnt how to write of individuals beyond the boundary too, to write of politicians and saints and scholars. People whose lives crossed mine began to pass away, and I found myself wanting to memorialise them. So much so that a contemporary of mine once remarked: 'you have to die before Guha will write about you'.

As it happens, I have written of cricketers who are still active, and of living non-cricketers too. Conversations with two civil-servant friends on the devaluation of the Bharat Ratna led me to consider how India had lost the capacity to autonomously appreciate and reward high achievement, especially high artistic achievement. Politics had overwhelmed our national discourse: a particularly narrow version of politics, which identifies the interests of the nation with the interests of the state. It seemed a good time to praise unacknowledged patriots and to polemicise against self-advertised super-patriots. It was time to resurrect an idea of India that was culturally sophisticated and socially inclusive, that loved songs rather than bombs; an idea of India as defined and elaborated by that once well-known Marxist-Gandhian, Jawaharlal Nehru.

In the end, though, I have to admit that the dead in this book outnumber the living. That is not the only reason why it may carry a whiff of the archaic and the antiquarian. For the ideas and individuals spoken of here have lost much of their sheen. Mahatma Gandhi has been supplanted by Guru Golwalkar, Karl Marx by Bill Gates. The Indians who tailor their lives to the thoughts of Golwalkar and Gates will, I fear, have to be remembered by other hands.

Comrades and Companions

An Anthropologist Among the Marxists

SOME years ago the columnist Bernard Levin wrote a piece in the London *Times* on the Communist Party of Great Britain's abject dependence, during the Second World War, on its Soviet counterpart. A good polemicist, Levin did not shirk from kicking a man when he was down. With the CPGB distintegrating, he now drew attention to its long history of mendacity, its consistent elevation of the interests of Soviet communism over the claims of the British nation. Levin wondered how such a party could have once commanded the allegiance of so many thinking people; its duplicity apart, the CPGB's chief ideologue in its heyday, Maurice Cornforth, was himself 'about as much of an intellectual as a pig in a sty'.

I do not know what response this attack evoked among readers of *The Times*, but when it was reproduced in *The Statesman* of Calcutta a torrent of letters descended upon the newspaper's offices in Chittaranjan Avenue. B.K. Ghosh-Dastidar wrote from Howrah that Mr Levin's dismissal of the British Marxist thinker had caused him acute personal pain: for he had learnt his philosophy from Cornforth's *Dialectical Materialism*, his politics from the man's *Theory and Practice of Revolution*. From another suburb of Calcutta, 24-Parganas (South), S.M. Karmakar characterised Mr Levin's article as, in effect, an insult to generations of Indians who, like himself, had been so deeply influenced by the life and work of their British comrades.

In its early years the Communist Party of India had the same relation to the CPGB as the latter had to the party of Lenin and Stalin. This perfectly mirrored the colonial relationship between India and Great Britain, and perhaps the spirited Bengali response to Bernard Levin's polemic might be seen as being of a piece with this larger history of servitude: many among the first generation of Communist leaders were Bengalis trained at Cambridge or Lincoln's Inn. But Indian Communists have long since asserted their independence of the mother country, even as the CPGB and its Soviet counterpart have come to lead a precarious existence on the edge of history's dustbin. So the letters of Mr Ghosh-Dastidar and Mr Karmakar must be seen in the context of the fact that the Indian state of West Bengal has the longest serving *elected* communist government in the world. In so far as thought and debate can flourish only in conditions of political freedom, it is Calcutta—rather than Peking, Hanoi or Havana—which is the intellectual centre of world Marxism.

II

I arrived in Calcutta in June 1980, three years after the Communist Party of India-Marxist had come to power in the state. The CPI(M) had broken away from the parent CPI in 1964 and was by now much the more powerful of the two. Of an impressionable age—twenty-two—I had come to begin a doctorate in sociology. That degree I came eventually to earn, but only after what was in effect five-and-a-half years of continuous fieldwork among Marxists.

In his reflections on fieldwork, the doyen of Indian anthropology, M.N. Srinivas, has talked of successful ethnography as having to pass through three stages. An anthropologist is 'once-born' when he initially goes to the field, thrust from familiar surroundings into a world about which he has very little clue. He is 'twice-born' when, on living for some time among his tribe, he is able to see things from their viewpoint. To those anthropologists fortunate enough to experience it, this second birth is akin to a Buddhist surge of consciousness for which years of study or mere linguistic facility do not prepare you. All of a sudden, you are able to see *everything* from the native's point of view—be it festivals, fertility rites, or the fear of death.

All ethnographers go through the first stage, a good many through the second. But an anthropologist is truly 'thrice-born' only when at last he moves away from the field, back to the very different world of the university. Here he reflects on his material, and is alerted to competing subjectivities by colleagues returning from their field-sites. The allegiance to one's tribe can never be entirely abandoned, but now one can at least hope to achieve partial objectivity: the mark of a scholar, as distinct from a partisan.

Bengali Marxism is an intensely lived yet deeply insular culture which has generated its own icons, texts, language, lifestyle and sectarian heresies. It is, in all these respects, akin to a tribe, a tribe inhabiting a mileu quite different from the worlds I was familiar with—principally, the cities of Delhi and Bangalore. I came, however, with the inestimable advantage of a surname well known to the tribe. My last name Guha, a surname most recognisably Bengali, is more usually rendered among the Tamils as 'Guhan'. But I had reason to thank the shorter form (a family peculiarity) because my new informants were utterly convinced, despite my disclaimer, that I could trace my ancestry to a long forgotten Bengali pilgrim in southern India.

My second birth as an anthropologist came roughly a year after I had moved from Calcutta, when I had mastered the language and technical apparatus of Marxism and, more crucially, was able to see the world exclusively through my tribal worldview. Like a good ethnographer, I participated actively in the binding rituals of the community, attending secret conclaves and writing in journals where I relentlessly hunted tribes hostile to my own. Moving out of Bengal upon the completion of my extended spell of fieldwork, I believe I have since attained thrice-born-ness, being now a safe distance from my tribe and exposed to the competing belief systems of the liberal, the Gandhian, and the right reactionary.

Living closely with another people, the ethnographer's characteristic, retrospective response is one of great affection, but tinged with critical distaste: a peculiar mixture that doubtless finds its echoes in these pages. But I also write with nostalgia for, like all tribes ever studied by anthropologists, Marxist intellectuals are on the brink of extinction. I count myself singularly fortunate in that, within the Calcutta of the early nineteen-eighties, I was able to study a culture which, in the decades to come, will be found entombed only in ethnological museums and university libraries.

III

My first field-site in Calcutta was the Indian Institute of Management, a spacious, well-laid out campus at the edge of the city, and at first sight a most unlikely place to find revolution in the making. The Institute's main task was to train young managers for such instruments of Western imperialism as the Imperial Chemical Industries and the First National City Bank. From its inception in 1961, however, the faculty had had a fair sprinkling of Marxist professors.

The two most distinguished Marxists at the IIM, while I studied there, were located in the Department of Economics. They had evidently not read the essay by Hans Gerth and C. Wright Mills on 'A Marx for the Managers', for in the classroom they taught the theory of the firm strictly by the principles of capitalist economics. But in coffee-room conversation, and in their written work, they talked frequently of 'smashing the apparatus of the Indian state'.

The two men—whom we might call Professors Sengupta and Basu respectively—had played a leading role in a famous controversy conducted in the pages of the *Economic and Political Weekly* (*EPW*) of Bombay which was then, as it is now, the pre-eminent independent Marxist journal of opinion in the country. Pursued over twenty-five years, this debate was concerned with the correct identification of the dominant mode of production in the Indian social formation. On this hinged the future of the Indian revolution itself; for, once the mode of production had been accurately characterised by the professors, the party of revolution would know precisely which classes to mobilise.

In the *EPW*, Professor Sengupta sided with those who argued that like pre-revolutionary China, contemporary India was essentially 'semi-feudal' in nature. This meant that only rich landlords were class enemies, and that poor and middle peasants, and even the odd kulak, could be recruited as tactical allies of the agricultural proletariat, theoretically the most reliable social group. Professor Basu, on the contrary, held that Indian agriculture was already well down the capitalist road, which implied that communist mobilisation must focus exclusively on landless labourers, since small to middling peasants, known to be notoriously indecisive, might easily be swayed to the other side. Both scholars based their conclusions on statistics generated by the agricultural surveys of the Government of India (data curiously held to be untainted by either landlord or capitalist bias): each accused the other of completely misunderstanding Lenin and Mao, the two holy authorities on the 'agrarian question'.

In my own department, we followed their polemics with bated breath. In the hierarchy of the human sciences, economics is to sociology as, in the Marxist lexicon, base is to superstructure. My teachers and I thus deferred in all important matters to these two professors of economics. Of course, we did not pretend to understand the debate, or dare to take sides. But in our rather less significant and politically inconsequential field of Marxist sociology, we had frequently to consult the two men. Thus we went to Professor Sengupta, who knew Russian, while studying Lenin's *The Development of Capitalism in Russia*; and to Professor Basu, who had been trained in Germany, while grappling with the many meanings of *Aufhebung*—a key concept in Marx's vocabulary which he had borrowed from Hegel.

As an apprentice sociologist, then, I learnt Marxism from mentors who in turn sat at the feet of Professors Basu and Sengupta. Outside the classroom my initiation was greatly aided by the magnificent collection of Marxist literature in the IIM library. This was perhaps one of the best (and in per capita terms least used) repositories outside the Anglo-American world—the complete works of Marx, Engels, Lenin, and Mao of course; seemingly endless shelves of glosses on them; and uninterrupted runs of such authoritative journals as the *New Left Review* and the *Review of Radical Political Economics.* Late into the evening I buried my eyes in these works, while students in adjoining cubicles looked with equal eagerness into *Fortune* and the Directory of the Bombay Stock Exchange.

My closest friend at the time was studying for a doctorate in economics under Professor Basu. Almost totally isolated in the student's hostel, we looked forward eagerly to nine o'clock, when the Institute bus arrived bearing members of the faculty, who mostly lived in the city. The two of us went into town rarely, and usually to College Street when we did. Here we spent our book allowance, in more or less equal parts, on stalls owing allegiance to the three leading Marxist groupings: the CPI, the CPI(M), and the Maoists. With bags laden, our excursions inevitably ended in the College Street Coffee House, a second home to all Calcutta radicals and an epicentre of the legendary Naxalite movement of the late nineteen-sixties.

IV

In 1984 I moved from the IIM to a position in the Centre for Studies in Social Sciences, situated at Lake Terrace in south Calcutta. This was part of a chain of research institutes set up in the early seventies by a Marxist professor of history, then serving as education minister in the union government, during the height of Prime Minister Indira Gandhi's 'left phase'.

The Calcutta Centre was housed in the residence of the great historian Sir Jadunath Sarkar, having been gifted to it by his widow. As his knighthood indicates, Sarkar was by no means a political radical. He was, however, a scholar of formidable powers, the author of standard histories of the Mughal period and of biographies of its emperors. An austere man who worked very long hours, he had in his personal possession scores of priceless Persian documents. Historians who came from outside to consult these manuscripts have written with feeling of Sir Jadunath's punctiliousness, his disdain for polite conversation and the awesome standards he set his disciples.

Jadunath Bhawan is a three-storey building off Rashbehari Avenue in what might be called Calcutta's Lake District: a dense, largely residential quarter, surrounded by vibrant markets, lying just north of two water bodies (the 'lakes') of perhaps five acres each—a tiny patch of nature in what is otherwise a completely built-up area. While the Bhawan's exterior is sturdy, even imposing, its rooms are small and dark, with paint peeling off the walls and a consistently damp smell all around. The windows let in a little light, but if one looked out of them, a depressing vista of grey and decrepit buildings met the eye. Through the openings also came, especially in winter, wafts of smoke from thousands of coal-fires lit in the neighbourhood. My wife, who came from leafy Bangalore to join me towards the end of my field-work, wondered how intellectual work could ever be carried out in such surroundings; yet the Centre numbered in its ranks half a dozen of the finest historians of modern India.

The scholars whom I joined in Jadunath Bhawan were, to a man, far to the left of the historian who once lived there, though they had inherited his austerity and love of scholarship. Politically speaking, they divided themselves neatly into three groups. A small core owed allegiance to the CPI(M), the ruling party in the state and source of half the Centre's funds. The rest bunched off into the CPI—then tied firmly to the apron strings of the Communist Party of the Soviet Union—and into the broad umbrella of the Naxalite movement, the Indian variant of Chinese Communism. The last were the only truly revolutionary group in national politics, upholding the banner of armed struggle but split nonetheless into a dozen or so competing factions.

Where fieldwork in the IIM had been interrupted and somewhat episodic, at the Centre it was concentrated and highly focused. Professors Basu and Sengupta had to live with Alfred Marshall in the classroom and Karl Marx outside, but my new colleagues were concerned exclusively with studying and arguing about Indian society from a left-wing point of view. Interpretations of Indian history were, of course, strongly flavoured by an individual's sectarian allegiances. When discussing current politics, the differences between the three groups were more readily apparent. The CPI, CPI(M) and the Naxalites still have extremely divergent analyses of the strategy for the present phase of the Indian Revolution, and—what is always of equally great significance for Marxists—the proper identification of the true Socialist Fatherland (Russia, China, Vietnam, Albania, or the Future).

Most of our research, however, pertained to the first half of the twentieth century. Here the discriminations were more subtle. At one level, the united CPI (which split only in 1962) was reckoned the parent institution of the three parties: all granted retrospective validity to its acts, refusing to condemn, for example, its support to the colonial government during the Quit India movement of 1942. But scholars still with the CPI tended to be least critical of the Indian National Congress, which was in their view the vanguard party of the Indian freedom struggle. This reluctance to criticise was partly in acknowledgement of the Congress' command over large sections of the masses, and in part, indubitably, owing to pressure from the Soviet Union, the superpower which had since 1971 been in a 'special relationship' with Congress-ruled India. The CPI(M) intellectuals, on the other hand, believed that the Congress was, above all, the instrument of the Indian capitalist class: having brought about the bourgeois revolution, it must now make way for the Next Stage of History, namely Socialism. The Naxalites were the group most hostile to the Congress: for them 1947 was a sham independence, and India was still a semi-feudal semi-colony ruled by Western imperialism in alliance with an indigenous comprador class.

On these characterisations depended, crucially, one's assessments of the Father and, I suppose, the Uncle of the Indian nation: M.K. Gandhi and Jawaharlal Nehru. Like most non-Bengali middle-class Indian homes in the shadow of the independence movement, my home had prominent photographs, at my parents' insistence, of those two men. Till I came to Calcutta I was utterly convinced of the saintliness of the one and the idealism of the other; beliefs that were to take a battering while doing fieldwork among Marxists.

In the CPI pantheon Nehru and Gandhi were greatly admired

figures; perhaps just a level below the perch occupied by Marx, Engels and Lenin. The CPI(M) was more critical. It faulted Gandhi for always acting in the class interests of the bourgeoisie, arguing that non-violence was promoted only to wean the masses from the revolutionary path. It was critical of him for professing the 'most reactionary and obscurantist of ideologies': against science, against reason, for religion. Nehru was allowed praise for his faith in Soviet planning but condemned for his weak-kneed approach and failure to use the power of the state to expropriate people of property.

The Naxalites loathed both men. A Maoist at the Centre was often found muttering imprecations at a veteran leader of the CPI who had forgotten himself so far as to write laudatory studies of *both* Congress leaders ('And he calls himself a Communist!'). Nehru I could not hope to defend, but for years I pleaded with this colleague to allow at least Gandhi the status of a genuine patriot and democrat, a status that Mao had once so graciously accorded Sun Yat-Sen.

To be a non-Marxist in this intellectual world was an act of courage; to be a Gandhian an act of heroism. One such hero in the Centre was the polymath historian Hiteshranjan Sanyal. Sanyal was a tall, shy man who, by the time of his tragic early death in 1988, had already done pioneering work in three very different fields: folk art and architecture, medieval religious dissent (*bhakti*), and twentieth-century peasant nationalism.

A formative influence, at once intellectual and personal, on Sanyal had been the anthropologist Nirmal Kumar Bose (1901–72). Bose had served as Mahatma Gandhi's secretary and interpreter while he travelled in rural Bengal in 1946–7, dousing the flames of communal passion. He was also the author of important studies of Gandhi's philosophy. While Bose wore his Gandhianism on his sleeve, Sanyal, unlike his teacher, was not a controversialist. But reading between the lines, one could see the Gandhian historian at work. He had in - fact spent years doing fieldwork in the villages of Medinipur District, studying the influence of Gandhi and his followers on peasant mobilisation during the three great nationalist upsurges. More indirectly, one could interpret Sanyal's work on *bhakti* as having its origins in an eminently Gandhian desire to see reform emerging from within Indian tradition. His masterful studies of pottery seemed to exemplify a fusion of the folk and the classical, and his work as a whole was a gentle indictment of those who insisted on a complete cleavage of the worlds of the elite and subaltern.

In his small, dark room adjoining mine, Hitesh Sanyal and I talked often of our shared idol, I having retained a sneaking admiration for the Mahatma. When Gandhi was mocked at seminars in the Centre, I would protest weakly; and Sanyal, puffing away thoughtfully at his pipe, would say not a word. This might just have been his reticence; or, more likely, as a Bengali intellectual he knew that open dissent was simply impermissible.

In the strict anthropological sense, Gandhianism could only be Sanyal's 'hidden transcript'. This became clear to me when I accompanied him on a visit to the well-known artist Rathin Mitra. In Mitra's flat overlooking Dhakuria Bridge we marvelled—against the roar of lorries and buses—at our host's portraits of the buildings Gandhi had lived in or otherwise made famous by his presence: from the Viceregal Lodge in New Delhi to the mud hut in Sevagram. As I remember that evening, I get the sense that the three of us, as we celebrated Gandhi, did so rather furtively—like truant schoolboys away without official leave.

V

Anthropologists studying village India have written of having had to take sides, willy-nilly, with one or other caste or faction. One might have taken residence in a Brahmin household, or early befriended the chief rival to the village headman; these chance alliances then having a determining influence on the course of research.

My own community, as I have noted, was sub-divided into three clans, each claiming common ancestors but now worshipping rival totems. Over the course of my fieldwork, I was to increasingly throw in my lot with the Naxalites. This was largely a matter of choice, for I was deeply attracted by their agrarian bias and their relatively greater openness to the ecological questions that preoccupied me in my own research.

Identification with the Naxalites led me to my third field site in Calcutta, the circle around the radical weekly, *Frontier.* The journal was run from one long room in the heart of the city, some six miles north of Jadunath Bhawan. The first time I visited the *Frontier* office, I was irresistibly reminded of a description in Leon Trotsky's autobiography of the journal *Iskra,* run in exile by a handful of Russian revolutionaries. *Frontier* was housed in the back of a building set apart from a small lane, itself hidden by a huge cinema house from the bustling main street. I felt palpably a part of an underground operation. This feeling was made more intense when, on entering the office, I was introduced to a lean, intense man with sunken eyes and a goatee. He could very well have been the young Lenin in Zurich.

The man in the goatee now runs *Frontier* with a devotion and meagre financial reward almost unequalled in the world of Indian journalism. At that time, however, he was assistant to the editor, Samar Sen, one of the more remarkable figures in the history of Bengal Marxism.

Samar Sen was born into a typically middle-class, *bhadralok* (literally 'genteel folk') family, a background he wryly caricatured in his memoirs *Babu Brittanta* (A Babu's Tale). Growing up between the wars, like many of his peers he became a fellow traveller of the CPI, the party then making strong progress among students of the University of Calcutta. Samar's radicalism was expressed most directly in his poetry. As a young college student, barely out of his teens, he wrote five slim volumes that are collectively held to constitute a paradigm shift in the trajectory of Bengali poetry. I have read the work only in translation, but in the opinion of knowledgable critics it was Samar Sen who first introduced wit into Bengali verse, while bringing at the same time an economy of expression, akin to prose, into a tradition of effusive lyricism.

Astonishingly, when he had turned twenty-five Samar Sen decided he would not write any more poetry. He never did. Sacrifice is deeply respected in both the Communist and Indian traditions, and the poet's act of renunciation assured him a unique status in the folklore of Indian Marxism. Thus a liberal economist who has never heard of Samar Sen recently described a Bengali intellectual to me as one who 'At fifteen has written his first poem. At seventeen has burnt his first tram. At nineteen has joined the Party. At twenty-one has left the Party. At twenty-three has written his last poem. At twenty-five has joined the World Bank—and at thirty has left it to rejoin the Party.'

The poetry apart, this is not a *curriculum vitae* that matches Samar Sen's. Always an ironic, detached man who personally stood apart from politics, he never at any stage openly identified with the Party. On renouncing poetry he became a journalist. For nearly twenty years he worked in the establishment press, for about half that time as a correspondent in Moscow.

When I first met Samar Sen, he had only a few years to live, and *Frontier*, started with the savings of the editor and his friends, had been going for a decade and a half. From the beginning, the weekly had appeared in quarto size on yellowing newsprint. Its austerity was a reminder of its modest origins and of the cause it came to hold.

Frontier was formed in the wake of the uprising at Naxalbari in north Bengal, when movements of landless peasants and tribals were erupting all over southern and eastern India. For a while it seemed that the country would go the way of China. The ruling classes were scared and a wave of business houses moved out of Calcutta.

In West Bengal the Naxalite movement was crushed through state repression, aided by fratricidal warfare among its cadres. At the helm of the anti-Naxalite operation was an Inspector General of Police, who called himself a Marxist, opposing the Maoists for their left-wing adventurism—clearly an infantile disorder. Withal, he was a hero among the historic enemies of the working class. The poet Dom Moraes has written of accompanying this policemen for lunch at the

Calcutta Club: when they entered the dining room, suited businessmen stood up and applauded vigorously.

Anyway, at the time of which I write the Naxalites were in complete disarray. In parts of Bihar and Andhra Pradesh they continued to work courageously among the most deprived sections of Indian society—tribals and low castes. Yet the Indian Revolution seemed as far away as ever, and a once-united movement had fragmented into many parts. These sects were largely agreed on the character of the Indian state—semi-feudal, comprador, *pace* Professor Sengupta of the IIM—but quarelled bitterly on the correct identification of the Soviet Union: was it social-imperialist, or merely state capitalist? They were equally divided on events in contemporary China. Some were pro Lin Piao, anti Gang-of-Four, pro Cultural Revolution; some anti Lin Piao, pro Gang-of-Four, anti Cultural Revolution. Other variations were permissible, but all were, of course, pro Mao himself.

As a respected forum above these divides, *Frontier* opened its pages to exchanges between different Maoist sects. The debates were fierce and highly personalised, though conducted in the cause of bringing about 'Party Unity'—which, curiously, was the name of the most obstinate sect of all. More valuably, the weekly carried reports of local agrarian struggles and of human rights violations by the state, which no bourgeois paper was likely to print. The editor's hand was most apparent, perhaps, in the journal's end pages, where new films, art and literature were written about without any necessary genuflection to the principles of socialist realism.

Without any prodding from its subject, a legendary aura had grown up around the journal's editor. It was rumoured that Samar Sen was not Maoist, but some kind of anarcho-Marxist. I actually never heard him talk politics. But one could infer his editorial policy from a line of Trotsky's he liked to quote: that there was no *Pravda* (truth) in *Izvestia* (news), no *Izvestia* in *Pravda*.

In his character, Samar Sen exemplified the simplicity of living so characteristic of the best kind of Indian Marxist. He lived in a tiny flat in southern Calcutta. Although the editor never burnt a tram, he travelled to his office in one—a journey of over an hour, each way, that he made daily till he was seventy and ailing. I remember him as a gentle little man with a shock of white hair on his head and round glasses on his eyes, a cigarette forever unlit upon his lips. In conversation he was incapable of anger or bitterness. The only time I saw him upset was when his friends planned a *festschrift* in his honour, a project he resisted with all his heart.

As an imaginative writer drawn almost against his will into radical politics, Samar Sen was a reminder that Marxist intellectual practice too could occasionally have an exquisite lightness of touch. His early renunciation of poetry notwithstanding, he retained an abiding love of literature, especially Russian literature. In a polemic I once wrote for *Frontier* I invoked as a model thinker for our times the radical theologian and environmentalist Ivan Illich. The editor had never heard of Illich; assuming I had made a mistake, he changed it in the proofs (without my knowledge, and rendering the sentence meaningless) to Ivan *Illyich*—a character from Tolstoy *I* had never heard of.

VI

My intellectual debt to Karl Marx is immense; my personal debt to Bengali intellectuals even greater. Looking back on my fieldwork I recall the distinguishing features of my tribe as a wonderful, unselfconscious austerity; a devotion to learning; and complete scorn for those seductions of intellectuals everywhere else, money and power. I carry memories too of dear friends I made in the field: memories, above all, of the two who are now absent—Samar Sen, a poet in politics, and Hiteshranjan Sanyal, a Gandhian among the Marxists.

But it is time to stand apart, to interpret Calcutta's intellectual life from the lofty perch of thrice-born-ness. Within anthropology there are two classic and somewhat competing techniques of interpreting primitive belief systems: the *functional*, that is, in terms of their contribution to individual self-esteem and collective solidarity; and the *structural*, namely the larger socio-historical context within which these beliefs inscribe themselves.

My own training orients me towards the second line of enquiry. In an essay on the nineteenth-century Bengali mystic Ramakrishna, the leading Marxist historian Sumit Sarkar has located the well-springs of the devotion of Ramakrishna's disciples to the acute boredom at work among Bengali clerks in British offices. Curiously, the Marxist intellectuals of Calcutta come overwhelmingly from the same social background as pilgrims who have visited Ramakrishna's abode in Dakshineshwar: the frustrated middle class. This is a status group, with a will to power but little opportunity to exercise it, that so dominated the early history of European socialism.

In some respects the composition of the Bengali Marxist elite confirms this sociological axiom, that socialism is only the class ideology of the petty bourgeois, alienated intellectual. For a more complete picture, however, one must also invoke factors distinctive to the region's political history. In two consecutive historical processes lie the key, perhaps, to understanding the affinity of the Bengali intellectual with Marxism.

The first is the consistent denigration by the British of the lack of physical prowess among the *bhadralok*. The Bengali, a high colonial official once remarked, 'has the intellect of a Greek and the grit of a rabbit'. This prejudice led to Bengalis being designated a 'non-martial race', a characterisation keenly felt by its victims. A number of historians have shown that the Bengali response to this slight took the form, on the one hand, of extolling physical exercise—as in the famous gymnasium movement of the late nineteenth century—and more strikingly so, by an adherence to political radicalism. From the nationalist terrorists of the early years of this century to the Maoist revolutionaries of the present day, the cult of violence has had a pervasive political influence in Bengal. Intellectuals in research institutes might not themselves manufacture bombs or behead class enemies, but their unmistakable admiration for these acts oriented them, inevitably, towards Marxism.

The second factor is the acute sense of political marginality among the Bengali elite. This dates at least to the year 1911, when the capital of British India shifted from Calcutta to New Delhi. Thereafter, the locus of the Indian freedom struggle shifted from west to east, especially with the advent of Mahatma Gandhi, a man who has not yet been forgiven in Bengal for thwarting the late challenge to his leadership of the Congress party by the Calcutta firebrand Subhas Chandra Bose. The Bengali middle class cannot reconcile itself to this loss of political power; and the rise to power of the CPI(M) must be interpreted, at least in part, as an assertion of regional feeling against the political centre.

Nothing better illustrates the uniquely provincial flavour of Bengali Marxism than the following, possibly apocryphal, anecdote. When Indira Gandhi was assassinated, her ashes were sent to different cities to allow public homage. While her ashes lay in Calcutta's Government House they were visited one evening by the state's finance minister. In the previous year this man had delivered no less than two hundred and sixty-two speeches on the discrimination against West Bengal in the release of funds from the central treasury. As the minister came out of Government House, he was asked how he felt when confronting the mortal remains of his most resolute political opponent. He replied in character: *Centre Kom Diye Che* (the Centre has again given us less than our rightful share).

Andhra Naxalite, Indian Democrat: C.V. Subbarao

WHEN the phone rang with the news of C.V. Subbarao's death the city around me grew more desolate as I lay awake all night with scores of memories of a departed friend. Subbarao in a Saturday meeting of the Peoples' Union for Democratic Rights, chastising a colleague for trying to turn a civil liberties group into a political sect; Subbarao on a public platform, speaking in his irrepressibly fluent broken Hindi; Subbarao in his cold, dark flat off Rajpur Road in old Delhi, brewing coffee and urging me to read Malcolm Caldwell's *The Wealth of Some Nations.*

One recollection made me chuckle despite my grief. With his friend, the writer Sumanta Banerjee, Subbarao had applied for a two-year fellowship to the Indian Council of Social Science Research. Both wanted a spell away from Delhi, to return to their roots: Subbarao wished to work on industrialisation in princely Hyderabad, Sumanta on the cultural history of Bengal. The ICSSR was then ruled by an eminence deeply suspicious of anyone or anything farther left of the *Patriot* newspaper. For reasons unstated, Subbarao's fellowship was granted but Sumanta's was not. The day the news came I met Subbarao in the coffee house of the Delhi School of Economics, his face wreathed in smiles. 'You see, I am only an *Andhra Naxalite*', he explained, 'so they [the screening committee] hadn't heard of me, but Sumanta is an *all-India Naxalite.*' The Bengali's allegiance to the Naxalites had indeed been more public, for he had left a senior position in *The Statesman* newspaper to go underground. In time he resurfaced, only to write a sympathetic history of the Naxalite rebellion. Sumanta's political past was thus well known to the babus in Delhi. (In the event, his fellowship was also granted—he used it to write a fine book on nineteenth-century Calcutta.)

Both words in Subbarao's self-description were operative. He had a great love of Telugu literature; aside from PUDR, the institution that meant most to him (at least in the years I knew him) was the radical cultural journal, *Srijana*, a journal brutally harassed by the Andhra Pradesh government. There was a period in the mid eighties when Subbarao was apparently always on the AP Express, rushing between New Delhi and Secunderabad to attend to both sets of commitments. Likewise, his political self had been deeply influenced by the Naxalite upsurge of the late sixties and early seventies. As a radical student leader in the Andhra University, Subbarao had been jailed for a long period during the Emergency.

This identity with the politics and culture of his home state suggests that an outsider like me, not steeped in the poetry of Sri Sri, Cherabandaraju and Varavara Rao, can provide only a partial appreciation of Subbarao. But of course, Subbarao was not '*only* an Andhra Naxalite'. In 1977 he moved from Andhra to Delhi, got a job teaching economics, and threw himself into the civil liberties movement. Through his work with the PUDR—from 1977 till the week of his death in January 1994—Subbarao did as much as anyone else in our time to deepen the meaning of Indian democracy.

Unlike other such groups, PUDR is not dominated by a single idea or individual. It works and thinks like a collective, but somehow, for many of us who are fellow travellers of that remarkable organisation, Subbarao most fully embodied its collective spirit. This may have been so only because he had been with PUDR since its inception, or because of his most likeable self, which attracted friends from all over. Of all the activists I have known, Subbarao stood out for his utter lack of self-righteousness. Obsessively committed to the 'cause', the activist is quick to pass judgement on those whose commitment is made less certain by considerations of family or career. In this respect Subbarao was exceptional. For him, it was enough that you cared—he was content with what you could give, at your time and in your own way.

In the end, it was his disregard of self that killed Subbarao. On the move, in the train, in a distant Bihar village one day and in a Delhi *dhaba* the next, the food he ate was made by diverse hands and often dubious in quality. Like a good Indian leftist he liked his rum and his Charminar cigarettes. Of these he had all too many. I remember a conversation I once had with a young PUDR woman worker at the Hindu College bus stop. We talked of Subbarao and I expressed my worries about those sixty cigarettes a day. The look on the face of the PUDR girl made it clear that my concern was misunderstood or, rather, misplaced: it appeared that to object to cigarette smoking was bourgeois puritanism.

I like to think that Subbarao would have appreciated my worry, for he would most emphatically preach against the personal frailties of his friends. Consider this story told me by the historian Amit Kumar Gupta. Gupta and his wife have only one son, who capped a fine academic career at Delhi by being awarded a Rhodes Scholarship. The parents took justifiable pride in the boy, till he wrote home from Oxford to say that he had fallen in love with a Chinese girl and was determined to marry her. Angry and hurt letters were exchanged, word of which reached Subbarao. At ten o'clock one night, Subbarao traversed the city to visit the Guptas, who live across the Jamuna, an hour and a half's bus ride away. Over several glasses of rum Subbarao finally convinced the couple that their objections sat oddly with their stated liberal-left beliefs, and in any case it did not matter much if their grandchild was to speak Mandarin rather than Bangla. His work done, Subbarao made to go. 'Why don't you spend the night at our flat', said Amit, 'it's already one o'clock'. 'It doesn't matter', answered Subbarao, 'this shall never be my city, but I know my way through it by now.' He was dead in a few months, but I was lucky enough to attend the reception organised by the Guptas for their son and his Chinese bride.

The morning I left home for Subbarao's funeral, my wife asked whether there would be any rituals. I answered in the negative, but in fact there were rituals, Communist rituals. His body was draped in a red flag, and a steely-eyed Naxalite stood guard over it. He was cremated to shouts of 'Comrade Subbarao Lal Salaam'. Yet the throng of admirers was not all from one end of the spectrum. There were, of course, some oustanding feminists associated with the PUDR, such as Uma Chakravarti and Urvashi Butalia. Also those left-wing historians, Sumit Sarkar and Dilip Simeon. But I also saw economists who are apolitical, such as Kaushik Basu and K. Krishnamurty, and sociologists who have been critical of Marxism, such as Dhirubhai Sheth and Shiv Visvanathan. In retrospect, Subbarao's funeral seems to have been the final public display of the spirit of intellectual community that once marked the University of Delhi.

II

At a memorial service, held fittingly at the Constitution Club in New Delhi, the advocate Gobinda Mukhoty remarked that 'when the history of the Indian democratic rights movement comes to be written, the name of C.V. Subbarao shall be placed alongside those of Jawaharlal Nehru, who established an Indian Civil Liberties Union in 1936, and Justice V.M. Tarkunde, who helped found Citizens for Democracy forty years later'. This was rich praise, richly deserved. In the twenty-three years of its existence the PUDR has done a great deal to enlarge our understanding of democracy. For much of this time, Subbarao served simultaneously as its moral conscience and its intellectual mentor, a guide to and a standard for its work. In his vision, democracy did not simply mean protection of liberty and freedom of expression. In a society as sharply divided as ours, the state has a moral as well as judicial responsibility to protect the rights of the disadvantaged, in particular their access to land, water, forests and the livelihood these resources provide them. It is also the responsibility of the state to act promptly and fairly in preventing or resolving disputes between communities; and to assure a dignified existence to the most vulnerable social groups, such as prisoners and refugees, who are otherwise unrepresented by trade union or political party.

This broader, and to my mind much fuller, understanding of Indian democracy informs the PUDR reports which Subbarao helped research and write, on such themes as environmental degradation and natural-resource conflict; on communal riots in a dozen states; and on the condition of prisons and the penal system more generally. Massively documented, yet presented in a deliberately understated and non-polemical tone, these reports are more credible than a good many academic monographs on the same subjects. Taken together, they provide an authoritative account of political and economic change in post-Emergency India, of the degradation of our democracy and of the scattered attempts to restore it.

C.V. Subbarao himself had an exceptional academic record, topping his university in both his degrees—physics and economics. His quality of mind is certainly reflected in the PUDR reports he helped put together, but Subbarao sometimes thought of taking time off to pursue his scholarly interests in a more sustained manner. In our last conversation he told me of his wish, now that he had turned forty, to spend the next few years on a thorough study of the political economy of environmental degradation. He might have written a landmark work on the topic, as indeed—were he to have put his mind to it—on a quite different topic, the social history of Telugu literature.

Subbarao had in fact an abiding respect for the vocation of the intellectual. A devoted teacher himself, he had scorn for those of his colleagues who felt that their involvement in social movements gave them, as he put it, 'the moral right not to take classes'. He had considerable respect for the Delhi School of Economics, which had fostered a culture of responsibility wherein teachers took classes, promptly corrected scripts, and attended seminars and staff meetings. With his fellow radicals, he was sceptical of much of the research done by the economists of the Delhi School; but unlike them he was fair-minded enough to acknowledge their work ethic.

Perhaps the roots of this respect for the university as an institution lay in one of his early experiences. When I joined the Institute of Economic Growth in 1988, he told me he knew one of my senior colleagues, the econometrician K. Krishnamurty. In my naivete I was surprised, for Krishnamurty was known to be quite non-political. Then he told me the story of his first meeting with the econometrician. In 1976, Subbarao had been taken in handcuffs from the Vishakapatnam jail to the university campus, to appear for his M.A. viva. When he entered the room Krishnamurty, who was the external examiner, asked the accompanying policemen to free his hands. At first they demurred, for a large student body had gathered outside the economics department upon hearing of Subbarao's arrival. 'Looking at this boy I can trust him not to run away', insisted the examiner. The handcuffs were finally removed for the interview: after which Subbarao returned to jail where, in time, he received word that he had come first in the university.

Subbarao's intellectual projects remain unfulfilled, but his example and ideas have long animated the work of the academics who came in contact with him. I remember two lessons in the ethics of intellectual practice that he handed me. In a polemic written for the *Economic and Political Weekly*, I had made a reference to '1950s Stalinists and 1960s Maoists'. When we next met, Subbarao noted that my crude stereotyping was itself a caricature of the argumentative style of those I had criticised. 'When you look long enough into the abyss', he remarked, quoting Nietzsche, 'the abyss stares back at you'.

On another occasion we appeared together in a panel discussion on state repression of tribals in Bastar. After a previous panelist had talked of the suppression of shifting cultivation by the Forest Department, I triumphantly held up an interview with the Naxalite leader Kondapalli Seetaramaiah in which he had characterised shifting cultivation as a 'primitive' practice that must be replaced by more 'modern' forms of agriculture. 'See this', I exclaimed, 'the Naxalites share the civilising mission of the Indian state.' I was at once corrected by Subbarao. 'Whatever Seetaramaiah may say or believe', he pointed out, 'the fact is that in Bastar the Naxalites are fighting for the continuance of shifting cultivation, working with the tribals and against the Forest Department. Look at their practice on the ground, not at their official ideology.' The warning was salutary, more so in an intellectual climate where, increasingly, lived experience counts for little, and 'representation' and 'construction' are all.

I must recall, too, an extended tutorial offered one lovely winter's day while drinking tea under the row of palm trees that run behind the lecture theatre of the Delhi School of Economics. Subbarao had just written much of a PUDR report on forest law, and I was just beginning doctoral research on forest policy. On pages of lined paper he outlined how the arguments of the report could be refined and elaborated, and the government's complicity in industry's decimation of forests more authoritatively documented. Sources of data were identified, and ways of analysing them suggested. Years later, I made the mistake of thanking him in the book that was the final outcome of that discussion. He came halfway across Delhi—to Teen Murti, where I then worked—to chastise me. Did I not know that socialists did not take individual credit? Did I not understand that our conversation under the palms was a product of intellectual curiosity and of personal friendship, and was not to have been formalised in this vulgar way?

After Subbarao died a manuscript of mine was found by his bedside table. He had agreed to read it, on condition that he should not be thanked. The printed book could not be improved by his comments, but it did carry as an epigraph this poem by his fellow Andhra Naxalite, Cherabandaraju. I need hardly state that the PUDR report where the poem first appeared did not mention the name of the translator.

Right

by Cherabandaraju

I will not stop cutting down trees
Though there is life in them
I will not stop plucking out leaves,
Though they will make nature beautiful
I will not stop hacking off branches,
Though they are the arms of a tree
Because—
I need a hut

(translated from the Telugu
by C.V. Subbarao)

Rooted Cosmopolitan: D.R. Nagaraj

THE writer and critic D.R. Nagaraj died in his forty-fifth year. A scholar he admired, Verrier Elwin, had once solemnly marked that number in a poem within his diary:

> Well, at least I'm still alive
> At the age of forty-five
> William Jones and Annandale
> Both to reach this age did fail.

To compare Nagaraj with William Jones is to offend both white man and brown. The British Orientalist will regard it as an insult to Jones' industry ('how many digests did your man compile?'). The Indian indigenist will see in it an affront to Nagaraj's politics ('but wasn't the Asiatic Society of Bengal complicit in the colonialist project?'). Worse still, the man putting their names together here does not read Kannada or Persian or Sanskrit. But he knew one, and knew enough about the other, to see them as akin in style of scholarship, in their love of learning and love of language.

I first heard of Nagaraj from the historian and autobiographer Sujit Mukherjee. I had asked Sujit about the doings of our friend Harish Trivedi, Professor of English at Delhi University. 'Harish has just been adjudged the second-best literary critic in India by U.R. Anantha

Murthy', said Sujit: 'He is now going around Delhi with a revolver looking for a fellow called D.R. Nagaraj.'

Soon afterwards I saw the finest critic in India in the flesh. The sight, I must admit, was not impressive. Nagaraj was reading a paper on Gandhi in the seminar room of the Nehru Memorial Museum and Library. The tone was low, the eyes did not stray from the text. In the high centre of intellectual power the scholar from Bangalore seemed out of his depth. After his talk he came up and shyly introduced himself. 'We have both dedicated books to T.G. Vaidyanathan', he said.

The book offered to Vaidyanathan I cannot read—it is in Kannada. But when I was next in Bangalore I located, in Premier Bookshop, a copy of Nagaraj's *The Flaming Feet*. It is a little book, and now a scarce one. Published in 1993 by his friend Siddhartha, on behalf of the Institute for Cultural Research and Action, it collects half-a-dozen essays on Dalit politics. Some of these draw on Nagaraj's specialist knowledge of Kannada society and Kannada literature. The first essay, however, is pitched at a higher level of generality. This is a brilliant analysis of the tension between the essentially spiritual programme of Gandhi and the political-economic project of Ambedkar. Nagaraj shows how their encounter was transformative for both. Through Ambedkar, Gandhi came to recognise the importance of economic rights. Because of Gandhi, Ambedkar internalised the significance of religion. The critic's achievement lies in tracing a chain of influence not admitted to by either party.

Nagaraj also shows how in the nationalist narrative Ambedkar's role had necessarily to be diminished. Among progressive Hindus 'a profound ethical halo' came to envelop the Mahatma's campaign against Untouchability. 'The Gandhian tales of sacrifice, courage, and struggle against the Hindu orthodoxy almost became a household talk in those areas where nationalist struggle was popular'. To set Gandhi against reactionary Shankaracharyas was to celebrate 'a hero's capacity to suffer spiritual isolation'. But 'in a play of such a script, the untouchables would never become heroes in their own right, they are just mirrors for a hero to look at his own existential angst and despair, maybe even glory'. The residues of this celebration reach into the present. For to invest the Gandhian programme with a 'legendary character' was to invite both 'ridicule and veneration'. The contemporary Dalit contempt for Gandhi flows out of this history. Once the oppressed castes came to more authoritatively represent themselves 'the case for patricide looked both genuine and unavoidable'.

Nagaraj used to joke that his admiration for Gandhi was essentially casteist. He was a weaver by caste, and so, in a manner of speaking, was the Mahatma. But his involvement with Dalit politics had also led him to a deep respect for Babasaheb Ambedkar. Nagaraj was unusual in his equal liking for two figures brought into sharp and continuing conflict by Indian politics, and more unusual still in providing fresh insight into two of the most written-about lives in Indian history. Before I had read five pages of his essay I knew I was in the presence of an altogether original mind. I knew how careless I had been in taking Nagaraj the seminarist as a proxy for Nagaraj the thinker.

In any case, it was only in public forums in Delhi that Nagaraj was diffident. In Karnataka he had an awesome reputation as an orator. The film-maker Girish Kaseravalli has remarked that although he heard Nagaraj speak many times he never came away thinking, 'I have heard him say this before'. I cannot easily forget, either, a five-minute talk he gave at a seminar in Manipal in April 1996. This was addressed to Dharampal, the old Gandhian who had been invited to inaugurate the seminar. Like some other despairing veterans Dharampal had recently walked into the arms of the Sangh Parivar. The occasion demanded deference, but Nagaraj's intellect and passion would not allow the betrayal to go unchallenged. Dharampal shifted uncertainly in his seat while he was called to account. How could the author of *Civil Disobedience and Indian Tradition*, the associate of Mira Behn and Jayaprakash Narayan, end up by defending in print the demolition of the Babri Masjid?

After I moved to Bangalore in 1995 Nagaraj and I would meet occasionally, and always in Koshy's Parade Cafe. Living in the largely English- and Tamil-speaking Bangalore 'Cantonment', I could never hope to enter his world, the Kannada-speaking 'City'. He moved himself with ease from one cultural universe to the other. His roots were so deep that he never sought to parade them or to casually dismiss 'cosmopolitanism'. The dedication of his first book to T.G. Vaidyanathan was an illustration of this. Nagaraj told me that the dedication was resented by his nativist friends, for Vaidyanathan—a legendary teacher of English at Bangalore University—had never learnt Kannada. Nagaraj's answer was that 'TGV' had lit up his mind, as he had lit up the minds of other boys who came to listen to him in English but spoke Kannada or Malayalam or Gujarati at home.

At my initiative our meetings became more frequent. In the month before his death we met three times in Parade's. The first time we discussed the Indian idiom of autobiography, of how the memoirs of Gandhi and Nehru and Shivram Karanth outlined various routes to, as he put it, the 'making of a historically determined but socially conscious individual'. When I suggested that Indians were not as revelatory in their self-testimonies, he offered as a counter-example the recent autobiography of the Kannada writer P. Lankesh.

The second meeting was more argumentative, an indication perhaps of our developing friendship. I held that the writings of scholars must be transparent and accessible. 'Accessibility' is not a value-neutral term, he responded. To ask for transparency was to privilege the native speaker of English over the others. 'Why do the translations of Habermas and Derrida keep intact certain key German or French terms? We must do *violence* to the English language, we must expand its structure and idiom much as postmodern novelists have.' As the debate intensified I pulled out my trump card. 'Obscurity is a cover up for lazy and imprecise thinking. To defend it is to defend the likes of Homi Bhabha and Gayatri Chakravorty Spivak.' I said this knowing that Nagaraj was on terms of intimacy with one or perhaps both. But his friendship with the King and Queen of Impenetrable Jargon did not, it seems, extend to literary kinship. His answer mixed puzzlement with pain: 'Surely you do not think *I* write like Spivak and Bhabha?'

At our last meeting we talked chiefly of his books. He hoped by the end of the year to complete his study of 'The Politics of Cultural Choices'. What next, I asked. 'I have written a book on Shaiva philosophy, focusing on the *vacanas* of [the twelfth-century poet-mystic] Allama Prabhu. But I want it first to appear in Kannada. Then I think I'll do a book on the Nation of Islam, on the links between black protest and the black literary imagination. I have already written an essay on Richard Wright and Toni Morrison. The next time I go to Chicago [he taught at the University every summer] I will try and meet Louis Farrakhan.'

The range of Nagaraj's ambition was immense. His learning and theoretical reach are both displayed in a small fragment I have seen of the projected book on cultural choices. This is the manuscript of a talk delivered in December 1996 at the Chicago Institute of the Humanities. To read it is to know that the larger work would have fundamentally altered our understanding of the caste system. A decent monograph can probably still be made up from the drafts that must lie in his computer. As it stands, *The Flaming Feet* is Nagaraj's only book in English. There are, besides, some published essays and reviews, aborted anticipations of what might have been. These include a sharp but by no means undeserved demolition of Kancha Ilaiah's book *Why I Am Not a Hindu*, and a lovingly qualified appreciation of Shiv Visvanathan's *A Carnival for Science*. More readily accessible in library or bookstore are introductions he wrote to a novel by U.R. Anantha Murthy and to the first volume of the collected works of Ashis Nandy.

Anantha Murthy's *Bharathipura* is about the attempts by a modernising Brahmin to transform his surroundings. Jagannatha, heir to the biggest estate in the temple town of Bharathipura, is radicalised while studying in England. When he returns the expectation is that he will manage his properties and sit comfortably atop the social and ritual hierarchy of the town, as generations of his family have done. Instead, he resolves to turn his world upside down by mobilising the oppressed Untouchables to enter and defile the temple.

Nagaraj's introduction to the English translation of *Bharathipura* (which was by P. Sreenivasa Rao) draws both on his close personal friendship with the author and his knowledge of Kannada literary history. Anantha Murthy's first novel, *Samskara*, was a 'product of Lohia-ite melancholy and rage against the caste system'. But this one had no such simple 'message'. At times it read like a critique of the social revolutionary who projects his ideas and hopes on a not-always-willing following. Indeed, 'the rebel's grandeur, misery and sentimental attachment to his cause . . . in a moment of crisis transforms itself into pure hatred of the *subjects* of his cause.' Some of the novelist's comrades in the socialist movement, seeking as always a clear political line, did not know what to make of the book. But Nagaraj asks us to see *Bharathipura* as part of an older tradition in the Kannada novel, in which political idealism is 'a matter of horror for the hero and amusement for the people', with heroes 'cured of their revolutionary excesses by the amused indifference of the people towards the project of emancipation.' The novel is thus 'essentially a critique of the limitations of the radical middle classes, claiming an exclusive and sympathetic right to change the nation.'

Nagaraj's prologue to Ashis Nandy's *Exiled at Home* presents a masterly survey of the major theories of colonialism. One school, associated with the likes of Franz Fanon and Edward Said, emphasizes conquest and subjugation. The second looks for the persistence despite political domination of a 'cultural soul'—the exemplar here is Ananda Coomaraswamy. The third, to which Nandy attaches himself, stresses the mutual transformation of ruler and ruled. 'When he is in the Fanonian or Freudian mode', writes Nagaraj, 'Nandy is melancholic. But the company of Gandhi makes him cheerful and enables him to see the transformative capacities of both the coloniser and the colonised'. Mischievously improvising on one of Nandy's own formulations, he suggests that 'if Nandy is Nathuram Godse, modernity is Gandhi—the assassin's relationship with his victim is both complex and multidimensional.' That the anti-modernist's vocabulary is forged in the crucible of modernity is both its strength and its weakness. What Nagaraj asks for now is a 'critique of the project of modernity from those intellectual, emotional, symbolic and semiotic structures which exist beyond its reaches.' Nandy, unfortunately, 'has difficulties in getting into the symbolic and philosophical universes of Nagarjuna, Shankara, Sarhapada or even pre-Enlightenment Christian thinkers and mystics.'

At the time of his death Nagaraj was working on an essay, to be delivered as the Sadat Hasan Manto lecture in Delhi, that hoped to make ninth-century Jaina texts on violence speak to the recent experience of anti-Urdu and anti-Tamil riots in Bangalore. But Nagaraj could do more than bridge the centuries. Alone among Indian intellectuals of my acquaintance, he combined a knowledge of his own linguistic tradition with a sure grasp of the theoretical idioms of the West. The cosmopolitan intellectual may get by with an Indian language on the street, but he has no real access to its philosophical or metaphorical depths. The 'vernacular' scholar might be steeped in Bengali or Tamil, but he is unsure or ignorant when it comes to the latest theories of the international academy. His knowledge of the West rests with what he read in college—with Leavis or Huxley if he is sixty or with Lawrence and Wells if he is eighty. Now Nagaraj was the pre-eminent scholar of Kannada culture, had a decent command of Telugu and passable knowledge of Hindi and Sanskrit, and even some Tamil too. He also knew as much as anybody about contemporary trends in anthropology, cultural studies, and history.

In his introduction to *Bharathipura* Nagaraj remarks that the storyteller in the novel displays 'a doggedness and determination *never* to leave his local habitat'. His own desire, it seems, was to make periodic and extended forays into the wider world without ever disavowing his local habitat. He would have continued to write on Kannada literature, but increasingly also on Indian history and global culture. With his learning, his linguistic skills, and his sheer intelligence, there is no saying what heights he would have reached.

I started by offering one comparison, and will end with another. The life of D.R. Nagaraj reminds me irresistibly of the life of the social activist C.V. Subbarao. Subbarao and Nagaraj were both born in the same year, 1954. Nagaraj had a familial intimacy with Subbarao's language, Telugu. Both had at one time been immersed in left-wing student politics. But so far as I can tell, they did not know one another.

Subbarao's contributions to the Indian civil liberties movement were of the same order as Nagaraj's contributions to Kannada literature. They were, in a word, immense. They will exercise the attentions of more than one future historian. Both men had accomplished a lifetime's work by the time they reached forty. I believe they knew this too. As the previous essay relates, shortly before he died Subbarao had decided to take long leave from activism to write a thesis on the political economy of ecological degradation. At a comparable stage in his life D.R. Nagaraj chose to write increasingly on national and global questions. After having their actions dictated to by political compulsions, both had at last decided to live for themselves. For Nagaraj to write on Kannada poetry or for Subbarao to lead an enquiry into a communal riot was simply a matter of social commitment and ethical obligation. But for Nagaraj to research the Nation of Islam or Subbarao to study political economy was to give in to intellectual ambition.

It is strange, uncanny even, how, so soon after these decisions were made public, they both died. No doubt a rationalist will scoff at this. He will say, with reason, that both men were utterly negligent with their health. Their fatal heart attacks were a consequence of years of bodily abuse, of smoking, drinking, relentless travel and erratic eating habits. I do not dispute this. Yet the thought remains—why would Nagaraj, like Subbarao before him, not be allowed to place self before society?

The Last Civilian: C.S. Venkatachar

VENKATACHAR was my grandfather's friend before he became mine. After years of service in the North, in secretariat and laboratory respectively, my grandfather and he both came home to retire in the Bangalore locality of Jayamahal. The civil servant and the scientist lived on adjoining streets and occasionally took walks together.

When Venkatachar befriended me in 1979, he was eighty and I twenty. Through an unsuccessful stab at an exam that he had once passed, I was coming to an appreciation of modern Indian history. Some of this history he had witnessed; some he had helped make. Thrown by profession and circumstance into the company of Nehru, Patel, Rajagopalachari, Rajendra Prasad and Mountbatten, deeply impressed by Gandhi—whom he often saw but never met—he now spent his time as an 'illustrious obscure' in Bangalore, seeking to understand more fully the momentous events of his century. His days were taken up with reading the latest monographs out of Cambridge, Berkeley and the Jawaharlal Nehru University. The books lay stacked on a glass table in his drawing room: sent to him for review, lent by libraries, or presented by the authors themselves. I was not ready to read them myself, but the digested summaries I was provided were attractive enough. Between the previews I would get Venkatachar to reach into the storehouse of memory and provide from his matchless range of experience an incident to supplement the findings of scholars in the archives.

A year of these conversations culminated in my securing admission to a Ph.D. programme in sociology at the Indian Institute of Management in Calcutta. I had hoped to work on Verrier Elwin, a character Venkatachar knew of mostly from hearsay. He took me to meet a famous sociologist he knew, who lived in the next colony. The distinguished scholar was unimpressed. 'Elwin was an *amateur* ethnographer', he said, 'I wouldn't waste my time on him. Besides, Calcutta is not known to be a *home* of Indian sociology.' I was devastated. We walked back in silence up the hill to Jayamahal, Venkatachar negotiating the bumps and scooters with his walking stick. He did not dispute the scholar's judgement, but the talks continued.

The interest generated by Venkatachar finally prevailed over the prudence advised by his friend. I moved to Calcutta, to begin my formal education in Indian society and history. Twice or thrice a year I would visit Bangalore and report on my progress. Over the years, Venkatachar's eyesight deteriorated, and the books disappeared from the glass table. He remained formidably fluent in five languages although, as one would expect, he had good days as well as bad. The tutorials were finally brought to an end by his death, on the 18th of June 1999, three weeks short of his hundredth birthday.

II

Cadambi Seshachar Venkatachar was born in a modernising Brahmin family of the old princely state of Mysore. They came from a *agraharam* near Hoskote but had, in his father's generation, moved to Bangalore. The boy was sent to an English-medium school in Chamarajpet and then to Central College. In 1918 he joined the Presidency College in Madras, for a B.Sc. in Chemistry. Living in an isolated princely state, he had not read a newspaper nor heard of Annie Besant, the partition of Bengal and the Montagu-Chelmsford reforms. In college Venkatachar remained resolutely non-political. 'I read no paper', he recalled. 'And in Madras, the Tamilian boys were very alert and used to read *The Hindu* from the first to the last page. I occasionally used to dip into it, but I never read it.'

The idea of appearing for the Indian Civil Service was implanted in him by a lecture given by S.G. Sengodayan, who had previously made the journey from Presidency College to the ICS. Venkatachar was excited by the fact that 'selection was based on merit and not on recommendation'. When his father offered to fund him, he sailed for London in the summer of 1921. He joined University College and swotted for a year. He got through the written tests comfortably and in his *viva voce* was asked what he thought was the place of the English language in a future India. It must stay, he answered, since it is the language of science and modernity.

Venkatachar was allotted the United Provinces cadre, but first proceeded for a year's training to Trinity College, Cambridge. There he learnt economics under the noted monetarist Geoffrey Crowther (a future editor of *The Economist*), and, less surely, Urdu from a retired colonel named Phillot who swore that the empire was degenerating due to the malign influence of Jews—such as Lord Reading, lately viceroy of India, and Edwin Montagu, secretary of state. As Venkatachar was to write in an unpublished fragment of autobiography, 'I carried no ideas from Cambridge about Britain's empire in India or how to rule it. My entry into the Civil Service was mainly a means of furnishing myself with a career with handsome emoluments and a pension at the end of it.' He did, however, carry the idea, conveyed by a don, that the ICS was 'a university in which you were never graduated; you went on learning by experience till the end of the career . . .'

In January 1923 Venkatachar took a train to Kanpur en route to Fatehgarh, his first posting. Travelling in the same carriage was Nisar Ahmed Sherwani, a member of a well-known UP Muslim family who had left his government job in answer to Gandhi's call. Here was one man leaving the portals of the Raj, another just entering it. Venkatachar had postings in Fatehgarh, Moradabad and Badaun before being seconded, in 1927, to the Indian Political Service. As assistant resident to the Central Indian States he made a routine call on the maharaja of

Chattarpur. He asked the little ruler if there was anything the paramount power could do to help him. The maharaja replied: 'All sorts of Englishmen come and ask me to show them the wing of the palace where E.M. Forster lived. I don't know, and don't care. I would be grateful if you would ask them to stay away.'

A more consequential meeting was with the Talcherkar family of Indore, among whom Venkatachar, in a daring act of inter-caste transgression, found a bride. However, the Political Service bored him. It was known in any case as a home for the indecisive and incompetent. In the words of a later viceroy, Lord Wavell, it was the place they sent soldiers who couldn't fight and civilians who couldn't rule. After writing a census report for Central India under the direction of J.H. Hutton (the most imaginative of all colonial census commissioners), Venkatachar asked for a transfer back to UP. He was sent to Gonda, a lush, swamp-filled district on the borders of Nepal, dominated by indolent *taluqdars*. The district administration, he remembered years later, 'was static, joltingly moved along with the changing time. Backward, it would not go; forward it would not move.' The governor of UP, Sir Malcolm Hailey, had in alliance with the Kanpur businessman and politician Sir J.P. Srivastava tried to bolster the landlords, creating a special rural development department to offer lollies to the tenants. The latter were unimpressed; they went over to the Congress, which under Jawaharlal Nehru and his circle promised far-reaching land reforms when they came to power.

In late 1937 Venkatachar was sent to Malaya as the Agent of the Government of India. He spent three years there, occupied for the most part with complaints of Tamil plantation labourers that they were less fairly treated than their Chinese conterparts. His conclusion, dryly communicated to New Delhi, was that 'the Tamils were certainly underpaid and discriminated against, but on the other hand the Chinese were invariably more hardworking and enterprising.'

Venkatachar was recalled to India just before the Malay Peninsula fell to the Japanese. In June 1941 he was appointed president, Court of Wards, headquartered in Allahabad, but responsible for the management of all the zamindari estates in UP. Two years later he took over as commissioner of Allahabad Division. The Quit India movement had recently been suppressed, but the War was still on. One of the commissioner's tasks was to pass on money and whisky to left-wing politicians, to bribe them into keeping the factory workers who followed them quiet. Another, more pleasurable task was to discover the full name of the scientist K.S. Krishnan, made a knight in the king's birthday list of 1945. By convention the recipient was not to know of the honour beforehand; moreover, the citation had to have the expanded initials. A brief conversation in Tamil, between commissioner and professor, revealed the details—Karaimanikam Srinivasa Krishnan.

Just outside Allahabad lay Naini jail. Lodged there at this time were Purushottamdas Tandon, Rafi Ahmad Kidwai, Lal Bahadur Shastri, Vijayalakshmi Pandit, and Kailash Nath Katju—that is, all the top leaders of the UP Congress except Nehru and Govind Ballabh Pant, who were locked up in Ahmednagar. Then they put the young Indira Gandhi in prison. 'What is the giddy idea of putting her in jail? She has just got married,' said Venkatachar to his superior, the chief secretary, Sir Francis Mudie—the words quoted as they appear in an interview conducted in 1984 by Dr Hari Dev Sharma of the Nehru Memorial Museum and Library. Mudie replied: 'Oh, I thought she may keep company with her aunt.' 'Don't you know,' replied the better informed Indian, 'that they are at daggers drawn with each other?'

Indira was soon released but then word came that Nehru himself was to be transferred to Naini jail. He was brought under escort by train, but the commissioner of Allahabad nonetheless arranged for the vehicle to be diverted to an isolated siding, away from an excited crowd that had gathered at the main station. Nehru was his usual charming self and, to Venkatachar's embarrassment, even offered to be handcuffed.

In retrospect, Venkatachar was fortunate in not having ever to 'repress' the nationalists. He reached the UP in January 1923, less than a year after Non Co-operation had been ended by the arson at Chauri Chaura. When the Civil Disobedience movement took place he was away in the states of Central India. During Quit India he was back in British terrritory, but in a politically uncontentious posting. In this way he never had to order lathi-charges or mass arrests of the men who would one day rule India.

Late in 1946 Venkatachar was appointed dewan of Jodhpur. The young maharaja of the state was negotiating with Jinnah, who promised him favourable treatment if he acceded to Pakistan, an idea he was soon disabused of. At this time the dewans of the four major Rajput states were all South Indians—K.M. Pannikar in Bikaner, V.T. Krishnamachari in Jaipur, T. Vijairaghavachari in Udaipur, and Venkatachar himself in Jodhpur. Working in concert they brought their masters into the Constituent Assembly, an achievement of incalculable worth. Nor did our man's contributions to national integration end here. Thus in 1948 Venkatachar moved to the ministry of states as joint secretary, succeeding V.P. Menon as secretary two years later. In all this he developed an abiding respect for Sardar Patel. For Patel 'was pragmatic and devoid of any meanness towards the Rulers . . . His directive to us was "Do not question the extent of the personal wealth claimed by them, and never ever confront the ladies of the household. I want their States—not their wealth".'

Venkatachar's last posting with the Government of India was as secretary to the president, Rajendra Prasad. Sometimes dismissed as an old-style Hindu conservative, Rajen babu was in fact a man of high principle and ability. Meeting him in April 1947, Alan Campbell-Johnson, Mountbatten's press attache, wrote of being 'impressed by his serenity and undoubted depth of mind and strength of character. He is essentially a moderate and conciliator, a man of the people whose good reputation has little to do with the demagogic arts, but is the outcome of long and loyal service to the Nationalist cause. He will undoubtedly have a key role to play in the new regime, whether in a united or divided India.'

Prasad's misfortune was the temperamental discord between him and his prime minister, Jawaharlal Nehru. Nehru wanted Rajaji and not him to be president in 1952; he was to be disappointed again in 1957, when the Congress Old Guard ensured that Prasad got a second term in preference to Sarvepalli Radhakrishnan, a man Nehru could more easily identify with. Venkatachar once told me a lovely story of how Radhakrishnan cornered him at a banquet and asked, accusingly, whether it was he who had inserted those verses from the *Gita* in the president's last speech. For command over Sanskrit was one of the advertised advantages of the vice-president—his superior was innocent of the language, but his superior's secretary, unfortunately, was not.

In an insightful essay on 'Relations between the Indian President and the Prime Minister' (*India Quarterly*, April–June 1971), Venkatachar wrote of how the first occupants of the two offices had set an unhappy precedent. Nehru, for his part, 'kept the president at arm's length and wanted no elder statesman to remind him of the truth of the advice which Lloyd George gave Winston Churchill during the latter's war-time prime ministership: "It is important for a prime minister to be surrounded by people who could stand up to him and say, not once but thrice, No".' Now Rajendra Prasad had the intelligence and experience to constructively disagree with the prime minister but not, it seems, the courage. He was, remarked his secretary, 'content to be informed at the pleasure of the prime minister and not to be "consulted" in constitutional terms; he faithfully performed whatever duties he was asked to do. He had his own ideas how he should "encourage" and "warn" the Cabinet; made even a couple of futile attempts in that direction but chose to efface himself due to his innate shyness, modesty and lack of confidence in himself to confront Nehru.'

'Outwardly there was deference to the president's functions; inwardly, they were largely ignored.' When in town Nehru would come to Rashtrapati Bhavan every Monday, and spend an hour alone with with the president. Venkatachar asked his boss about the content of these conversations. Rajen babu replied sadly: '*Idhar udhar ki baat karte hain, phir chale jaate hain.*' The Constitution certainly anticipated a more active role for the head of state, but the precedent set in the 'fifties continued for a very long while. Venkatachar commented, in 1984, that 'the result is that the president now chosen is one who would, sort of, be amenable or subservient to the overwhelming authority of the prime minister.' Since then, of course, the decline of the one-party state and the instability of governance by coalition have, willy-nilly, made of the president of India something more than a rubber-stamp.

Venkatachar retired from the ICS in January 1958, after thirty-five years in service. Nehru sent him as high commissioner to Canada, where he befriended Lester Pearson. 'Tell me', said Pearson, 'why does your great prime minister have a blind spot as far as Mr Krishna Menon is concerned?' In Ottawa Venkatachar once threw a party for Lord Mountbatten and—more daring by far—once accompanied Morarji Desai to a night-club. For the high commissioner, 'the evening was quite nerve-wracking as I kept wondering how he, a renowned puritan, would react to the typically sybaritic atmosphere of the club—particularly when the striptease act came on. As it was the evening went off peacefully.'

After Canada Venkatachar declined governorships, vice-chancellorships and the like, choosing to spend his retirement amidst his books and his flowers in Bangalore. He could be scathing about ex-civilians who hovered around the powerful. In about 1983, L.K. ('Lord Keynes') Jha was asked to carry some letters addressed by Mrs Indira Gandhi to Ronald Reagan and Margaret Thatcher. Venkatachar was disgusted that this former governor of the Reserve Bank had, out of fear only of offending the prime minister, become a postman.

III

I would, when I could, take with me to Venkatachar such friends as had some genealogical connection with him and his world. One of these was Keshav Desiraju, a Cambridge man and serving UP civilian who also happened to be a grandson of Sarvepalli Radhakrishnan. The old man was delighted, more so as he was then reading the very fine biography of the late president by his son, S. Gopal, Keshav's uncle.

He retold with relish the tale of how Radhakrishnan had disallowed the commissioner of Benares, Nethersole, from sending the police into the campus of the Benares Hindu University, a hotbed of nationalist politics and provider of the bulk of the second-rung leadership of the Quit India movement. When taken to task for 'inaction' by his boss, Sir Malcolm Hallet, Nethersole answered: 'Sir, you might be the governor of the United Provinces, but the vice-chancellor of the Hindu University is a Fellow of All Souls and a Fellow of the British Academy besides.' Venkatachar praised Gopal's biography but went on to complain of a previous work of his. 'I was disappointed by your uncle's life of Nehru,' he told Keshav. 'Why did he have to praise Panditji by diminishing others? Why was he so critical of Rajaji? After all, Rajaji was a great *South* Indian.'

Venkatachar once remarked, in print, that it was 'a pity that such a great man of penetrating wisdom as Rajaji persistently refused to write anything of himself and of his long political life.' Yet he always rejected suggestions that he write his own memoirs. He believed that these, especially if written by civil servants, tended to be self-serving tales of the 'I was right and the minister was wrong' variety. But through the sixties and seventies he did author a series of learned reviews and essays for newspapers and journals. These writings are rich in historical understanding but notably free of anecdote or personal remembrance.

In his articles Venkatachar was to challenge two sacred cows of Indian nationalism. One was the Quit India movement, a 'maladroit move' that contributed greatly to Partition. In 1939 Congress 'tactically weakened itself in severing the link with Government'; when Gandhi inaugurated Quit India three years later, 'in fighting the British he was fighting the Muslims by proxy.' Of course there was the cynical judgement of the historian D.D. Kosambi that the 1942 movement provided 'the glamour of jail and concentration camp to serve to wipe out the so-so record of the Congress ministries in office, thereby restoring the full popularity of the organisation among the masses.' Venkatachar believed that his hero, Rajaji, was vindicated in his opposition to 1942, for responsible governance was likely to be more rewarding, in the long run, than irresponsible (if heroic) resistance. Reviewing a typically gushing book by an American scholar on this 'spontaneous anti-imperialist revolution', he remarked tartly that 'by any judgement—biased or unbiased—the Quit India movement must be deemed to be a failure.'

The scholar-civilian also trained his critical eye on non-alignment. He conceded that the policy of equidistance from the United States and Soviet Russia had a moral charge as well as a utilitarian purpose—it allowed India to extract economic concessions from both superpowers. But perhaps its greatest use was its lack of precision. It could mean anything to anybody. 'The doctrine was exciting for the new nations for it was so eminently expandable . . . Who and what is Non-Aligned is a question without answer. That is its gratifying aspect.' Alas, as 'India discovered in 1962, non-alignment is not a comprehensive insurance policy to cover all sorts of risk or threat to national security.' The philosophy was more bombast than substance. It had not kept India out of the Cold War; it drew her into the 'Disneyland fantasy' of *Hindi-Chini bhai bhai.* On Republic Day 1968, Venkatachar published in the *Deccan Herald* a long essay with the title, 'Is Neutralism Still the Best Foreign Policy for India?' 'Contrary to her own economic interests and national well-being', he wrote, 'India had to adopt anti-western overtones.' Three years later, the fig-leaf of neutralism was finally discarded, but not in the direction Venkatachar had hoped. Mrs Indira Gandhi signed the 'Indo-Soviet Friendship Treaty', whose true costs to our econmic interests and well-being have not yet been calculated.

Venkatachar wrote with penetration on the recent past as well as the evolving present. Possibly his best, and certainly his best-known, essay was published in a volume on *The Partition of India: Policies and Perspectives, 1935–47,* edited by C.H. Philips and Mary Doreen Wainwright.* This analysed, in magisterial fashion, the push and pull

*Allen and Unwin, 1970.

factors that led to the creation of Pakistan. Among the former he numbered the pro-Hindi and anti-Urdu literary-political movement gathering pace since the late nineteenth century; the Congress' arrogance towards the Muslim League; its serious underestimation of the abilities of Mohammed Ali Jinnah; and its gross overestimation of the support it itself commanded among the poorer Muslims of the subcontinent. The latter included the long search, pre-Jinnah, for a Muslim homeland, based on an enduring suspicion of what the Hindus would do to Muslims in a majoritarian state; the opportunism of Muslim civil servants and businessmen seeking a government and market they could dominate without fear of competition; and the emotional appeal of faith—fatally discounted by Marxist-influenced thinkers such as Nehru.

Venkatachar was incisive in his explanation of Partition, yet completely unsentimental about the happening itself. There was no nostalgia for Akhand Bharat, a United India. History, he said categorically, 'does not show Jinnah as a tragic figure nor geographical partition as a tragedy.' From his early experiences in Badaun, where with an energetic police officer he had forestalled a serious riot during Moharram, Venkatachar knew that there were serious cleavages among Hindus and Muslims in northern India. 'The idea that the British were all the time involved in dividing' he dismissed as 'nationalist rhetoric'. We divided, and they ruled, as Maulana Mohammed Ali once remarked. The transfer of power he regarded as a 'multiple success-story', the creation of two sovereign states through the graceful withdrawal of the Empire.

Impressive too is Venkatachar's assessment of that most controversial figure in the history of free India, Jawaharlal Nehru. Watching disinterestedly from the sidelines, the civil servant had seen the great man at work as both rebel and ruler. In the first incarnation, he saw how the young prince drew to the Congress both the educated middle classes and sections of the peasantry. Only Nehru, apart from Gandhi, could put party before self and unite the various factions of the Congress. Unlike the Mahatma, however, he had 'a clear concept of a modern

State.' It was not enough to drive the British out—one needed as well a 'vision of an independent India'.

Venkatachar could be sharp in his criticisms of Nehru's personal arrogance. This had once alienated Jinnah, and after 1950 had inhibited Rajendra Prasad from playing the role accorded him by the Constitution. Again, if some senior ministers of free India displayed 'the servility of amoral invertebrates', this was because their boss commanded that they behave thus. At the level of ideology, Nehru followed the Fabians in believing that economics always dictated how individuals and groups behaved. He was also too soft on communism, unable to distinguish the romantic universalism of the *Manifesto* written by Marx and Engels from the hard-headed foreign policy of Russia or China.

For all this, there was no gainsaying the attractiveness of the larger vision, no denying the enduring gains. Consider this judgement, as true and wise today as when it was offered in 1973:

> The survival of India as a democratic State—at least in its present form—is his greatest achievement. Another great achievement is the liberalisation of the Hindu social structure through the modification of the Hindu code. He took India out of the mainstream of Hindu orthodoxy without changing the Indian character. He was the most determined practical moderniser of present-day India.
>
> Nehru's socialism was largely derivative from Britain's Fabian Socialism and from strands of Marxist thought particularly related to the Soviet system of planning. His economic thinking was geared to outmoded rigid ideologies. By contrast his political thinking was flexible. He strengthened the democratic spirit—in the absence of strong democratic opposition to his unchallenged authority—by a scrupulous respect for the freedom of the press and for the independence of the judiciary.

Note, finally, Venkatachar's warnings about Hindi imperialism. He spoke the language well, as well possibly as any Tamil ever has done, yet he greatly resented its imposition on South India. The chief proponent of language chauvinism, the Jana Sangh, he saw as a threat to liberal political structures and values. 'The Hindus of the Gangetic valley', he wrote in January 1970, 'have not fully broken through the feudal-bureaucratic society of the Islamic past. The impact of modern forces has been less effective in the North in comparison with the coastal and peninsular parts. Entrepreneurial talent is scarce; there is not much avidity for science and technology.'

There was a battle on hand between the Hindi atavism of the North and the 'revolutionising forces of modernism'. A decade later, Venkatachar worried that this struggle 'may indirectly hasten the gradual wearing of the liberal, democratic, legal structure of the Indian state. In the Hindi-speaking heartland, we see definite signs of the emergence of atavistic Hinduism prepared to fight the only enemy with which it is familiar: Islam . . .'

One must have misgivings about Venkatachar's unwillingess to write the two major books that were within his grasp—the first, reflective and anecdotal, on the last days of the Raj; the second, prescriptive and analytic, on the political-administrative structure of a free but imperfectly democratic India. He did, of course, contribute greatly to the works of others. That prolific and once-esteemed historian, K.M. Pannikar, always ran his drafts past his friend of Rajputana days. When I published my own first book in 1989, Venkatachar occupied pride of place in the acknowledgements. I read the sentence out to him: 'C.S. Venkatachar, possessed of a scholarly detachment quite remarkable in a former civil servant of the Raj, first introduced me to the study of Indian society.' The ninety-year-old chuckled and shuffled slowly to a shelf. He pulled out a book, opened a page, and indicated a footnote for me to see. The book was *Reorientations*, published back in 1964 by the historian of slavery and empire, Hugh Tinker. The footnote acknowledged his debt 'to C.S. Venkatachar, possessed of a singular detachment for a former ICS official . . .'.

The Buddha of Parade's: P.K. Srinivasan

WHEN I moved to Bangalore in the summer of 1995, my neighbour in Delhi asked why. 'It has India's finest second-hand bookshop', I answered, 'my favourite cricket ground, and . . . P.K. Srinivasan'.

The proprietorship of Select Books shall pass from father to son, the management of the Chinnaswamy Stadium from secretary to scheming secretary, but P.K. Srinivasan, who appeared as indestructible as either, died in January 1996 without naming a successor. Perhaps there can't be one. Thus an obituarist wrote of how the veteran journalist stood by the values of learning and integrity, while his epigones lived in a world increasingly shadowed by materialism. Another friend put it better. P.K., he said, spent his money on booze and books, not booze and bonds.

For very many years P.K. Srinivasan was perhaps Bangalore's best-known English-language journalist, and unquestionably the best-loved. When he died his old newspaper, the *Deccan Herald*, refused to print an obituary, although they remembered to carry the chief minister's message of condolence. Some may see in this an astonishing gracelessness, others merely the mark of the times. I myself know a rising young editor with a D.Phil. from Oxford who claims he hasn't read a book since he returned to India. Journalists, he says, don't need them any more. P.K. Srinivasan thought otherwise, but then he didn't have a college degree: two reasons for us to remember him, even if the *Deccan Herald* would not.

II

Born in 1925, P.K. Srinivasan ('Srini' to his peers, 'P.K.' to the rest of us) was a Thia from Malabar who grew up in the English-and-Tamil-speaking world of Cantonment Bangalore. He studied briefly at Madras Christian College, dropping out in his second year. When the British left India he was away in Kuwait, working for an oil company. A year on a rig left him with an abiding distaste for physical exercise and a sense of guilt at being away when his country became free.

When P.K. returned to Bangalore in 1948, the Garden City— actually a town, then, and truly green—had just acquired its first English newspaper. Its editor was Pothan Joseph, a man who oversaw more periodicals than has Khushwant Singh, and rather better ones too. At various times Pothan Joseph ran Mohammed Ali Jinnah's *Dawn*, Ghanshyam Das Birla's *Hindustan Times*, and Ramnath Goenka's *Indian Express*, never bowing to those imperious proprietors. But he also kept his distance from his staff, by maintaining (to quote his follower) 'a bamboo curtain which separated the editorial sanctum from the sub-editorial menagerie.'

When P.K. Srinivasan joined the *Deccan Herald* as a sub, Pothan recognised in him a rare animal and allowed him entry into the sanctum. The young man shared his love of booze and books, and became a protégé. The editor himself wrote a column called 'Over A Cup of Tea', a title he had carried over from one of his previous publications. When I bought a copy of Pothan's collected columns from the Select Bookshop, I showed it to P.K., who chuckled richly. 'And never was a newspaper column more grossly misnamed', he remarked, adding, 'Pothan's pieces were composed over the evening Scotch rather than the morning cuppa'. 'Why the euphemism?' I asked. 'It was probably Pothan's way of cocking a snook at the Gandhians', answered P.K.:

'His brother (the distinguished Kerala Congressman George Joseph) once made him spend a week at the Sabarmati Ashram—he spent the rest of his life making up for that.'

When I first began to read him, some twenty years ago, P.K. was writing a widely-read column on foreign affairs. *His* column had no title, but was at least more honest about the writer's predilections, being accompanied by a photograph of P.K. smoking a pipe.

P.K.'s conversation was peppered with Pothanisms, stories about and remarks made by an editor legendary in his own time. When a lesser-gifted follower published a desultory biography of Pothan Joseph, P.K. wouldn't comment, but I was with him when an old-timer came up and said, 'Srini, you should have written that book.' In his admiration of Pothan, and otherwise, P.K. remained a young man of the nineteen-fifties who never grew up. His moral world was that of Nehruvian liberalism, his mental world shaped by the pre-eminent English writers of the period—Graham Greene, Evelyn Waugh, Kingsley Amis, and other such: the politics of the *New Statesman* mixed with the literary tastes of *The Listener*, ripened in this case by the music of Kundan Lal Saigal.

III

P.K. Srinivasan spent three decades in the service of the *Deccan Herald*; this tenure was interrupted twice. In the early seventies he was invited to join the staff of the chief minister of Karnataka, Devraj Urs. Urs was a reform-minded politician whose achievements included progressive land legislation. His social inclusiveness was also reflected in his staff—for aside from P.K., who served as press adviser, these included a Sikh, Chiranjeev Singh (personal secretary) and a Christian, Christopher Lynn (secretary to the chief minister). I guess they spoke English to one another. P.K. was warmly nostalgic about those days, whose clubbishness furthered, amongst him at any rate, a pre-existing fondness for alcohol. There is a story of P.K. lying in a chair in the chief minister's antechamber, stone drunk, prior to a visit by Mrs Indira

Gandhi. It is said that Urs himself helped his assistant to his feet and to the shower.

However, Urs soon fought with Mrs Gandhi for other reasons and lost his job. P.K. now rejoined the *Deccan Herald*, but difficulties at home led him back to the bottle. His condition deteriorated till he finally left Bangalore for an ashram in Coorg. He might have spent his remaining days there, except that a year or two after he reached Coorg a stray visitor brought along a copy of his old newspaper. As chance would have it, that issue had an essay by the literary critic T.G. Vaidyanathan defending Adolf Hitler. I did not know either man then, and cannot locate that particular day's paper. I know of the article's contents only at second and third hand. It appears that TGV had reminded his readers that Hitler was a vegetarian, and a caring soul who did not forget to solemnise through marriage his long-standing affair with Eva Braun days before he shot her and himself. This attempt to un-demonise the wickedest man of the century had the inestimable consequence of bringing P.K. back into circulation. He wrote a sarcastic rejoinder entitled 'Dear Uncle Adolf', and shortly afterwards was back at his desk at the *Herald*'s office on Mahatma Gandhi Road.

P.K. did as much as anyone else to make the *Herald* the leading English newspaper in Karnataka. However, the newspaper's new management could not fathom the columnist's popularity or his principle, and, in circumstances never satisfactorily explained, P.K. left his long-time employers in disgust. He had devotees elsewhere, one of whom offered him a weekly column carried in the southern editions of the *Economic Times*. Here he ranged over a broad terrain constituted by literature and nostalgia, and less often by politics. His tone was affectionate and understated, an exception being a sharp attack on Ashis Nandy, a scholar he otherwise admired, for essaying a dialectical—but in his view diabolical—defence of sati. More characteristic was a remembrance he wrote of Philip Spratt, the sometime Communist revolutionary, biographer of Gandhi, and dissecter of the Hindu personality, who in the 'fifties lived in quiet obscurity in Bangalore. This contained a wonderful cameo of the young P.K. following the elderly

Spratt at a distance, both men on bicycles, down the lanes of Fraser Town and into a corner cafe. Here the khadi-clad Englishman sat down to consume an *idli-wada-kapi*, his sole companion a volume of Freud dug out of his bag.

By Spratt's standards P.K.'s tastes were distinctly epicurean; by the standards of today's journalists hopelessly ascetic. Thrice a week he held court at Koshy's Parade Cafe on St Mark's Road, surrounded by a crowd of lawyers, writers, actors, film-makers, granite dealers, bank managers and plain old drunks. The architect Nikhil Arni, a member of P.K.'s outer circle, once called him the 'Buddha of Parade's'. The image was apt, for like the Nepali prince P.K. was a gentle colossus; broad of build, placid in countenance, wise but not judgmental, helping his followers work their way out of darkness into enlightenment. Admittedly, the audience he commanded was confined to a small coffee house; it didn't extend to the whole of this world, or the next.

Parade's appeal for P.K. lay in the quality of its coffee and the discounts it offered on its whisky, but not on these alone. For the cafe lay, and still lies, underneath the only halfway decent library in Bangalore, run by the British Council. P.K. came to it on Tuesdays, after giving his copy to the typist at the *Economic Times* (he remained, till the end, an ink-and-nib man); again on Friday, after receiving and correcting the typescript for errors; and once again on Sundays, to read at leisure the words in print. By now the cycle had been abandoned for an autorickshaw which brought him from his home in Fraser Town to Mahatma Gandhi Road. From the *Economic Times* he would make his way to the British Council and Parade's, stopping en route at the Premier Bookshop and Variety News. With the books or magazines he bought he would settle in the cafe and await his visitors.

Between 1980 and 1995 I was not based in Bangalore, yet a frequent visitor to it. I came to the city to visit the girl I loved and to do research with colleagues at the Indian Institute of Science. An incremental attraction, always, was P.K. Srinivasan. It was best to catch him early, on the stately walk from M.G. Road to Parade's, to check thus on what he was reading, to help him carry his books and help him cross the ever-busier St Mark's Road. He liked one of the tables that ran along the restaurant's wall, rather than one located at the centre. These tables had couches on one side and stiff-backed chairs on the other. He would sit on the sofa—which by unspoken custom was always his—and look benevolently upwards at the person across him. To catch P.K. early was to have to oneself half-an-hour of the most urbanely genteel conversation, before its disruption by the arrival of the drunk and disorderly.

On Sunday mornings a competing durbar was held in distant Rajaji Nagar, at the home of T.G. Vaidyanathan. TGV's salon served coffee and opened at nine a.m., whereas P.K. never reached Parade's Cafe before noon. This gave the young and energetic time to attend both gatherings; both rich in argument and allusion, although at Parade's the arguments were less one-sided and the allusions less multi-cultural. On several occasions in the early nineteen-nineties it was my very great pleasure to transport TGV, after his own shop closed, to converse with P.K. at Parade's. Their fight over Hitler forgotten, they had a genuine affection for one another, as well as an old-fashioned absence of envy. Fittingly, when P.K. died and an admirer endowed a prize in his memory—for the best work by a Bangalore writer—it was won by Vaidyanathan. Chiranjeev Singh flew over from Delhi to make the presentation, while in his acceptance speech TGV wondered how P.K. could have stayed so many years in journalism and not made a single enemy. As for myself, I go to Parade's once or twice a week, but, five years after he has gone, still cannot enter it without looking first for my friend's comfortingly ample presence on the couch against the wall.

The Use and Abuse of Gandhi

Gandhi's Editor: K. Swaminathan

BEHIND every great thinker lies a lesser being who shall translate, collate, annotate or otherwise facilitate his work. James Boswell accompanied Dr Johnson around the pubs of London, committing to memory, and thereafter to print, every word uttered in the cups. It fell to two later Englishmen, Ernest Jones and James Strachey, to make—as biographer and translator respectively—the work of Sigmund Freud accessible to a wider public. Friedrich Engels, being German, took his duties most seriously—subsidising the writing of Karl Marx's books, reviewing them when they appeared, even assuming the paternity of an illegitimate child to save his friend's marriage.

It is a happy accident that the men who thus served Mahatma Gandhi came from the four corners of the land. Mahadev Desai, who joined Gandhi first, was, as a fellow Gujarati, well placed to accompany him on his village tours, to handle his correspondence, to translate his autobiography and other works of truth. When Mahadev died in prison in 1942, his almost automatic successor was the lean and energetic Punjabi, Pyarelal, secretary to the Mahatma in the last, tormented decade of his life. In 1946-7 his place was briefly taken by the Calcutta anthropologist, Nirmal Kumar Bose, who worked with Gandhi when he walked through the riot-torn villages of eastern Bengal.

Mahadev Desai translated Gandhi's works, and himself wrote narrative accounts of the Bardoli and Ahmedabad satyagrahas. Bose, for his part, wrote the autobiographical *My Days with Gandhi*, whereas Pyarelal contributed weighty studies of Gandhi's *Early Phase* and *His Last Phase*. These works are read and remembered, but it was the lot of a man who hardly knew Gandhi in the flesh to finally and authoritatively place all his words before the world. This was the Tamilian and scholar Krishnaswami Swaminathan.

II

Born in 1896, a son of the man who first translated Valmiki's Ramayana into Tamil, Swaminathan was educated at P.S. High School, Mylapore, Presidency College, and the University of Oxford. He then commenced a successful career as a teacher of English, first at a small college in Chidambaram and thereafter at his old college in Madras. Like other intellectuals of his generation, he moved easily between his native tongue and the foreign one. A lover of Tamil literature, he also published a popular play, *Kattai Vandi*, written—to judge only from its title—in the fashionable mode of social realism.

Swaminathan was the first of three brothers of distinction. Next to him in age was K. Venkataraman, a world authority on synthetic dyes and founder-director of the National Chemical Laboratory in Pune; younger still was K. Sanjivi, one of Madras' best-known teachers and practitioners of medicine. In 1957 Sanjivi was offered a professorship at the newly created All India Institute of Medical Sciences in New Delhi. He wished to go, but his eldest brother had just suffered a nervous breakdown. Commanded by the family to stay back and nurse him, Sanjivi refused the job. For this act of brotherly love his reward was to see a fully restored Swaminthan march off to Delhi to take up a position of his own, as Chief Editor of the *Collected Works of Mahatma Gandhi*. The capital welcomed the scholar, but Madras itself was well pleased with the exchange: not joining the AIIMS enabled Sanjivi to establish that extraordinary and still-vigorous institution, the Voluntary Health Service in Adyar.

Swaminathan was the third man appointed to oversee this most ambitious programme in Indian publishing history. First to join had been Bharatan Kumarappa, younger brother of the Tamil nationalists J.M. and J.C. Kumarappa. Bharatan died not long after and was succeeded by the veteran Congressman Jairamdas Daulatram. Daulatram left in two years, preferring the sinecure of a governorship to the business of deciphering and authenticating scrips and scraps written in a hand untidy in three languages. When Swaminathan took over, only four volumes had appeared, covering the first three comparatively insignificant decades of Gandhi's life. By the time he retired, twenty-eight years later, the story had been brought down to the 30th of January 1948.

That Swaminathan stayed in Delhi as long as he did was due not least to some sensible advice from C. Rajagopalachari. In 1960, before the professor left Madras, he called on the statesman, who urged him to be more tolerant of the *babus* and *netas* than he had been of his British superiors in the Indian Educational Service. 'Remember you are serving Gandhi, not the Delhi Government', said Rajaji. 'Don't submit your resignation, as you used to do again and again in Madras. The Nawabs in Delhi will *accept* your resignation'. And so, as Swaminathan was to recall, 'I never yielded to the temptation to resign, and have, like Casablanca, clung to my post for a quarter century while fires raged and storms blew all around me.'

It is fair to say that none of Gandhi's secretaries, or either of the previous editors of the *Collected Works*, would have carried off the job as successfully as Swaminathan did. All five would have been careful and conscientious, but care and conscientiousness required, in this case, to be matched by scholarship, the ability to assess and measure words, to place them in context, to identify their significance in the life of the man and his time. The professor of English had the intellectual apparatus, but also the doggedness and persistence to supervise a job which, as one of his admirers described it, turned out to be a neck-and-neck race between the editor's age (in years) and the number of volumes published by him: Swaminathan won, narrowly, by 94 to 90.

The Collected Works of Mahatma Gandhi will inspire many works of exegesis. I have beside me a typescript of a book by an Australian historian on Gandhi's religious thought, based wholly on the *CWMG*—to use the abbreviation that increasingly peppers the footnotes of scholarly articles, books and theses. The industry of Swaminathan and his colleagues has also been mined in recent studies by Judith Brown, Bhikhu Parekh, Partha Chatterjee and Rajmohan Gandhi, all but the last of which were made possible only by a near-*total* reliance on the *CWMG*.

III

A man not given to overstatement, H.Y. Sharada Prasad, has called K. Swaminathan the 'most eminent book editor of our times'. Swaminathan was also the most reticent of editors for though he, better than anyone else, knew and understood the most original thinker of the century, he never really told us what he thought of him. Swaminathan published little on Gandhi in his own name, but what he did leave behind makes one wish he had been more forthcoming. A lecture of 1984, in memory of K. Santhanam, contains a series of biting but not unfair assessments of some highly-esteemed scholars of Gandhi. Thus Judith Brown 'regards Gandhi as a lover of power using politics to increase his own stature.' Raghavan Iyer 'studies Gandhi *in vacuo* and tries to relate him to the political and moral thinkers of the West with little regard to what he learnt from the poor people whom he loved and served.' Eric Erikson, 'who wrote a brilliant and wholly satisfying book on "Young Man Luther", analyses Gandhi into shreds and patches, all because he was totally ignorant of Gandhi's cultural background, the living creative poetry of Vaishnavism, which none can deny and none can destroy.' On the other side the editor did commend the thousand-page tome of A. Ramaswami, a 'meticulous scholar now dead and forgotten because he committed the atrocious sin of writing in Tamil instead of in English.'

Swaminathan remarks, in the same lecture, that the 'Gandhi story is inexhaustible, like the Ramayana and Mahabharata combined, and like these epics it is equally amenable to reverent study and mercenary exploitation.' As regards the latter he had in mind, most of all, 'that 'sensation-monger and wizard of the box office'—Richard Attenborough. For 'Attenborough's Ben Kingsley disguised as Gandhi is a stuffed dummy set up for floral offerings, which could equally serve, and has actually been used, for target practice by the opponents of non-violence who abound in America, Iran and elsewhere. There is no Rama without Sita, Lakshmana, Bharata, Hanuman and so on. [But] Attenborough's Gandhi is a Titan among dwarfs, an eagle among sparrows, a mere caricature unrelated to reality.'

It is noteworthy that Swaminathan does not refer to Gandhi as the 'Mahatma': he seemed, like Ananda Coomaraswamy before him, to reserve the title for men whose quest was *wholly* spiritual, such as Sri Ramakrishna and Ramana Maharishi. In any case, he sought to make the Mahatma mortal, seeing him as but the first among equals in the struggle for truth and non-violence and against racism and imperialism. 'Charismatic leaders', he writes, 'momentary meteors like Hitler, Mussolini and Khomeini, gain followers and lead movements by making others feel weak, helpless and dependent on those towering tyrants. But as V.S. Srinivasa Sastri, Gandhi's life-long friend and frequent opponent, used to say, "Gandhi does not want blind or timid followers; he wants clear-eyed, courageous fellow travellers. He does not want hero-worshippers; he wants fellow-worshippers of Truth with him".'

In his Santhanam Memorial Lecture of 1984 the editor went back seventy years to relate how he briefly met his master on Gandhi's first visit to Madras, in April 1915. Gandhi was staying at the home of the editor and publisher G.A. Natesan, and Swaminathan was one of the students called upon to attend on him. His duties included 'mending his quill pens because he would not use nibs, then all imported, filling his ink-stand with swadeshi ink and going with him on foot or by tram to the Roman Catholic Bishop's house in San Thome, the Anglican Bishop's house near St George's Cathedral, the Mahajana Sabha Hall [in] Mount Road, Ranade Hall, Mylapore, . . . George Town, Royapettah and various other locations.' Five years later Swaminathan attended on Gandhi again. This time the Mahatma was on the look-out for able-bodied (if non-violent) soldiers, but after choosing some other young men he rejected Swaminathan with these words of cold comfort: 'You may not join me now, but I shall call you when I need you and you are ready.' When the call finally came, forty years later, the student was better prepared, for, as Swaminathan confessed, he had in 1920 been the type of youth 'who talked sedition and planned strikes without mustering courage to declare them.'

In 1988, their main task completed, Swaminathan and his Chief Deputy Editor, C.N. Patel, were persuaded by Orient Longman to bring out a *A Gandhi Reader*. This selection of seventy small passages gives a clue to what kind of opus Swaminathan might have written on Gandhi, had he been so inclined. The *Reader* includes statements on women, untouchability, non-violence and satyagraha, but more surprisingly perhaps a dozen tributes to men and women of his acquaintance. The people so honoured include several of his friends and co-workers in South Africa—Maganlal Gandhi, Haji Hossein Dawood, and the Reverend Joseph Doke (who was also Gandhi's first biographer)—as well as two Englishwomen, Emily Hobhouse and Florence Winterbottom, who had helped mediate between browns and whites. We find, too, commemorations of those who were Gandhi's peers and forbears in the nationalist movement—Chittaranjan Das, Annie Besant, Tilak, and Gokhale. Also remembered are exemplars of social groups who were sometimes (but in Gandhi's view wrongly) perceived as a threat by the dominant Hindu—hence the printing of tributes to the Muslim nationalist Dr M.A. Ansari, the Christian nationalist S.K. Rudra (Principal of St Stephen's College, Delhi), and the anti-colonial Englishman C.F. Andrews. It is thus that Swaminathan gently dusts Gandhi off his pedestal, by revealing his gift of friendship and the range of associations and identifications he lived and died for.

But it was language, as much as life, which attracted the English professor to a man who had not studied English beyond his own matriculation. It is in the preface to *A Gandhi Reader* that we find why Swaminathan so cheerfully spent half-a-lifetime sorting out his words, and why we might do likewise too. 'Gandhi's literary style', he remarks,

> is a natural expression of his democratic temper. There is no conscious ornamentation, no obtrusive trick of style calling attention to itself. The style is a blend of the modern manner of an individual sharing his ideas and experiences with his readers, and the impersonal manner of the Indian tradition in which the thought is more important than the person expounding it. The sense of equality with the common man is the mark of Gandhi's style and the burden of his teaching. To feel and appreciate this essence of Gandhi the man, in his writings and speeches, is the best education for true democracy.

The civil servant and scholar C.S. Venkatachar once compared *The Collected Works of Mahatma Gandhi* to the Qutb Minar, that other monument to industry and efficiency, that marvel likewise of clarity and longevity. But to find a suitable analogue for the editor one needs, I think, to reach further back still. Working away with his loving long pen, Swaminathan was to Gandhi what Ganapati once was to Vyasa, transcribing and setting into order a narrative of astonishing length and complexity, running out of breath only when his master ran out of words.

IV

I have written above of Swaminathan the editor and scholar. That is how the world shall remember him, but to me he was also a revered great-uncle, my mother's mother's mother's brother. The *mama* is, at least in South India, the most intimate of relations aside from one's parents, and Swaminathan was my *mama* thrice over.

As a young boy, growing up in a town near Delhi, I was obliged always to touch my great-uncle's sandal-clad feet on our visits to the city. The gesture was not motivated exclusively by respect, for one usually got a ten-rupee note in exchange. Years later, I developed an interest in Gandhi. I was now based in the capital, but Swaminathan had moved back to Madras. On a trip South I saw him in his ancestral home in Alwarpet—a home with the splendid name of Dharmalayam. We discussed the Mahatma, with he stressing the Vaishnava roots of his thought and practice and me arguing that the core of Gandhi could be separated out from his religion, that faith was not necessary to understand or to follow him. Our conversation was academic and professional and before I left I did not touch his feet. But he gave me a gift nevertheless. This was his biography of Ramana Maharishi, published and sold like hot cakes by the National Book Trust. As he handed over his present my great-aunt muttered, in Tamil, 'Don't give the boy the book—it is wasted on him.'

The study of Ramana, I am ashamed to say, still lies unread on my shelves. But soon after I returned to Delhi I began a correspondence with my nonagenarian uncle-turned-friend. Like his master, his preferred mode of communication was the postcard. His p.c.'s would instruct me to meet one or other friend of his, such as the philosopher Ramchandra Gandhi, a man he loved dearly, both for the brilliance of his mind and the wild eccentricity of his personal habits. Or they would carry a gentle admonition: 'Learn Tamil and lead a simple life.' Or they would carry a patriarch's humorous counsel. So, when my son was born and named Keshava Dhananjaya, he wrote to say that 'In olden [i.e. British] days, K.D. meant Known Depredator, professional thief. The initials may have lost their meaning *now*. But be careful. Make sure that the baby doesn't wear a bad label. Krishna [i.e. Keshava] was a butter-thief . . .'

As this correspondence was being carried on, Lal Krishna Advani's *rath* began moving through northern India, spreading riots and burning bodies in its wake. In October 1990 I published an attack on Hindu chauvinism in a Delhi newspaper in which I remarked that the Sangh Parivar seemed determined to borrow the worst elements of Christianity and of Islam. Their faith, I claimed, was the Hinduism of 'shakti', or power, whereas what India truly needed was the religion of 'bhakti', or devotion.

With the easy self-confidence of youth I clipped my article, made a xerox and mailed it to Swaminathan. Three weeks later came a four-page handwritten reply. 'The clubbing together of medieval Islam and medieval Christianity', remarked the scholar-Gandhian, 'is wrong and misleading. Christianity ceased to be medieval and fanatic with the Protestant Reformation and all Christian Churches—British, Roman and Greek Orthodox—are now quite friendly to and co-operating with the Hinduism of Ramakrishna, Vivekananda, of Sri Aurobindo, Sri Ramana and Gandhiji, of Jyoti-Ramalinga and Narayana Guru. There is no conflict between this Neo-Hinduism and modern Christianity'. Christianity, he insisted, 'is a growing and humanistic religion', whereas Islam 'tries to freeze a mode of thinking and code of conduct appropriate to 7th Century Arabia.'

The distinction between *shakti* and *bhakti* made by me, further pointed out Swaminathan,

> is an outrageous perversion of the Truth, our dharma, which is not bhakti but shakti and shanti. Gandhi embodied the shakti of our religion as Ramana embodied the shanti. The Truth is like the Sun, it is Shiva, it blinds the eye that sees it. Shanti is like the moon, cool, calm, lovely, harmless. Ramachandra is chandra, the light of Shiva. But he is also Shakti, Agni, soul-force, Narayana, the light and WARMTH in each human heart, the agni used for cooking food and misused for burning houses. . . . Gandhi was not an exponent of bhakti, but a messiah of shakti. He taught us (as Jesus taught the Jews) that love is light and only love can overcome the dark evil, hate. God is a symbol, not a diabol . . .'

Swaminathan tried hard, but in the end unsuccessfully, to suppress his impatience with the illiteracy born, in my case, out of political correctness. 'From lofty ivory-towers', he commented in a devastating aside, 'our scholars look not for Light, but only dollars.' Yet he was as disturbed as I with the intolerance of the men who claimed to speak on behalf of Hinduism. 'All the "Monkey" devotees of Gandhi and Rama', he wrote bitterly, 'are now SOLIDLY behind Advani.' In a later letter, he remarked on how 'since 1969 our netas have bribed, bullied and misled the voters by appealing to the *asura* also within us. Midas and Godse threaten to triumph over Jesus and Gandhi.'

As I was to find out, other and more powerful Hindus in Delhi were hearing likewise from Swaminathan. The President of India,

R. Venkataraman, had been his student at Sri Meenakshi College, Chidambaram; whereas the respected diplomat-politician, G. Parthasarathi, had studied with him at Presidency College, Madras. In 1990 and 1991 Swaminathan addressed a series of letters to both men asking that they intervene in solving, peacably and with honour to both parties, the dispute at Ayodhya. Parthasarathi commanded no influence any more, whereas Venkataraman was unable or unwilling to exercise it. In December 1992 the monkey hordes finally succeeded in demolishing the masjid at Ayodhya. The act outraged the patriot, the Gandhian, and the Hindu, and Swaminathan, of course, was all three.

I did not see or hear from Swaminathan in his last months, which from all accounts were spent in extreme agony, mental as well as emotional. Since his death, in May 1994, I have had more reason than before to dip into the Gandhi volumes that he put together. Meanwhile, the destroyers of Ayodhya have moved into the offices of the Government of India. I recall, with especial feeling, the first line of his wonderful, admonitory letter of November 1990: 'Gandhism *alone* can overcome Godse-ism.'

Gandhi's German: Herbert Fischer

IN a little apartment off Lubecke Strasse in central Berlin there is a 'Gandhi Informations Zentrum' run by two knowledgeable followers of the Mahatma. Christian Bartolf is a scholar of pacifism and a counsellor to young German males who conscientiously object to military service. His colleague Peter Ruhé is a former computer engineer who has an extensive collection of Gandhi photographs. The walls of their Centre are lined with books, the file cabinets taken up with photo-negatives and xeroxes of letters written to Europeans by Gandhi. Outside India and the great American universities, theirs is perhaps the finest collection of Gandhiana.

The German interest in Gandhi is strong, and most of it is recent. It owes itself to the process of rethinking and researching that followed the Second World War. From the turn of this century until 1945 the Germans were among the most violent of modern people. However, after the end of the War they sought to lose themselves in civilian production and consumption. They vigorously and collectively pursued affluence, till a section of the young began to dissent. From the nineteen-sixties, the environmental movement provided the focal point for a more general reappraisal of the military-industrial complex. Germany was a front-line state in the Cold War: indeed, it was the only nation to have two sections, one on either side. Nowhere else was the opposition to nuclear arms and nuclear energy as strident. Simultaneously, and in common with other Western countries, there was also a reaction against the excesses of consumerism, and a growing interest in spiritualism and the simple life.

It was two German thinkers, Ivan Illich and Wolfgang Sachs, who provided the most penetrating critiques of industrialism. Their analyses of modern technology and its dehumanising effects on human life were inspired by Gandhi. Meanwhile, the Gandhian legacy found institutional expression in the Green Party, with its commitment to pacifism, to inter-generational and inter-national equality, and to the participation of women in public life. The Germans Greens have, of course, drawn from other sources as well, but they are nevertheless the most Gandhi-like of any political movement of our time.

But I recall here an older German connection to the Mahatma. The German connection begins with Herman Kallenbach, the architect of Jewish extraction who, in May 1910, gifted Gandhi 1100 acres near Johannesburg to establish an ashram. Kallenbach had previously spent time in a Trappist monastery, and he was to pass on to the Indian some of the skills he learnt there, such as shoe-making and carpentry. Their friendship continued for thirty-five years and was ended only by the German's death. A separate volume in the *Collected Works* reproduces the 250 letters written by Gandhi to him.

Much later, in the nineteen-thirties, Gandhi had a brief correspondence with a German Protestant priest named Dietrich Bonhoeffer. The National Socialists had just come to power, and Bonhoeffer thought of organising non-violent resistance against them. He wrote to Gandhi, asking that he come to India and learn the techniques of satyagraha. The Mahatma invited him over, but in the end Bonhoeffer decided to work among radical Christians in the United States. By the time he returned to Germany it was too late to dislodge the Nazis by non-violent means. Bonhoeffer, who was a man of much character and charisma, met a tragic end when he was executed in 1944 for his part in a failed plot to assassinate Hitler. What, one wonders, would have been the fate of a satyagraha campaign against the Nazis led by a Gandhi-trained Bonhoeffer in 1933 or 1934?

Herman Kallenbach finds an honourable place in the Gandhi biographies. Dietrich Bonhoeffer's connection to the Mahatma is little known, although his final sacrifice is warmly remembered in his country. But I now wish to write of a German unhonoured in his land and ours, who was withal a close associate and disciple of Gandhi. His name is Herbert Fischer, and he lives a life of dignified retirement in Berlin. For a couple of years in the mid-thirties Fischer was part of Gandhi's inner circle. He worked for the All India Village Industries Association (AIVIA), a key Gandhian institution, and saw or talked to the Mahatma at least once or twice a week.

As a young man in Nazi Germany, Herbert Fischer read about Gandhi in a magazine called *Tao*, published in Switzerland by Werner Zimmermann. Zimmermann was an admirer of Tagore and generally of things Indian, whose journal carried news of our national movement. Fischer was already oriented towards vegetarianism and organic farming, and from what he read in *Tao* the Mahatma seemed to combine the simple life with anti-authoritarian politics. In 1935 he wrote a letter addressed to 'Mahatma Gandhi, India', asking to be allowed to work with him. A reply came back, explaining the harsh ashram regimen, and adding that he was welcome if he could abide by it.

When Fischer finally arrived in Sevagram, late in 1936, Gandhi was not at home. He had left with his entourage for the annual Congress meeting, being held at Faizpur, in the Khandesh region of Maharashtra. The German found his own way to Faizpur, to be greeted by Gandhi with the words, 'So you have come.' He did not speak more, but told Fischer to report to J.C. Kumarappa, General Secretary of the AIVIA. This was the first Congress ever held in a village, to mark which the Gandhians had set up a Khadi and Village Industries exhibition. Fischer worked here by day, and stayed in the dormitories by night. Somewhere in between, his jacket was stolen, his passport and papers with it. The German Consulate in Bombay said they would give him a new passport on condition he returned to his country and joined the military. He refused, returning to Wardha instead.

For the next year-and-a-half Fischer worked with the AIVIA, focusing on the problem of rural co-operation. From the beginning, he was treated not as a visitor but a co-worker. Certainly the colonial police saw him as such, for in a report on Fischer they noted that 'he is a regular wearer of khadi'. When he could he cycled the seven miles from Maganwadi, the AIVIA's headquarters, to Gandhi's ashram in Sevagram. There he and his master had friendly arguments. Gandhi, ever the attentive host, ordered that Fischer be served an egg a day, which he believed necessary for the European body. The visitor demurred, arguing that even cold-blooded Germans could remain vegetarian. A more weighty disagreement was political. Gandhi thought that Fischer should return home and commence a satyagraha campaign against the Nazis. The German answered that Hitler 'was not Judge Broomfield' (the English judge who had called Gandhi a great saint while being forced to sentence him). Although they disagreed on the universal efficacy of non-violence, Gandhi never forced Fischer to go back to Germany. However, in 1938 he asked him to move to Itarsi in Madhya Pradesh, to begin work among hand-weavers. It was here that Fischer met his wife, a Jamaican nurse working in a mission hospital. Itarsi was then a major railway junction, the place where one changed trains when travelling from Allahabad to Wardha. It was thus Fischer's privilege to take care of Jawaharlal Nehru while he went to or returned from meetings of the Congress High Command. Nehru would not wait in the 'waiting room': rather, he would command the German to take him for a contemplative walk in a nearby forest.

On 4 September 1939 Great Britain was finally, and officially, at war with the Nazis. All 'enemy aliens' were rounded up by the Raj, including our white-skinned German-born Gandhian opponent of Hitler. For the duration of the war, Fischer, his wife, and their baby son circulated among various internment camps in central India. From

Jabalpur they were moved to Ahmednagar, then to Deolali, and finally to Purandar. This last was a 'parole' camp, with no barbed wire, and with internees allowed to cycle the twenty-five miles to Poona, on condition they returned before nightfall. Fischer used the unprecedented liberty to commute the Gandhian way to the library of the Servants of India Society. Based principally on his research there he was to write a book on agricultural co-operation.

During the war Gandhi wrote several times to the viceroy, asking for the release of the Fischers. They were eventually set free in June 1946, a full twelve months after the cessation of hostilities in Europe. Gandhi now wrote to George Abell, the viceroy's secretary, asking that Fischer be allowed to visit him. The next month the German family made their way to the hill town of Panchgani, to see Gandhi. They had a long and emotional conversation, and before they left the Mahatma had typed and signed this personal testimonial: 'I have known Mr Herbert Fischer and his wife for a long time. Mr Fischer was for some time in the Village Industries section of my constructive activities. The Fischers belong to the Quaker Settlement at Itarsi. They are a simple godfearing family and lovers of humanity.'

Fischer now felt that the time had come for him to return home, to help rebuild a destroyed but de-Nazified Germany. His native area of Saxony lay near the Czech border, in the eastern sector of a now divided land. Although no Communist, Fischer respected the Reds for having been in the vanguard of the resistance against Hitler. He worked for some years in rural reconstruction, and in the early fifties was posted as the DDR's Trade Representative in New Delhi. He and his wife travelled around India meeting, once more, J.C. Kumarappa and other Gandhians. To his sorrow Jawaharlal Nehru kept his distance, perhaps out of fear of offending the richer and more powerful West Germans. Later, in the nineteen-seventies, Herbert Fischer returned to India as East Germany's first full-fledged ambassador to our country.

Much of what I have related here I learnt when I interviewed Herbert Fischer in his apartment a couple of years ago. It was a cold and wet day, and although his directions were precise I was defeated by the Berlin transport system and my own lack of German. Somewhere I took a wrong train, and then the wrong overbridge. When I finally reached his home he relieved me of my jacket, set it to dry on a heater, and gave me a coat of his own. He was tall and erect, an old man of soft movements and a quiet grace. We spoke, over cups of Indian tea, of his days with Gandhi but also of the troubled unification of his native Germany.

Previously I had only Fischer's spoken words to go by, but I have now obtained a copy of an extended essay written by him and published by the Gandhi Informations Zentrum in Berlin. This is called *Mahatma Gandhi, personlich erlebt* (Mahatma Gandhi, as seen in person). I do not read German, but fortunately have a father who does. It is on his translation of the original work that the following paragraphs are based.

Herbert Fischer's essay combines close observation with sharp analysis. It gives, as no other work I have seen, a vivid feel of the annual Congress session as held in that party's pomp: the 'huts erected from light bamboo mats on bare fields', the 'discussions [which] took place in the open on a raised platform' such that 'everyone could hear what the leaders said', and, above all, the magnificent presence of the Mahatma: 'After the sessions, during the meals and at other functions, there was always a great rush. A path for Gandhi could be found with difficulty. Everyone wanted to see him from near, or touch him. A man threw himself on the floor to touch his feet, even though he was in danger of being trampled upon by the crowd. Such worship of a living man I had not so far seen. I had to think back to the New Testament for a similar instance.'

Fischer also offers a sketch, rich in quotidian detail, of the Gandhian Ashram built by J.C. Kumarappa in Maganwadi.

> It had a few solid buildings and a number of huts whose walls were made of bamboo mats coated with clay and cowdung . . . After some time, I got a hut about two-and-half metres by two-and-a-half metres in dimension. It had no window as the outer wall was half-a-metre below the roof,

> thus allowing light and air into my "room". Instead of a cupboard, there was a cord drawn from one end of the room to the other, where I could hang my belongings. The floor consisted of earth covered with cowdung. This made it firm, warm in the cold season, [and] termite proof . . . Each week the person in the hut had to replace the cowdung.

On Sunday, their day of rest, the workers at Maganwadi would walk or cycle over to Sevagram. Fischer clearly studied Gandhi with attention and fascination, for he provides an indelible portrait of his room and routine. Thus, after early morning prayers and the obligatory walk, the Mahatma

> withdrew to a corner of his room, the only one in the house which was surrounded on all sides by a two-metre wide verandah. The long sides each had two doors, the others one apiece. All six doors were always open and there was continuous coming and going. The other corners were also used. When I once came in, I saw a young man reading aloud from Nehru's autobiography, which had just been published. In another corner a beginner was playing a musical instrument. Gandhi's wife came in from time to time to fetch a lid or cooking vessel. All this did not distract him . . . [H]e sat on the floor on a grass mat covered with a khadi sheet, with a white cushion at the back. On his thigh he held a board which served as writing support. Next to him was a desk barely half-a-metre high, in which he kept paper and writing material. If his secretary or a visitor came, they sat before him. To save time he shaved while talking—naturally without a mirror—or he did his spinning. Only during very important conversations did he content himself with just listening and speaking.

Gandhi, writes Fischer, was addicted to argument. 'For him, a requirement was debate with those of different opinion. This helped him to check his own train of thought.' Fischer likens him to a chess player. 'As a chess player considers in advance the opponent's next move and his own, so it appears to me that Gandhi made his move with reference to the expected answer. He did not play chess or other games for passing time, for time was too precious for him and life itself offered an interesting pastime!' He presents Gandhi's thought as constantly evolving and adapting. As he says with regard to the Mahatma's decision to kill a poisonous snake in the ashram, 'he did not bind himself in literal interpretations [in this case, of *ahimsa*], but decided each situation on humanitarian grounds.' Gandhi was often reproached for being inconsistent but, as Fischer sagely notes, 'there was consistency in his inconsistency, as his words and actions were determined by the prevailing conditions.' In other words, he changed his mind as the facts themselves changed.

Herbert Fischer's thirty-three page pamphlet on Mahatma Gandhi is chock-full of information and insight. We learn here why Gandhi wore a watch despite his stated opposition to industrial technology, and why he came to drink goat's milk. We get a first-hand account of why he attracted so many talented disciples: as an American misisonary quoted here said, Gandhi 'seems to me a mixture of my own father and Jesus Christ.' Fischer remarks upon the importance of women in Gandhi's thought and political practice. There is an intimation of his precociousness as a conservationist ('to eat more and need more, to Gandhi was theft').

All in all, *Mahatma Gandhi, personlich erlebt* is almost unique in the literature for its mixture of authentic experience and historical wisdom. It ought to be available in English, and in Indian languages too. In other times the Central Government might have funded the translation themselves. Not now, however, when—as Herbert Fischer sorrowfully writes—'extreme right-wing Hindus worship Gandhi's murder and his murderer. How frightening that the "Father of the Nation" can be so disgraced [by] his own country's worship of force . . .'.

The Green Gandhian: J.C. Kumarappa

FORTY-FOUR years ago, in the last week of May 1956, a grand Sarvodaya Sammelan was convened in the temple town of Kanchipuram. Heirs and disciples of Mahatma Gandhi, some in government and some well out of it, came together to assess the state of the Gandhian movement in post-independent India. Gandhi's 'spiritual' successor Acharya Vinoba Bhave, inaugurating the conference, celebrated five years of the Bhoodan movement, which had just reached its climax with the donation of 800 whole villages in Orissa. The former governor-general and Madras chief minister C. Rajagopalachari, speaking next, worried about the rise of atheism, and hoped that Vinoba's mission of God would help return the wayward to their old faiths. Jayaprakash Narayan, the firebrand socialist tamed by his *jeevan daan* (life-gift) to Vinoba's land-donation movement, paid tribute to his new leader as 'an embodiment of purity and holiness'. The president of the Republic, Dr Rajendra Prasad, offered his benediction to Bhoodan, this 'great revolutionary movement' which 'will be fruitful not only to India, but to the world'. The Congress president, U.N. Dhebar, bringing up the rear, spoke of how the 'three greatest disciples of Gandhiji', working separately but complementing one another, were realising their Master's ideal: 'One is Dr Rajendra Prasad who occupies the throne of Rashtrapati, taking the country on the path of cultural advancement. Another (Jawaharlal Nehru) sits as the prime minister striving every minute for world peace. And the third is our "our Baba" (Vinobaji) who has undertaken the task of establishing a new order of society in India.' India was fortunate indeed, said Dhebar, 'because the nation that is gifted with the dynamic power arising out of the fusion of these three energies need fear nobody on earth.'

Missing from this communion of Gandhians was a man who, in the Mahatma's own lifetime, had been as close to him as any of the speakers at Kanchipuram. J.C. Kumarappa, born in 1892, was an economist trained in London and New York who joined Gandhi in 1929. For more than two decades he helped run two key swadeshi institutions, the All India Village Industries Association and the All India Spinners' Association. Immersed in rural India, a student of rural life in relation to the natural environment, this Tamil Christian had written two pioneering if now forgotten works of Gandhian economics: *Why the Village Movement* (1938) and *The Economy of Permanence* (1945). He had also drawn others of his family into the nationalist movement; an elder brother, Dr J.M. Kumarappa, who was a respected professor of social science in Bombay, and a younger brother, Bharatan, in time to be appointed the first editor of the *Collected Works of Mahatma Gandhi.*

In May 1956 J.C. Kumarappa was living near Madurai, but could not be bothered to take the train to Kanchi to join his erstwhile comrades. He shared none of their self-satisfaction, for in his view none of the Holy Trinity praised by U.N. Dhebar had carried the Mahatma's work very far. A man of independence and integrity, angular, proud and obstreperous as Tamils so often are, Kumarappa had in fact quarrelled publicly with each one of them. He berated Rajendra Prasad for living in Herbert Baker's viceregal palace instead of the mud hut which Gandhi had thought most fitting for the president of a free India to dwell in. He denigrated Jawaharlal Nehru for leading India down the suicidal path of industrial development, away from the Mahatma's own dream of a 'village-centred economic order'. (Nehru returned this hostility, with interest, being wont to refer to Kumarappa's outfit as the All India Village Idiots Association.)

As for Baba Vinoba, Kumarappa knew this embodiment of purity and holiness to be utterly lacking in common sense. In the very early days of Bhoodan, he had warned Bhave not to take the *sarkari* route of setting targets—so many lakh acres to be collected before 31 March—but rather, to work patiently at making the land already collected productive and sustainable. With decades of experience behind him, Kumarappa urged that the Bhoodan movement create properly staffed committees to work on rural reconstruction in specific areas. But Vinoba hoped instead for an inner spiritual awakening among the land grantees, and responded by disbanding the committees that already existed, foredooming Bhoodan to failure.

While his former friends patted one another on the back at Kanchi, Kumarappa was hard at work in his ashram in T. Kallupatti, tucked away in the south-western corner of Madurai district. Despairing of the *jeevan-daanis* he had begun an interesting correspondence with S.K. Dey, an able and energetic public official who had just been appointed the minister of community development in the union cabinet. 'Community Development' was one-half of the price paid by the Government of India (the Khadi and Village Industries Commission being the other half), committed as it was to rapid industrialisation, to settle its conscience with having allowed Gandhiji to be named as the Father of the Nation. Dey, who had made his mark rehabilitating refugees from West Punjab, was—unlike all other cabinet ministers before or since—willing to hear out men wiser than he. He thus invited criticisms from Kumarappa, whom he admired as one of the 'very few people left today with the baptismal fire still intact'.

The old Gandhian indeed came out burning. At Dey's suggestion, he undertook a survey of rural development work in 27 villages of Madurai, taking himself from place to place, by bus and bullock-cart, in the months of April and May 1956. His 'Report on Rural Development Work in Madurai District' was despatched to the minister on 9 June. This report needs to be disinterred from the Manuscripts Section of the Nehru Memorial Museum and Library in New Delhi and presented in the public domain. For the excerpts presented below will show that its diagnosis of the ills and potential remedies of village work is as pertinent now as it was then.

Kumarappa's criticisms of the Community Development programme were unforgiving. Most of its funds, he said, were taken up on unproductive schemes like road-building. Moreover, the 'persons who have co-operated [with the Government] belong to a small section of the public, though moneyed and influential'. But the Harijans 'are notoriously neglected,' the poor 'are still standing apart suspiciously'. 'Generally speaking,' he summed up, 'the atmosphere around officials and *gram sevaks* is not one of love for rural people and their life but one of their own employment and advancement.' The insensitivity of public officials was compounded by their brief, handed down from above, which was completely at odds with the physical realities of Indian agriculture. The variety of swadeshi which Kumarappa himself promoted emphasised local rather than national self-reliance, working towards what he called the 'economy of permanence' (roughly synonymous with what we less elegantly term 'sustainable development'). As he once remarked: 'If we produce everything we want from within a limited area, we are in a position to supervise the methods of production; while, if we draw our requirements from the ends of the earth it becomes impossible for us to guarantee the conditions of production in such places.' Proof of his far-sightedness in matters ecological is provided by the following remarks in his Madurai report:

On water conservation: 'The irrigation tanks are as a rule silted up and eroded. . . . If these tanks are desilted four or five feet, much of the cry for water will cease and the farmers can get two or three crops a year where even getting one is a gamble today. Attention to these tanks will give us control over floods and reduce erosion. If properly advised and guided, I am sure, the villagers will gladly extend their co-operation in such schemes. . . . This is a programme that will quickly raise the production of food several fold and thereby better village conditions in a very short time.'

On fertiliser over-use: 'There are no facilities [in the agricultural demonstration centres] for soil and water analysis. In the absence of these, no artificial or chemical manures should be used. Now such fertilisers are being supplied at favourable rates. They may prove ruinous in the end. At present the Government seems more anxious to dispose of their fertilisers than to observe the ill effects of their use indiscriminately on all kinds of fields in the course of years.'

On forest protection: 'Water supply depends on an efficient forest policy. The Government is overanxious on the revenue production of forests rather than their being a conserving ground for water. Every village should have its common lands properly taken care of.'

On the protection of artisans: 'Welfare of villagers rests on the occupations open to those who are not fully employed on the land. [Village] industries provide the necessary complement to work on land. A few stray attempts are being made to help with the ghani, khadi work, bee-keeping, etc. But these are not considered an essential feature of the development [work] and suffer from a lack of emphasis. . . . All village industries will have to be resuscitated to put life into rural parts.'

J.C. Kumarappa's ear-to-the-ground practicality contrasts starkly with Vinoba Bhave's intellectual loftiness, his spiritual and at times almost ethereal approach to Gandhism. Baba Vinoba was more comfortable discussing Adi Sankara than soil fertility, Vedanta instead of water conservation. Which is why when land was donated to him, he knew not what to do with it. But our Tamil economist differed equally with the dominant thrust of economic development in the 'fifties, the Nehru–Mahalanobis model of prosperity through steel plants and atomic power. State socialists and Gandhian spiritualists were anathema to him, and he to them. Out of date and unwanted in his own time, he might yet be reclaimed by us. For while the environmentalists of today are unaware of his name and work, they are only taking up where he left off. High on their green agenda figure the things Kumarappa talked of in his 'Report on Rural Development Work in Madura District' of 1956 and in numerous other writings of the 'forties and 'fifties: soil fertility, water conservation, forest protection, resource recycling, handicraft production—all this not by government patronage but through the renewal and revitalisation of decentralised 'community' systems for the management of water, pasture and forests.

J.C. Kumarappa, even more than M.K. Gandhi, was a prophet and pioneer of the contemporary environmental movement. But while Medha Patkar and Chandi Prasad Bhatt might not know of these connections, Kumarappa's name does adorn one of the very few functioning Gandhian institutions in India today. In the summer of 1996, I paid a visit to the Gandhi Niketan Ashram in T. Kallupatti, where Kumarappa lived between June 1953 and January 1960. Winner of the Jamnalal Bajaj Award for 1981, the Ashram runs a High School for 3000 village children, half of them girls in sparkling green sarees. There is also a Dr J.C. Kumarappa Institute for Rural Technology and Development, which runs courses in weaving, leather-work, pottery and beekeeping, and whose students come from as far afield as Manipur. Nicely maintained too is Kumarappa's mud hut, set in a small garden of neem and sapota trees, its one spacious room converted into a library.

All in all, the Ashram in southern Madurai is a living memorial rather than a dead museum, honouring through its work Gandhi and one of his finest followers. Curiously, though, at the entrance to the hut-turned library hangs a photograph of J.C. Kumarappa with Vinoba Bhave, captioned 'Two Saints'. Down the lane, a newish building bearing the name 'Nehru Hostel' is home to the outstation students of the Dr J.C. Kumarappa Institute. Thus have two of Kumarappa's ideological adversaries been turned into his consociates in the tasks of civilisational renewal. An illustration, perhaps, of Hinduism at its synthesising and assimilating best—or worst.

The Bhadralok's Gandhi

MORE than a hundred years ago, in the winter of 1896–7, Mohandas K. Gandhi travelled through the cities of India. He was then on sabbatical from the struggle in South Africa, and in most places was warmly received. Pherozeshah Mehta chaired a meeting for him in Bombay, where the young lawyer—not yet thirty—spoke of the problems of Indians in Natal and the Transvaal. Both Gokhale and Tilak gave him an 'affectionate welcome' in Poona and helped convene a meeting presided over by the great Sanskritist R.G. Bhandarkar. He next proceeded to Madras, which, as he was to gratefully recall, went 'wild with enthusiasm'. His pamphlet on the Indian question in South Africa 'sold like hot cakes', while his lectures were sponsored by two local stalwarts, G. Parameshvaran Pillai of *The Madras Standard* and G. Subramaniam Iyer of *The Hindu*.

From Madras Gandhi proceeded to Calcutta, where his reception was all too different. He first met Surendranath Bannerjee, who passed him on to Raja Pyarimohan Mukarji and Maharishi Debendranath Tagore. When both those gentlemen gave the lawyer a 'cold reception', he thought he might try his luck with the press. He called at the office of the *Amrita Bazaar Patrika*, but the person he met there took him to be a wandering Jew. He next made an appointment with the editor of the *Bangabasi*. This man kept Gandhi waiting for an hour; when he was finally allowed in and made his presentation, he was dismissed with these words: 'Don't you see our hands are full? There is no end to the number of visitors like you. You had better go. I am not disposed to listen to you.'

Gandhi's first brush with the *bhadralok* of Bengal set the tone for subsequent encounters. On the 1896–7 visit he was, admittedly, little known, but even when he assumed the leadership of the freedom struggle, even after he was venerated by elites and subalterns in all corners of the empire, the *bhadralok* would not take to him. In 1939, when there were proposals for countrywide celebrations of his seventieth birthday, it fell to Satishchandra Dasgupta to organise the eastern end of the *tamasha*. Dasgupta, a veteran khadi worker and authority on the cow, was deeply disappointed by the response. Writing in the journal *Rashtravani*, he complained that 'it is in Bengal that Mahatma Gandhi has been marked down by the intelligentsia as the worst and implacable enemy. Anyone going through the daily papers of Bengal could not but have been struck by the unanimity of anti-Gandhi feeling.' But Dasgupta would not give up hope. 'May God grant Bengal', he wrote, 'clearer and clearer understanding' (of the greatness of Gandhi).

God would not, or more likely could not. Move on another fifty-five years, to the publication of a new biography of Rabindranath Tagore. The authors are Krishna Dutta and Andrew Robinson, one a Bengali by blood, the other Bengali by inclination. Dutta and Robinson examine, as they must, Tagore's arguments with Gandhi, but do so in an extraordinarily one-sided way, taking upon themselves the roles, simultaneously, of prosecutor, judge, jury, and hangwoman. Poisonous remarks about Gandhi pepper their narrative: indeed, in one sentence alone they call him 'narrowly-read', 'reactionary', 'anti-scientist', 'Indian chauvinist', and, most astonishing of all, a 'stay-at-home'.

Between that unnamed editor of *Bangabasi* and Messrs Dutta–Robinson lies a long unbroken history of *bhadralok* resistance to Gandhi. Recall the famous argument between M.N. Roy and V.I. Lenin in the early 'twenties, when the Russian recognised the power and promise of Gandhi's movement, but the Indian dismissed him as a tool of the bourgeosie. Roy's characterisation became the Marxist orthodoxy, resurfacing two decades later in the attacks on Gandhi in the influential book *India Today*, authored by the Bengali Londoner Rajni Palme Dutt. Roy himself abandoned Marxism but continued to hold Gandhi in low esteem. Like that other great critic of the Mahatma, George Orwell, it was only his martyrdom that made Roy moderate his life-long distrust of the man.

The reasons for the *bhadralok* hatred of Gandhi have been many and various. One thinks that envy, the fact that a man he considered of lower intelligence than himself had the masses in his thrall, was at the root of M.N. Roy's dislike of Gandhi. But Roy also had his less subjective reasons, which were more widely shared. For the progressive, especially Marxist, intelligentsia of Bengal, Gandhi was too enamoured of tradition and too prone to religious imagery to be a reliable guide to the new society. There was also his philosophy of non-violence, which sat uncomfortably with a people who wished above all to wish away their typification by the British as a 'non-martial race'. While they rejected satyagraha, the *bhadralok* supported swadeshi; only they said, with reason, that they had thought of it long before Gandhi. In any case, *bhadralok* icons cultivated body-building and bomb-throwing, not fasting and satyagraha. This is true even when the critic had not the body or the bombs, as with Nirad Chaudhuri, whose outbursts against Gandhi are directed chiefly at ahimsa. (This worship of violence also lay behind the attacks on Gandhi, and Gandhi statues, by the Naxalites in the sixties.) There are even Bengalis who complain that it was due to Gandhi that cricket and not football became India's national game.

The greatest of Gandhi's *bhadralok* adversaries was, of course, Netaji Subhas Chandra Bose. Bose admirers will tell you of the deep deception practised on him by the Mahatma, which led to the Bengali being ousted in 1939 from the Presidency of the Congress, an office Bose had won in a fair election. That episode certainly does not do much credit to Gandhi, but it must also be said that he had no reason to love or trust Bose. For some years prior to the struggle over the Congress Presidency, Bose had made public his low opinion of

Gandhi's intellect and leadership qualities. He thought that the old dog had had his day, and must make way forthwith for the young lion—himself.

Bose's challenge to Gandhi brought together the various strands of *bhadralok* criticism—envy, rationality, the belief in science and violence. In his book *The Indian Struggle*, published in 1935, he criticised Gandhi for being beholden to capitalists, and for 'exploiting many of the weak traits in the character of his countrymen which had accounted for India's downfall to a great extent'. The traits encouraged by Gandhi were India's 'inordinate belief in fate and the supernatural—her indifference to modern scientific development—her backwardness in the science of modern warfare, the peaceful contentment engendered by her latter-day philosophy and adherence to Ahimsa carried to the most absurd length.' His fair-minded biographer, Leonard Gordon, writes that 'Bose felt that in her struggle against the British, India needed a strong, vigorous, military-type leader—perhaps even himself—not a hesitating, confused, reformist guru.' Gordon also notes that Bose's 'outspoken criticism of colleagues was not to do him any good in the future.'

For all his reservations, Bose always called Gandhi 'Mahatma'—not, it must be underlined, with mocking irony, but with respect. Other critics, in Bengal and elsewhere have tended to refer to him, especially in print, as 'M.K. Gandhi'. Indeed, the refusal to use the honorific has united revolutionary Marxists with right reactionaries. Between 1921 and 1947 nationalist newspapers would speak only of the Mahatma, but their colonialist counterparts, as for instance *The Times of India* and *The Statesman*, would write only of M.K. Gandhi, no doubt on the grounds that that was how he was referred to in the police and prison records of the Raj. After 15 August 1947 these newspapers guiltily abandoned the less respectful usage, in part to curry favour with the new Congress rulers and in part in response to pressure from readers.

When *The Telegraph* was founded in 1982 under the auspices of a publishing house with impeccable nationalist credentials, it yet made it its practice to refer always to the Mahatma as 'M.K. Gandhi'. Was this, one wonders, simply a republican reflex, or did it also owe something to a long history of *bhadralok* aversion? The example of Netaji, who did not allow doctrinal and other disputes to come in the way of due respect, is a good one for *The Telegraph* to follow. It would also have before it the example of Gurudev, the man who first approved, sanctified and made popular the title by which Gandhi was thenceforth known. If the greatest of all Bengalis thought to call the greatest of modern Indians 'Mahatma', this should be good enough for the rest of Bengal, *bhadraloks* and all.

Gandhi's Ambedkar

MAHATMA Gandhi was not so much the Father of the Nation as the mother of all debates regarding its future. All his life he fought in a friendly spirit with compatriots whose views on this or that topic diverged sharply from his. He disagreed with Communists and the *bhadralok* on the efficacy and morality of violence as a political strategy. He fought with radical Muslims on the one side and with radical Hindus on the other, both of whom sought to build a state on theological principles. He argued with Nehru and other scientists on whether economic development in a free India should centre on the village or the factory. And with that other giant, Rabindranath Tagore, he disputed the merits of such varied affiliations as the English language, nationalism, and the spinning wheel.

In some ways the most intense, interesting and long-running of these debates was between Gandhi and Ambedkar. Gandhi wished to save Hinduism by abolishing untouchability, whereas Ambedkar saw a solution for his people outside the fold of the dominant religion of the Indian people. Gandhi was a rural romantic, who wished to make the self-governing village the bedrock of free India; Ambedkar an admirer of city life and modern technology who dismissed the Indian village as a den of iniquity. Gandhi was a crypto-anarchist who favoured non-violent protest while being suspicious of the state; Ambedkar a steadfast constitutionalist, who worked within the state and sought solutions to social problems with the aid of the state.

Perhaps the most telling difference was in the choice of political instrument. For Gandhi, the Congress represented all of India, the Dalits too. Had he not made their cause their own from the time of his first ashram in South Africa? Ambedkar however made a clear distinction between freedom and power. The Congress wanted the British to transfer power to them, but to obtain freeedom the Dalits had to organise themselves as a separate bloc, to form a separate party, so as to more effectively articulate their interests in the crucible of electoral politics. It was thus that in his lifetime, and for long afterwards, Ambedkar came to represent a dangerously subversive threat to the authoritative, and sometimes authoritarian, equation: Gandhi = Congress = Nation.

Here then is the stuff of epic drama, the argument between the Hindu who did most to reform caste and the ex-Hindu who did most to do away with caste altogether. Recent accounts represent it as a fight between a hero and a villain, the writer's caste position generally determining who gets cast as hero, who as villain. In truth both figures should be seen as heroes, albeit tragic ones.

The tragedy, from Gandhi's point of view, was that his colleagues in the national movement either did not understand his concern with untouchability or even actively deplored it. Priests and motley *shankaracharyas* thought he was going too fast in his challenge to caste—and why did he not first take their permission? Communists wondered why he wanted everyone to clean their own latrines when he could be speaking of class struggle. And Congressmen in general thought Harijan work came in the way of an all-out effort for national freedom. Thus Stanley Reid, a former editor of the *Times of India*, quotes an Indian patriot who complained in the late thirties that 'Gandhi is wrapped up in the Harijan movement. He does not care a jot whether we live or die; whether we are bond or free.'

The opposition that he faced from his fellow Hindus meant that Gandhi had perforce to move slowly, and in stages. He started by accepting that untouchability was bad, but added a cautionary caveat—

that inter-dining and inter-marriage were also bad. He moved on to accepting inter-mingling and inter-dining (hence the movement for temple entry), and to arguing that all men and all *varnas* were equal. The last and most far-reaching step, taken only in 1946, was to challenge caste directly by accepting and sanctioning inter-marriage itself.

The tragedy, from Ambedkar's point of view, was that to fight for his people he had to make common cause with the British. In his book, *Worshipping False Gods*, Arun Shourie has made much of this. Shourie takes all of six hundred pages to make two points: (i) that Ambedkar was a political opponent of both Gandhi and the Congress, and generally preferred the British to either; (ii) that Ambedkar cannot be called the 'Father of the Constitution' as that implies sole authorship, whereas several other people, such as K.M. Munshi and B.N. Rau, also contributed significantly to the wording of the document. Reading *Worshipping False Gods*, one might likewise conclude that it has been mistakenly advertised as being the work of one hand. Entire chapters are based entirely on one or other volume of the *Transfer of Power*, the collection of official papers put out some years ago by Her Majesty's Stationery Office. The editor of that series, Nicholas Mansergh, might with reason claim co-authorship of Shourie's book. In a just world he would be granted a share of the royalties too.

Practised in the arts of over-kill and over-quote, Shourie is a pamphleteer parading as a historian. He speaks of Gandhi only as 'Gandhiji' and of the national movement only as the 'National Movement', indicating that he has judged the case beforehand. For to use the suffix and the capitals is to simultaneously elevate and intimidate, to set up the man and his movement as the ideal, above and beyond criticism. But the Congress' claim to represent all of India was always under challenge. The Communists said it was the party of landlords and capitalists. The Muslim League said it was a party of the Hindus. Ambedkar then appended a devastating caveat, saying that the party did not even represent all Hindus, but only the upper castes.

Shourie would deny that these critics had any valid arguments whatsoever. He is in the business of awarding, and more often withholding, certificates of patriotism. The opponents of the Congress are thus all suspect to him, simply because they dared point out that the National Movement was not always as national as it set out to be, or that the Freedom Struggle promised unfreedom for some. But how did these men outside the Congress come to enjoy such a wide following? This is a question Shourie does not pause to answer, partly because he has made up his mind in advance, but also because he is woefully ill-informed. Consider now some key facts erased or ignored by him.

That Ambedkar preferred the British to the Congress is entirely defensible. Relevant here is a remark of the eighteenth-century English writer Samuel Johnson. When the American colonists asked for independence from Britain, Johnson said: 'How is it that we hear the greatest yelps for liberty among the drivers of Negroes?' Untouchability was to the Indian freedom movement what slavery had been to the American struggle, the basic contradiction it sought to paper over. Before Ambedkar another outstanding leader of the lower castes, Jotiba Phule, also distrusted the Congress, in his time a party dominated by Poona Brahmins. He too preferred the British, in whose armies and factories low castes could find opportunities denied them in the past. The opening up of the economy and the growth of the colonial cities also helped many untouchables escape the tyranny of the village. The British might have been unwitting agents of change; nonetheless, under their rule life for the lower castes was less unpleasant by far than it had been under the Peshwas.

Shourie also seems unaware of work by worthy historians on low-caste movements in other parts of India. Mark Juergensmeyer has documented the struggles of untouchables in Punjab, which, under its remarkable leader Mangu Ram, rejected the Congress and the Arya Samaj to form a new sect, Adi-Dharm, which was opposed to both. Sekhar Bandyopadhyay has written of the Namasudras in Bengal, who, like Ambedkar and his Mahars, were not convinced that a future Congress government would be sympathetic to their interests. And countless scholars have documented the rise of the Dravidian movement in South India, that took as its point of departure Brahmin domination of the Congress in Madras: the movement's founder, E.V. Ramaswami 'Periyar', also fought bitterly with Gandhi.

The leaders of these movements, and the millions who followed them, worked outside the Congress and often in opposition to it. Enough reason perhaps for Shourie to dismiss them all as anti-national. Indeed, Shourie's attitude is comparable to that of white Americans who question the patriotism of those blacks who dare speak out against racism. For asking blacks to stand up for their rights, men of such stature as W.E.B. Du Bois and Paul Robeson were called all kinds of names, of which 'anti-American' was much the politest. Later, the great Martin Luther King was persecuted by the most powerful of American agencies, the Federal Bureau of Investigation, whose director, J. Edgar Hoover, equated patriotism with acquiescence to white domination.

Much of the time, Shourie writes as if there is a singular truth, with him as its repository and guarantor. Time and again he equates Ambedkar with Jinnah as an 'accomplice of Imperial politics'. He dismisses all that Ambedkar wrote about Hinduism as 'caricature' and 'calumnies'. Not once does he acknowledge that there was much truth to the criticisms. There is not one admission here of the horrendous and continuing sufferings of Dalits at the hands of caste Hindus that might explain and justify Ambedkar's rhetoric and political choices. For Shourie, the fact that Ambedkar disagreed long and often with Gandhi is proof enough that he was anti-national. He even insinuates that Ambedkar 'pushed Gandhi to the edge of death' by not interfering with the Mahatma's decision to fast in captivity. Of the same fast other historians have written, in my view more plausibly, that by threatening to die Gandhi blackmailed Ambedkar into signing a pact with him.

Somewhere in the middle of *Worshipping False Gods*, the author complains that Ambedkar's 'statues, dressed in garish blue, holding a copy of the Constitution—have been put up in city after city'. However, this aesthetic distaste seems rather pointless. For the background to the statues and the reverence they command lies in the continuing social practices of the religion to which Shourie and I belong. If caste lives, so will the memory of the man who fought to annihilate it. The remarkable thing is that fifty years after independence, the only politician, dead or alive, who has a truly pan-Indian appeal is B.R. Ambedkar. Where Gandhi is forgotten in his native Gujarat, and Nehru vilified in his native Kashmir, Ambedkar is worshipped in hamlets all across the land. For Dalits everywhere he is the symbol of their struggle, the scholar, theoretician and activist whose own life represented a stirring triumph over the barriers of caste.

Shourie's attacks on Dalits and their hero follow in quick succession the books he has published attacking Communists, Christians, and Muslims. Truth be told, the only category of Indians he has not attacked—and going by his present political persuasion will not attack—are high-caste Hindus. Oddly enough, this bilious polemicist and baiter of the minorities was once an anti-religious leftist who excoriated Hinduism. To see Shourie's career in its totality is to recall these words of Isaac Deutscher, on the communist turned anti-communist:

> He brings to his job the lack of scruple, the narrow-mindedness, the disregard of truth, and the intense hatred with which Stalinism has imbued him. He remains sectarian. He is an inverted Stalinist. He continues to see the world in black and white, but now the colours are differently distributed . . . The ex-communist . . . is haunted by a vague sense that he has betrayed either his former ideals or the ideals of bourgeois society . . . He then tries to suppress the guilt and uncertainty, or to camouflage it by a show of extraordinary certitude and frantic aggressiveness. He insists that the world should recognise his uneasy conscience as the clearest conscience of all. He may no longer be concerned with any cause except one—self-justification.

II

Ambedkar is a figure who commands great respect from one end of the social spectrum. But he is also, among some non-Dalits, an object of great resentment, chiefly for his decision to carve out a political career independent of and sometimes in opposition to Gandhi's Congress. That is of course the burden of Shourie's critique but curiously, the very week his book was published, at a political rally in Lucknow the Samajvadi Party's Beni Prasad Verma likewise dismissed Ambedkar as one who 'did nothing else except create trouble for Gandhiji'. This line, that Ambedkar had no business to criticise, challenge or argue with Gandhi, was of course made with much vigour and malice during the national movement as well.

I think, however, that for Ambedkar to stand up to the uncrowned king and anointed Mahatma of the Indian people required extraordinary courage and will-power. Gandhi thought so too. Speaking at a meeting in Oxford in October 1931, Gandhi said he had 'the highest regard for Dr Ambedkar. He has every right to be bitter. That he does not break our heads is an act of self-restraint on his part.' Writing to an English friend two years later, he said he found 'nothing unnatural' in Ambedkar's hostility to the Congress and its supporters. 'He has not only witnessed the inhuman wrongs done to the social pariahs of Hinduism', reflected this Hindu, 'but in spite of all his culture, all the honours that he has received, he has, when he is in India, still to suffer many insults to which untouchables are exposed.' In June 1936 Gandhi pointed out once again that Dr Ambedkar 'has had to suffer humiliations and insults which should make any one of us bitter and resentful.' 'Had I been in his place', he remarked, 'I would have been as angry.'

Gandhi's latter-day admirers might question Ambedkar's patriotism and probity, but the Mahatma had no such suspicions himself. Addressing a bunch of Karachi students in June 1934, he told them that 'the magnitude of [Dr Ambedkar's] sacrifice is great. He is absorbed in his own work. He leads a simple life. He is capable of earning one to two thousand rupees a month. He is also in a position to settle down in Europe if he so desires. But he doesn't want to stay there. He is only concerned about the welfare of the Harijans.'

To Gandhi, Ambedkar's protest held out a lesson to the upper castes. In March 1936 he said that if Ambedkar and his followers were to embrace another religion, 'We deserve such treatment and our task [now] is to wake up to the situation and purify ourselves.' Not many heeded the warning, for towards the end of his life Gandhi spoke with some bitterness about the indifference to Harijan work among his fellow Hindus: 'The tragedy is that those who should have especially devoted themselves to the work of [caste] reform did not put their hearts into it. What wonder that Harijan brethren feel suspicious, and show opposition and bitterness.'

The words quoted in the preceding paragraphs have been taken from that reliable and easily accessible source: the *Collected Works of Mahatma Gandhi.* The hundred volumes of that set rest lightly on my shelves as, going by other evidence, they rest on the shelves of the man who compiled *Worshipping False Gods.* Perhaps the most perverse aspect of an altogether perverse book is that Shourie does not once tell us what Gandhi said or wrote about his great adversary. A curious thing or, on reflection, a not-so-curious thing: for if that scholarly courtesy was resorted to, the case that Ambedkar was an anti-national careerist would be blown sky-high.

One of the few Gandhians who understood the cogency of the Dalit critique of the Congress was C. Rajagopalachari. In the second half of 1932, Rajaji became involved in the campaign to allow the so-called untouchables to enter the Guruvayoor temple in Kerala. The campaign was led by that doughty fighter for the rights of the dispossessed, K. Kelappan Nair. In a speech at Guruvayoor on the 20th of December 1932, Rajaji told the high castes that

> it would certainly help us in the fight for Swaraj if we open the doors of the temple [to Harijans]. One of the many causes that keeps Swaraj away from us is that we are divided among ourselves. Mahatmaji received many wounds in London [during the Second Round Table Conference of 1931]. *But Dr Ambedkar's darts were the worst. Mahatmaji did not quake before the Churchills of England. But as representing the nation he had to plead guilty to Dr Ambedkar's charges.*

As it was, the managers of temples across the land could count upon the support of many among their clientele, the *suvarna* Hindus who agreed with the shankaracharyas that the Gandhians were dangerous revolutionaries who had to be kept out at the gate. Unhappily, while upper-caste Hindus thought that Gandhi moved too fast, Dalits today feel he was much too slow. The Dalit politician Mayawati has, more than once, spoken of the Mahatma as a shallow paternalist who sought only to smooth the path for more effective long-term domination by the *suvarna*. Likewise, in his book *Why I am Not a Hindu* Kancha Illiah writes of Gandhi as wanting to 'build a modern consent system for the continued maintenance of brahminical hegemony'—a judgement as unfair as Shourie's on Ambedkar.

Whereas in their lifetime Gandhi and Ambedkar were political rivals, now, decades after their death, it should be possible to see their contributions as complementing one another's. The Kannada critic D.R. Nagaraj once noted that in the narratives of Indian nationalism the 'heroic stature of the caste-Hindu reformer', Gandhi, 'further dwarfed the Harijan personality' of Ambedkar. In the Ramayana there is only one hero but, as Nagaraj points out, Ambedkar was too proud, intelligent and self-respecting a man to settle for the role of Hanuman or Sugreeva. By the same token, Dalit hagiographers and pamphleteers generally seek to elevate Ambedkar by diminishing Gandhi. For the scriptwriter and the mythmaker there can only be one hero. But the historian is bound by no such constraint. The history of Dalit emancipation is unfinished, and for the most part unwritten. It should, and will, find space for many heroes. Ambedkar and Gandhi will do nicely for a start.

What Gandhi Was Not: Vinoba Bhave

WHEN the Emergency was promulgated in June 1975, Mrs Indira Gandhi got support from an unexpected quarter, the Labour Party in England. Out of a mistaken sense of loyalty to Jawaharlal Nehru, whom they had worshipped, men like Michael Foot convinced themselves that there was indeed good reason for Nehru's daughter to lock up all her political opponents—those 'seditious, reactionary, anti-national elements'—censor the press, and put in place a reign of fear and terror. It took an honest British socialist, E.P. Thompson, to debunk the 'Foot line' that Mrs Gandhi was acting just as her father might have done. For, unlike the Labour politicians, Thompson visited India during the Emergency and could judge exactly how far the country had deviated from the robust democratic traditions that Nehru had helped establish. In a brilliant essay, 'The Nehru Tradition', Thompson asked the question, 'How could Nehru's daughter do this?' His answer, in part, was that in the ways that mattered, the lady was not her father's daughter at all.

Michael Foot should have known better, as might have Vinoba Bhave, who was in some ways the most surprising domestic supporter of the Emergency. Just as the Labour Party's certificate helped bolster Mrs Gandhi's sagging image overseas, the silent support of Gandhi's spiritual heir helped justify and consolidate her rule at home. Bhave came to be known derisively as the *sarkari sant*, a sad comment on the man and on the movement he was chosen to lead.

As it happened, the twentieth anniversary of the Emergency in June 1995 also coincided with the centenary of Vinoba Bhave's birth. To mark this event, Bhave's memoirs, *Moved by Love*, were published in English translation. They show him to be a pious, puritan, and self-righteous man, devoid of humour and the capacity for self-criticism. The book could more appropriately have been called *Moved by Myself*. It is littered with anecdotes showing Bhave as more virtuous than the people around him—as a glutton for hard work (at the spinning wheel or with the broom), as a master of self-denial (of food and sex), and as exceptionally adept at picking up new tricks. Here is a typical example of the way in which the author gives himself not merely pats but thumps on his own back. 'Someone asked me why I was studying four languages', he writes, 'and I replied—because I couldn't find a fifth!'

Gandhi once remarked: '*No* man can be actively non-violent and not rise against social injustice no matter where it occurred.' He should have made an exception for this particular disciple. In 1948, for example, Bhave was approached by Dalit refugees from Pakistan who had been promised land by the Government of India but never actually given it. They wanted to undertake satyagraha, but he convinced them not to. Twelve years later, in Indore, Vinoba himself lauched a satyagraha—to remove cinema posters! 'Wake up, women of Indore!', he screamed: 'Don't put up with all these posters for one day longer. Tear them down! Burn them!' This last was a strange exhortation for a man of non-violence. His lopsided sense of priorities might explain why, when Bhave was visited by the chief minister of Maharashtra during the Emergency, his only concern was to get him to approve a ban on cow-slaughter.

Reading Bhave's memoirs, one is continually struck by the contrast between his life and way of thinking, and Gandhi's. Bhave never made a blunder, while Gandhi readily admitted even to Himalayan ones. Bhave writes: 'I am by nature a hard-hearted sort of man. No one's death grieves me, no one's birth gives me joy, no one's sickness causes me much anxiety.' Gandhi wept when friends died, and, more remarkably, at the thought of Hitler's Luftwaffe bombing Westminister Abbey. The intellectual and moral influences on Gandhi were varied—starting with his mother's Vaishnavism and enriched with the Sermon on the Mount and the writings of such great Western thinkers as Ruskin, Tolstoy and Thoreau. But Bhave seems never to have broken out of his roots. As a Maharashtrian Brahmin, he acknowledges only Hindu influences on his thought: the Vedas, the Gita, the Vishnusahasranama. Even in their appearance, master and disciple made a study in contrast. Gandhi, clean-shaven with spectacles planted on his nose, looked like Everyman (only uglier), whereas Vinoba sported a long white beard and an absurd black head-scarf—he wanted to be a *baba*, and look like one.

Assessing Vinoba Bhave's life as a whole, it comes as no surprise that in 1975 and 1976 he came to value the rights of cows more than the rights of humans. Indeed, well before the Emergency he had driven the Gandhian movement into a *cul-de-sac*. To the disgust of other Gandhians like J.C. Kumarappa and Mira Behn, Bhave showed little interest in rural reconstruction, in concrete programmes of afforestation and soil conservation, in the improvement of artisanal technology and the promotion of ecological agriculture.

His admirers, such as are left today, point to the Bhoodan movement, to the time when Bhave was able to persuade landlords in several states to donate land to the landless. But that movement was in fact wrecked by the initiator himself. Once the land was donated he never bothered to organise any follow-up, did nothing to make sure that the land would in fact be farmed productively and usefully by the landless. His followers organised Bhoodan committees, but Bhave decided one day to abolish them all. In his memoirs he is proud of this act of eccentric destructiveness. 'Even if the disbanding of the committees had brought the work to a standstill all over India', he writes (and it did), 'I would still have regarded it as a right step. It is my basic principle that organisations can never create revolutions.' To this we may answer that Gandhi recognised the value of organisation and of patient, hard work in one area or one department. But the evidence of the Bhoodan movement does not support Vinoba's 'basic' and rather absurd principle either. Thus Vinoba would not stay more than one night in any village, nor would he encourage other workers to do so. As Hallam Tennyson, an Englishman sympathetic to the movement, has pointed out, the consequence was that 'many villages developed factions and disagreements leading to disillusion and the rapid flickering out of the Bhoodan spirit.'

Vinoba was a Sanskrit scholar and dialectician but an utterly shallow thinker. Writing in the nineteen-sixties, another commentator on Bhoodan, V.S. Naipaul, measured the distance between Vinoba and the Mahatma in clipped and characteristically precise tones:

> The stoic call to action becomes, with Bhave, an exercise in self-perfection, an act of self-indulgence and holy arrogance. He will not see his duty through to the end; it is the duty of fire only to burn. He separates, in a way the Mahatma never did, the private religious act from its social purpose. . . . Bhave goes back again and again to the scriptures: their rediscovery becomes an end in itself. So, in the name of reform, the Mahatma and goodness, Bhave slips into reaction.

His defenders might argue that in 1975 Vinoba was an old man of eighty who could scarcely have led a popular satyagraha against the Emergency. To this it might be answered, first, that there was no reason for him to support it, and second, other men of his vintage took the honourable path. Jayaprakash Narayan and Morarji Desai, who were well into their seventies, were only two among a large number of Gandhians who were jailed for their opposition. Then there was Acharya J.B. Kripalani, a full ten years older than Vinoba, and a man of such towering moral stature that even Mrs Gandhi did not dare put him in prison. Kripalani spoke out and fought against the Emergency even when he was ninety and ailing. Having gone through a series of complicated operations in hospital, he was visited by his doctor. The patient was drowsing, but as the doctor put a stethoscope on his heart he stirred and said, 'There is no Constitution there—all that I have left are Amendments.'

Such was the quintessentially Gandhian spirit that Vinoba Bhave, the *sarkari sant*, could not and would not display when it mattered, between June 1975 and March 1977.

The Gandhi Who Loved the West

WHAT do a prominent hawk and a well-known dissident activist have in common? K. Subrahmanyam, the hawk, lives and works in New Delhi; once an adviser to governments, he now uses the columns of *The Times of India* to urge his countrymen to be nuclear, stay nuclear. M.D. Nanjundaswamy, the activist, is based in Bangalore: once a professor of law, he now heads a farmers' organisation called the Karnataka Rajya Raitha Sangha, which mobilises peasants against exploitation by the city and by multinationals.

One is an establishment figure, the other a protest organiser. One moves in and out of the corridors of power; the other in and out of the jails of the Government of India. These two men are separated by their styles of work and their ideologies, by their prejudices as much as by their affinities. What, possibly, could they have in common? But consider the following events of the last week of January 1996:

1. A debate was under way on whether India should sign the Comprehensive Test Ban Treaty (CTBT), a treaty promoted by the United States and designed to prohibit the further testing and manufacture of nuclear weapons. Some strategists believed that India should sign, so as to ease the tension with its close neighbour and fellow 'nuclear threshold' state, Pakistan. Others disagreed, claiming that a nuclear deterrent was the price of eternal

vigilance, its possession alone deterring Pakistan from advancing across the border. As the argument proceeded, K. Subrahmanyam pulled out a trump card. Not to sign the CTBT, he argued, would be in the glorious Indian tradition of resistance to Western imperialism. To have atom bombs, and not to allow others to put curbs on their production and testing, would be 'in consonance with the tenets of Gandhi', it would, indeed, be 'a Gandhian approach of non-cooperation with nuclear imperialism'. (*The Times of India*, 24/1/1996)

2. A parallel and in some ways more significant debate concerned the liberalisation of the Indian economy, the moves to open it out to Western capital and multinational firms. Manmohan Singh, the finance minister and architect of these reforms, was the hero of millions of middle-class Indians who hoped that his initiatives would allow them to lift their country out of its stupefying poverty, indeed to become Singapore writ large. But Singh was a villian to others, notably intellectuals and activists from left-wing traditions; they thought liberalisation would stifle indigenous industry and destroy indigenous agriculture, thus making India even more dependent on the West. M.D. Nanjundaswamy, a thinker of the latter persuasion, had for some time been mobilising his Raitha Sangha against the entry of foreign firms. His first target was a seed-producing firm (Cargil), his second a pharmaceutical company (W.R. Grace), his last that paradigm of the American way of life, Kentucky Fried Chicken or KFC. The KFC restaurant in Bangalore, the first of a projected chain, was consistently picketed by farmers of the Raitha Sangha. In a daring action, some 200 activists entered the restaurant, smashed window-panes and furniture, yelled at customers and chefs, scattered leaflets, and departed. Nanjundaswamy, who planned the raid but was not physically part of it, called a press conference. The attack on KFC, he said, 'was just to tell the entire world that multinational corporations will not be tolerated here.' He then explained why they chose

> 30th January for the action: 'This is how we observe Mahatma Gandhi's death anniversary to tell the whole world Gandhiji is still alive'. (*Deccan Herald*, 31/1/1996)

Gandhi has his uses, or should one say misuses, for both these men deftly twisted the seer out of context. True, as Subrahmanyam pointed out, Gandhi was a celebrated fighter against imperialism; but would he have regarded Indian scientists who manufactured bombs as anti-colonial patriots? Hardly likely, since the Mahatma once remarked that 'he who invented the atom bomb has committed the greatest sin in the world of science.' True, as Nanjundaswamy insisted, Gandhi was a passionate believer in swadeshi, economic self-reliance, but would he have countenanced the issuing of threats and the destruction of property? Impossible, for it would be inconsistent with his belief in non-violence, in the intimate connection between means and ends.

Gandhi is for most Indians the ultimate touchstone of moral authority, playing a part in public discourse roughly equivalent to that of Thomas Jefferson in the United States or the Qoran in Islamic countries. It is thus hardly surprising that he is quoted on every side of every major debate in India today. What is distinctive about contemporary invocations of Gandhi, however, is that they are almost always allied to attacks on the West. The hawk and the farmers' leader are at one in this sense too, using Gandhi only to abuse the West.

More than fifty years after the British departed, the theme of Western domination never strays far from the pages of our newspapers. Right-wing Hindu conservatives who worry about the corrosion of our traditional culture by MTV and its ilk; left-wing nationalists, who believe foreign capital will undermine development and increase poverty; mandarins in government who are concerned at the possibility of American political domination in a new unipolar world—all these, and more, sense a 'foreign hand' at work, undermining the unity, self-reliance, and integrity of India. The colour of this foreign hand is always white, although its precise nationality is sometimes hard to establish.

Indigenism is rampant in India today, as evidenced by the fashion codes of my own tribe, the intellectuals. There was a time when most of us were Marxists; now most of us are multiculturalists. The categories of culture and civilisation have replaced the categories of class and capitalism as the prisms by which social scientists view the world. Where there is scholarship there is polemic, and nowhere is this shift more clearly marked than in the changing vocabulary of abuse. Thus, in the golden age of Marxism a writer you disagreed with was dismissed as a lackey of capitalism or a running dog of imperialism. Now, in the brown epoch of multiculturalism, the offenders are accused of being Eurocentric or of exhibiting cultural arrogance. The class struggle between capitalists and workers has effortlessly been transformed into a 'civilisational' struggle between the West and the Rest. There is, in this respect, a curious affinity between bitter ideological opponents—and not just in India. In the world of American academics, for instance, Harvard's Samuel Huntingdon, shouting for the West, and Columbia's Edward Said, screaming for the Rest, both seem to view civilisations as exclusive, oppositional, and largely incapable of learning from each other.

Those who think in these broad civilisational terms very easily place Gandhi east of Suez, in an ideological as much as in a physical sense. Thus British Tories berate him for not recognising the superiority of their culture, while Indian indigenists celebrate him for offering what they think is a 'civilisational' alternative to Western domination. Tories and indigenists both fall back on what is perhaps the most famous of Gandhi stories. On a visit to London in 1931, for a conference determining India's political future, Gandhi was asked by a British journalist what he thought of Western civilisation. 'I think it would be a good idea,' he replied. Beyond this over-quoted witticism, it might be thought that there is good reason for the nativist to believe that Gandhi would be on his side. For in his politics he worked tirelessly to free his country from foreign rule; in his economics he promoted swadeshi, hand-spun khadi over Manchester mill-made cotton; and in his ethics he drew deep nourishment from the Vaishnava traditions of his native Gujarat. It is thus that Indian politicians and intellectuals, when looking for an indigenous alternative to Western imperialism, run straight to Gandhi.

Was Gandhi then a quintessentially Indian, even Hindu thinker? Marx's most famous disciple, Lenin, once remarked that his master's thought was a synthesis of German philosophy, British political economy, and French historiography. I rather suspect that a similar inventory of influences would reveal Gandhi's thought to be a distinctively Indian blend of Russian populism via Leo Tolstoy, American radical democracy through Henry David Thoreau, and English anti-industrialism from John Ruskin. This Hindu's intellectual debts were most certainly Western in origin. What's more, he said so himself—witness the guide to further reading appended at the end of his best-known work, *Hind Swaraj* (1909): six books by Tolstoy, two each by Thoreau and Ruskin and works by Plato, Mazzini, Edward Carpenter and others. The only Indians in the list are Dadabhai Naoroji and Romesh Chander Dutt, who wrote not on the glories of Hindu culture but on the economic effects of British rule in India.

Testimony to Gandhi's cultural broadmindedness and his love of many things Western might be found in his close friendships with Englishmen and South Africans, in his loving engagement with Christianity, or in his concern for the survival of England and English civilisation in the dark days of the Second World War. When his closest white friend, Charles Freer Andrews, died in 1940, Gandhi wrote that while the numerous misdeeds of the English would be forgotten,

> not one of the heroic deeds of Andrews will be forgotten as long as England and India live. If we really love Andrews' memory, we may not have hate in us for Englishmen, of whom Andrews was among the best and noblest. It is possible, quite possible, for the best Englishmen and the best Indians to meet together and never to separate till they have evolved a formula acceptable to both. The legacy left by Andrews is worth the effort. That is the thought that rules me whilst I contemplate the benign face of Andrews and what innumerable deeds of love he performed so that India may take her independent place among the nations of the earth.

The cognoscenti are familiar with this quotation, but I now want to offer as clinching proof a little-known story that to my knowledge has never found its way into the Gandhi anthologies and Gandhi biographies. The *dramatis personae* in this tale are an Indian, Yusuf Meherally, and an American, Bertram D. Wolfe. Both were well known in their day but seem to be forgotten in ours. Meherally was a freedom fighter, a founder-member of the Congress Socialist Party and sometime Mayor of Bombay. Wolfe was an early, brave and rigorous left-wing critic of Stalinism, the writer of *Three Who Made a Revolution* and other books.

In 1946 Yusuf Meherally visited the United States. He was dying of tuberculosis and had come to rest from his labours in India. The past ten years had been spent mostly in prison, yet Bertram Wolfe, his host in New York, found his friend in an unusually mellow mood. On earlier visits Meherally had been full of righteous indignation at the evils of colonialism, but this time round he was even willing to offer the British some praise. Wolfe was puzzled at this change, this one-hundred-and-eighty degree shift in tone and attitude. He asked for an explanation. 'They are leaving', answered Meherally, 'any day now we will be free. Gandhiji says that now that they are going, we must remember the best of British civilisation—the rule of law, their sense of fair play, and so on. We should remember it, and keep it.'

Half a century later, this advice seems as sensible as when it was first offered. I am no partisan of Pepsi and KFC, but I do know that the best of Western civilisation is still on offer, and we are yet to get hold of it. The most humane of their governments—say Finland and Norway—treat their poor and their women more fairly. The best of their scientists, in Germany and the United States, turn their research to practical consequence and human betterment; ours accumulate strings of research papers, many of dubious quality, and chairmanships of committees. Their industrialists often donate their surplus money to foundations funding the arts; ours more often put it away in Swiss bank accounts. Their public officials are, by and large, honest, hard-working, and efficient. In the isolated instance when they are caught with their hand in the till, they are brought to book by the courts, the legislature, and the media. Consider, by way of contrast, the fact that not a single Indian politician has ever been convicted and been sent to jail for corruption—despite the majority of them undoubtedly being guilty on this score.

The distressing thing is that those Indians who admire the West do so for the wrong reasons. Many of us prefer Madonna to Ravi Shankar, Danielle Steele to R.K. Narayan, T-shirts to *kurtas*, Kentucky Fried to *tandoori*: choices that seem to me indefensible on aesthetic or other grounds. Professionals warm to the artefacts of a high-consumption lifestyle, the vacuum cleaners and Ford cars which are dispensable and irrelevant to a society such as ours. No one sees where we can properly emulate the West: in crafting public institutions that capably, consistently, and impersonally serve the society they are part of. They have, and we require, law courts where judges cannot be bought; universities where teachers take classes and students are not perenially on strike; systems of transportation that are safe and reliable; hospitals where rich and poor alike are served with courtesy and promptness.

A large, mature democracy, an old, self-renewing culture—this is what India aspires to be. Does it not then possess the confidence, the dignity, to take what it wants from the West and quietly ignore the rest? That, precisely, is what Japan has done, what Singapore has put into practice. Back in the nineteen-forties, Yusuf Meherally and Mahatma Gandhi knew when it was time to stop talking of 'Western imperialism'. We, who have never seen the inside of a British prison, do not.

Internationalists

Memories of E.P. Thompson

IN 1978 E.P. Thompson published *The Poverty of Theory*, his attack on the work of the French philosopher Louis Althusser. Two years later I arrived in Calcutta to begin a Ph.D. A Left Front government was in power and the atmosphere was clouded over with socialisms. Thompson versus Althusser, the young and moralising Marx versus the mature and scientific one, revolutions rooted in the peasantry compared with those led by workers, the merits of Stalinism, Eurocommunism and post-Mao Chinese Marxism—such was the stuff of scholarly dispute. The debates permeated down from professors to doctoral students and more slowly across to the seat of state power, the happily named Writers Building. The Left Front, bowing to the wind, had inducted three or four academics into their Ministry. For the first time in the history of modern Bengal, it seemed that ideas mattered.

I am not Bengali and the place where I studied, the Indian Institute of Management, lay at the other end of Calcutta from the Secretariat. But I read Thompson, responding immediately to the strong moral centre of his work. From *The Poverty of Theory* I moved on to *Whigs and Hunters*, an account of the enclosure of common lands to breed deer for the king's pleasure. Poachers had protested the monarch's 'Black Act' by stealth and in disguise; while I was reading the book in 1981–2, the papers were beginning to notice the rather more open protests to a new forest act tabled in the Indian Parliament.

Thompson's work, like nothing else, formed a bridge between

history and sociology, between eighteenth-century Britain and twentieth-century India. I came to form part of an invisible college of beginning historians who circulated hard-to-get copies of his articles through the subcontinent. A friend in Madras wanted a copy of Thompson's essay 'The Moral Economy of the English Crowd'; another in Delhi, unknown to the first, had it. I picked up an ink-stained copy, had a second made by an ancient photocopier, put this in my bag and boarded the Grand Trunk Express, checking below my berth every half-an-hour until we reached Madras. I handed over the prize; the return offering came not long after. The Madras papers had reproduced an article published in London about a film featuring Thompson in conversation with C.L.R. James (another, slightly lesser hero of ours). My friend posted me the report; I read it and snipped out the photograph. Later, on a visit home I came across an aunt riffling through my wallet. In search of a photograph of my girlfriend, she found instead a photo of two old and foreign men, one white, the other black.

II

While I was reading Thompson and making my way as a scholar through the 'eighties, he himself had abandoned history for the peace movement. His Indian admirers were divided on this. Those who owed allegiance to the ruling party of Bengal, the Communist Party of India (Marxist), complained he did not clearly state that the Americans were 'objectively' responsible for the Cold War becoming hot. When Thompson visited India in 1986, carrying the message of the Campaign for Nuclear Disarmament, the CPM crowd heckled him at his meetings and abused him in their party journals for playing into the hands of Western imperialists. But all of us, within and outside the party, felt slightly cheated. After *The Poverty of Theory*, we had waited patiently for his book on Blake and the promised synthesis of his studies in eighteenth-century social history, which already had a title, *Customs in Common*. What we got were screeds against capitalist exterminism and Stalinist totalitarianism.

When the Cold War ended in 1989, Thompson argued that the CND was owed some credit, a claim ferociously denied by the victors and their ideologues. Thankfully, towards the end of the struggle he had begun his return to history. I had an early indication of this, for in 1987 I submitted an essay on colonial forestry to the journal he helped found, *Past and Present.* There were five referees, all anonymous, but the first sentence of one report gave Thompson away. 'The machinery of this article creaks somewhat self-consciously', it began—the style was unmistakable, and a more obvious clue came hot upon the heels of the first: 'There is a puzzling omission in the author's account of environmental destruction by the British—shikar. For a fictional account of the savagery of white hunters, he should read the novels of Edward J. Thompson, especially his *Siva's Hair*'.

Siva's Hair was, as I found out, based in Bengal, where its author, E.P. Thompson's father, had spent many years as an educational missionary. He was an associate and biographer of Tagore and, later, a friend of Nehru and Gandhi and a supporter of freedom for India. But the younger Thompson's empathy with India and Indians had, at least in the beginning, little to do with whose son he was. In the early nineteen-sixties, when the Bengali historian Partha Sarathi Gupta wished to consult the elder Thompson's papers, he was told by Eric Hobsbawm that 'Edward is embarrassed by his father'. When Gupta went to meet him, he found the son unwilling to discuss the father but most interested in the development of the communist movement in Bengal.

For much of his life E.P. Thompson was instinctively pro-Indian and just as instinctively anti-American. Meeting him at a party in New York, the writer Dick Margolis found him distant and stand-offish, very much conscious of being the great man. Thompson's mother was American, but his feelings towards the country of her birth had strictly political origins. To the upper-crust Englishman's prejudice against an upstart culture was added the socialist's aversion to economic and political imperialism. India, by contrast, was an ancient civilisation and, through Gandhi and Nehru, in the vanguard of the resistance to colonialism. Thompson also thought that socialist causes lost in the West might yet be won, and less violently, in the Third World. 'India is not *an* important country', he once wrote, 'but perhaps *the* most important country for the future of the world . . . All the convergent influences of the world run through this society: Hindu, Moslem, Christian, secular: Stalinist, liberal, Maoist, democratic socialist, Gandhian. There is not a thought that is being thought in the West or East which is not active in some Indian mind.'

This appears in an essay written in 1977, following Thompson's first visit to India. He had come over to present copies of Nehru's letters to his father to the Nehru Memorial Museum in New Delhi, and to take back copies of his father's letters to Nehru in return. It was the middle of Indira Gandhi's Emergency, advertised by the Labour Party in Britain as a move which saved India from anarchy. Mrs Gandhi received Thompson in person at the Nehru Museum. But the historian was not fooled. Meanwhile, a group of young scholars opposed to the Emergency, and from another institution bearing Nehru's name, the Jawaharlal Nehru University, had contacted him. A secret meeting was arranged: not, of course, at the university but in a private house. Here Thompson was made to answer for the betrayal of Indian socialism by its British parent. 'Why has the British labour movement abandoned us like this?', they asked. 'Why did Michael Foot support the Emergency?' As Thompson recalled it, 'Twenty pairs of pained, angry, estranged, and brave eyes waited for my answer. I did not have one to give.'

One of those pairs of eyes was owned by Neeladri Bhattacharya. Neel was then a graduate student; when I came to know him, a decade or so later, he had become a Reader in History at JNU. In 1991 I was preparing to spend a term at Oxford when I got a last-minute phone-call from Neel. 'While you are in England you must go and see E.P. Thompson', he said. I was astounded. 'Me, see *Thompson*? Where is he, and who am I? When I went to Adelaide you didn't ask me to meet Don Bradman.' 'You must contact him', insisted Neel, 'He knows of you—he has read your *Past and Present* article. Besides, he is lonely and ill, and he likes Indians. Here's his address.'

After I reached England I was uncertain whether to contact Thompson. I overcame my diffidence, finally, persuaded by Neel's caveat: 'besides, he *likes Indians.*' I wrote to his home in Worcester; his reply came by return of post: 'Dear Mr Guha, I have just come home after an extended stay in hospital. I tend to be irritable—you may as well see a bear in the zoo. Yours sincerely, E.P. Thompson.' It made me wish I had never left India. Within a week, though, came a more conciliatory letter: 'Dear Mr Guha, I am now feeling much better. If you are free and have the time, do come to Worcester to see us. May I suggest lunch on Thursday the 13th? You can take the 10.20 train from Oxford, and return by the 4.30. Please take a taxi from the station: ask for Upper Wick. Dorothy and I look forward to our meeting.'

On Thursday the 10.20 was late by almost an hour. To kill time I wandered into a used bookstore near the station and picked up a copy of Nirad Chaudhuri's *A Passage to England.* When I boarded the train I found a nearly empty compartment: the only occupants, at the far end, were three women. Their conversation and laughter wafted across: they were evidently American. I read my Chaudhuri fitfully, thinking more of what Thompson might say, and over what he might not.

When the train reached Worcester station I got into a taxi as instructed. The Thompsons lived outside Worcester, but the route lay through the town. We passed the cricket ground, with the Cathedral overlooking it. A match was in progress. On another day I would have stopped and looked in, for the ground was reputed to be one of the prettiest in England, and a great Indian cricketer, the senior Nawab of Pataudi, had often played there.

After a couple of false turns the taxi found the house, 'Wick Episcopi'. It was set in an acre or two of farmland, with sheep grazing in front, a line of hills visible from the back. It seemed very much the residence of a traditional English country gentleman. The owner confirmed this impression, for when I knocked and he opened the door, he had a collie at his heels. 'You came by yourself?', he asked. 'Dorothy decided to go and fetch you, along with the Americans who are also coming.'

He invited me in and I sat down, putting my book on the table next to my chair. 'You read Nirad Chaudhuri', muttered Thompson, 'bloody reactionary.' 'True,' I answered, weakly, 'but a master of English prose'. Dorothy duly arrived, with the giggling Americans. One of them was the widow of a writer-friend of the Thompsons. She had phoned that morning asking to come, with her friends, leaving the Thompsons no option. As Dorothy laid lunch the three ladies insisted on being photographed with the bear in the zoo, one by one and then, with me holding the camera, all together.

Over lunch Thompson was silent, while Dorothy asked the writer's wife whether his books were still in print and who was reading them. The meal ended, Thompson announced he was taking me to the attic to see his father's papers. I jumped out of my seat, eager to grab him for myself. He walked up ahead of me, painfully, the effort clearly marked out upon his face. Dorothy, watching from the foot of the stairs, asked whether he was sure he wanted to take me up four flights. 'Yes, *yes*', he answered impatiently, for it was clear he too wanted to get away from the Americans.

When we got to the top he sat down, took a minute or two to get his breath back, and began riffling through a box of index cards. 'Now let me see, what was the name of the chap you said you were writing a life of? Elwin. No letters from him here. But here are some from that other recreant priest, C.F. Andrews. And these letters are from his, and my father's friend, Tagore. After I finish my little book on my father and Tagore, I shall donate these papers to the Bodleian.' As he went through the cards I asked him the question I had been preparing to ask for a dozen years: 'Why is it that you often quote Nehru but never Gandhi? I've been a bit puzzled about this, for I think your historical and political work are closer in spirit to Gandhi.' The answer was unexpectedly tame and beside the point: 'I suppose the reason is that I have two dozen letters of Nehru in my collection, and only one of Gandhi's.'

The next year I was back in England, and wrote to the Thompsons. His health had improved somewhat; the Tagore book was in press, *Customs in Common* had been published, and the Blake was almost done. Visitors, or at least Indians, were welcome. 'Why don't you come and spend Sunday afternoon with us,' he wrote. 'Spend the night too, and we will put you on a train to reach London before the archives open. I have always felt bad about the *three* [the word underlined by him] Americans who ruined your last visit.'

At the Paddington bookshop the title which caught my eye was Auberon Waugh's memoir, *Will this Do*? I read the Waugh in the train, riveted by the irreverence and easy elegance of a very different kind of country gent from the one I was going to visit. Before we reached Worcester I put the book away in my bag, for I was not about to expose my admiration for a *British* reactionary to Thompson's eyes. I thought I would finish it at night, and in bed.

As the train pulled into the station I spotted Thompson, looking incredibly old and bent, draw himself up from a bench, a walking stick in one hand, a book in the other. It was more normal for Dorothy, who was in sturdier health, to meet visitors off the train—but this was his way of making up for the last time. We got into the car: each change of gear was a struggle. Tea and Dorothy relaxed him, and soon we were talking of mutual friends spread out over the world—the Spanish socialist Juan Martinez Alier studying the resistance of native Americans to shrimp-farming in Ecuador; the Indian feminist Radha Kumar trying to keep the peace with Helsinki Watch in Bosnia. I was carrying a message from an editor-friend at Oxford University Press in New Delhi: he had edited *Alien Homage*, Thompson's book on his father and Tagore, and hoped Thompson would come for the release. 'Wouldn't it be nice to go to India?', said Thompson, slowly rocking back and forth in his chair, addresing the dog at his feet, 'Wouldn't it be nice to go to *India*?' For a moment Dorothy was alarmed. 'No, Edward', she said firmly, 'not this winter. Maybe next year, if the doctor allows it.'

That night I pulled out pyjamas from my bag but left the Auberon Waugh inside. Somehow, it didn't seem right even to touch the book in the home of these great radicals. Just before we turned in, Thompson had offered me a book of his own: the recently published *Customs in Common*, but I had already bought this in London. 'Remind me before you go to give you a book of my poems', he said. Next morning I was too polite to remind him of his promise but, as Dorothy and I prepared to leave for the station, he surprised me by revealing that he already had a book of *mine*. 'Incidentally, I've been sent a copy of *This Fissured Land* for review. You said last night that you wanted to write a tribute to my work: the notion that I might have had a little (!) influence in India is very pleasing. But you might give up the idea after you read my review.'

III

It was an honour to know E.P. Thompson, and a greater honour to be chastised by him in print. The review of *This Fissured Land* (which is an ecological history of India, written with Madhav Gadgil) appears to have been the last review he wrote. I sensed early what its tenor would be, for he had written to a common frend that he 'was flattened by the weight of the first chapter.' I offer two extracts from his published review here, not to draw attention to the book but to illustrate the qualities of Thompson the historian and Thompson the internationalist. The offending first chapter presented a theory of ecological change, of which he remarked that it was 'not so much wrong as boring and sometimes even banal, with pseudo-tables and diagrams which plot the obvious, as if the authors distrusted the power of words. Books ought not to be presented in this way, since the general reader, or student, may close them unread before entering upon the real territory of discourse.'

Thompson gave us a slap on the wrist for our style, and a spank on the bottom for our tone. He said he laid down the book 'in a state of depression. Is it absolutely necessary that so much ecological writing should be so deeply depressing? Maybe it is, and should be. Yet despite all exploitation and abuse, that vast area of fissured land, from the Himalaya to the tip of the peninsula, is so rich still in so many resources and species that one wonders if one might be permitted a glimmer of utopian encouragement. Might the downward drift not yet be turned around?'

This was a man who knew he was dying writing about the future of a land that was not his own. I am reminded of a remark by George Steiner, to the effect that the collapse of Marxism has 'left a black hole in the history of hope.' It is true that Marxists have themselves forgotten how to hope. After the break-up of the Soviet Union, a group of leading British Marxist scholars published a volume of essays with the gloomy title, *After the Fall.* Such are the men who once accused the author of *The Poverty of Theory* of being an inward-looking Little Englander.

When I read his review I wrote to Thompson in defence of our theoretical chapter. At least, I said, none of the authorities we cited was French. The letter must have reached him days before he died. I heard of his death in strange circumstances. The news was buried in a corner of page 11 of *The Times of India.* Like most of my friends, I had missed it in the morning. But the Director of the Nehru Museum, where I worked, had not. Chairing a seminar by a French scholar in the afternoon, he prefaced a comment thus: 'As E.P. Thompson, the man whose death the papers reported today, once said . . .'. I was numbed, but had to sit through the rest of the seminar. As soon as it was over, I came out of my office and could not stop myself weeping. Without thinking, I started walking home, and after a little while I found myself outside the gates of the memorial to Mahatma Gandhi, the place where he was shot on 30 January 1948, and which stands exactly halfway between where I lived and my office. I went into the memorial and sat under a tree to collect myself: it seemed somehow the right place to remember Thompson, even if he would not have seen the connection.

Whatever the theory, in practice Thompson was a truly international person. Memorial meetings were held for him in parts of the world where his critics are unknown and will remain unhonoured. Three were held in Delhi alone, and friends kept me posted on meetings in Helsinki, Barcelona and Melbourne, as well as on a dozen or more convened in his detested United States. About a fortnight after Thompson died, I came across a professor of sociology sitting in the cafe of the Nehru Museum, hunched over a scrapbook of newspaper cuttings. I stopped and asked him what he was reading. It was an essay written by Thompson in *The Times* during (and on) the Falklands war. This was his way of remembering the historian, whom he called 'a frame of reference for all of us on the left'.

In December 1993, the mourning over—Thompson had died in August—a copy of the *London Review of Books* arrived at my home in New Delhi. I had subscribed to the *LRB* when I had some spare pounds, saved in Oxford in 1991. Finding it too parochial, I allowed my subscription to lapse. No issue had arrived for over a year, and then this one suddenly popped up in the post. Inside its pages was an affectionate memoir by Thompson's old sparring partner, Perry Anderson. Now Thompson had begun *The Poverty of Theory* by saying: 'I commenced to reason in my thirty-third year, and, despite my best efforts, I have never been able to shake the habit off'. But what rational explanation was there for my receiving this particular issue of the journal? A computer glitch, erasing the information about unsent pounds and unposted issues? Or simply a thoughtful and knowledgeable office secretary who knew that if an Indian, even one Indian, had once subscribed to the *London Review of Books*, he deserved as of right a free copy of an issue containing a tribute to E.P. Thompson? At any rate, I had not been sent copies for a whole year before that, and have not received any since.

In the summer of 1994 I was once more in England. Almost the first person I met was David Hardiman, the author of three fine Thompsonian works on the social history of Gujarat. I had known Hardiman to complain that at *Past and Present* meetings the great man looked past him—an imaginative and established interpreter of his historical method—while in search of any Indian who might be up at Oxford. But now, on seeing me in the India Office Library, Hardiman burst out in excitement: 'Do you know what is on the inside flap of *Witness Against the Beast*? A photo of Thompson reading your book.' Dropping my papers, I took the tube to Dillons in Gower Street. They only had the paperback of Thompson's posthumously published book on Blake. This had no photo of any kind. Maybe David Hardiman had seen the hardback, I thought. Dillons helpfully suggested Blackwell's bookshop in Oxford. I was in Blackwell's the same evening and found a copy of the hardback. The photograph was indeed there, of Thompson reading *This Fissured Land*, the book's jacket and title clearly visible. My joy was tempered by the first friend I showed it to. 'Can't you see Thompson is frowning', he remarked, 'he's probably reading your first chapter.'

The Other Side of the Raj: Mira, Spratt, Elwin and Haldane

THE middle years of the nineteen-twenties are reckoned to be a quiet time in Indian history. They form an unnoticed and largely unwritten-of interlude between the non-co-operation movement, which ended in flames in Chauri Chaura in February 1922, and the civil disobedience movement, which took off at Dandi on the 6th of April 1930. Gandhi himself dignified the lull by writing his autobiography in between extended sessions at the spinning wheel. Lesser nationalists, meanwhile, were arguing over whether to enter the legislative councils set up by the Raj. The *charkha* and council entry lack the appeal of protest and satyagraha; little wonder, then, that historians tend to pass by the years that separate the two great mass campaigns of Indian nationalism.

There are few dissertations and fewer books set between 1925 and 1927, the years when two extraordinary Englishmen, and one Englishwoman, came to make their home in India. Each was fired by the struggle of a subject people against their country, and each came to play a more than modest part in this struggle. At a time when a passport was not merely a badge of convenience, each exchanged their certified membership of the most powerful empire on earth for an uncertain status in a nation still struggling to come into its own.

It was the lady who came first. Madeleine Slade was born in 1892, the daughter of a naval officer. While her father was away on foreign postings she grew up in the English countryside, riding, hunting, and playing the piano. As a teenager she accompanied him to Bombay, where her time was passed in a whirl of parties and holidays in the hills. Her first real interest was in music, particularly German music, and still more particularly the music of Beethoven. After reading Romain Rolland's little book on the composer and his big novel, *Jean Christophe*, she went to Villeneuve to meet him in the autumn of 1924. She found the writer scanning proofs of his latest work, *Mahatma Gandhi.* Miss Slade had not, at this time, heard of a man likened by Rolland to Jesus Christ. But she bought the book when it appeared and knew at once that the 'call was absolute'. Prudently, she decided to prepare by practising spinning and weaving. In May 1925 she sent Gandhi samples of wool she had spun. Gandhi replied that it was 'excellent', and asked her to come 'whenever you choose'. Sailing from Marseilles on October 25th, she landed in Bombay on the 6th of November and took the night train to Ahmedabad.

Philip Spratt arrived in India fifteen months later, and by an altogether different route. Ten years younger than Madeleine Slade, he was the son of a London schoolteacher with Nonconformist leanings. In 1921 this lower-middle-class boy won a scholarship to Downing College, Cambridge. Elements in the University were fired by the Russian Revolution, and Spratt joined them. From the Labour Club he moved on to the Communist Party of Great Britain, selling their publications outside factories and on railway platforms. On graduating he was asked to go to India as a 'messenger and reporter'. S.A. Dange, Muzaffar Ahmed and others had just started the Communist Party of India and, in true colonial style, the CPGB wanted to control and regulate it. Spratt was instructed to tell the CPI to form a separate Workers and Peasants Party as a legal cover, and to work more diligently at capturing the trade unions (led at this time by moderate reformists such as N.M. Joshi). He arrived in Bombay early in 1927, moving on to Delhi, Kanpur and Lahore, in search of workers and of communists to lead them.

Yet another adventurous Englishman, Verrier Elwin, landed in Malabar in September 1927, making his way up the peninsula to Poona, his chosen home. An exact contemporary of Spratt, also born in 1902, he entered Merton College, Oxford, the year the Communist joined Cambridge. The son of a bishop who died when he was six, Elwin embarked on a brilliant Oxford career, claiming first-class degrees in English and Theology. Ordained on coming down, he appeared ready to follow his father up the hierarchy of the Church of England. To his friends' surprise and his mother's shock, he decided to join the Christa Seva Sangh, a small, struggling sect seeking to 'Indianize' Christianity.

Having come to India with scarcely a backward glance, these three foreigners threw themselves into the life of the land. Madeleine Slade became, as 'Mirabehn', an intimate, devoted and occasionally fanatical follower of Gandhi. She cooked for him, cleaned for him, prepared his food and washed his clothes. When Gandhi was jailed she took over the editorship of *Young India*, till the police came for her too. Other Gandhians (including, it is alleged, his wife Kasturba) sometimes found her possessiveness tiresome, but to the Master she was as close and as trustworthy as a daughter. In 1931 he took her to the Round Table Conference. She came wearing a *khaddar* sari and sandals, insisting that England was to her now a foreign country. When a London reporter asked whether she'd become a Hindu, she replied: 'No. But there was once Christ and the Buddha, and now there is Gandhi.' In 1934 she made a successful tour of the United States, carrying the Mahatma's message to a land always willing to believe the worst about the British, especially when communicated by someone who had once been British. The following year Gandhi chose her to find a suitable site for his new ashram. He had asked her to look for the poorest village in Wardha, India's poorest district. Mira settled on Segaon, soon to be renamed Sevagram, where Gandhi and his secretariat then relocated.

Elwin, meanwhile, had been following a less steady but certainly more colourful route. Visiting Sabarmati for an inter-religious meeting in January 1928, he too fell under the Mahatma's spell, allowing himself to be adopted as his English son, much as Mira was the daughter. He came to see Gandhi as Christ personified, and satyagraha as having biblical sanction. Through books such as *Truth about India* and the *Dawn of Indian Freedom*, as well as dozens of newspaper articles, he addressed two rather different constituencies: the British public which needed to be convinced of the justness of India's cause, and the community of Indian Christians which, with few exceptions, had made clear its preference for the Raj over the Congress. In time Elwin left the Christa Seva Sangh, itself an enclosed ashram of hermits, in search of poor Indians whom he could more directly serve. He decided on the tribals—at the time a group neglected by reformers and nationalists. Thus in 1932 he moved with his companion Shamrao Hivale to a remote village in the Mandla district. Life with the fun-loving, hard-drinking, khadi-hating and sex-obsessed Gonds made him view the Mahatma in a new light. His personal affection remained, but the Gandhian credo he rejected as unsuitable to the tribes, more so when he married a Gond girl and refused to practice *brahmacharya.* Through the 'thirties and 'forties, while Shamrao ran schools and a hospital, Elwin wrote a series of landmark books on the culture and predicament of the tribes. At least two of these, *The Baiga* (1939), and *The Muria and their Ghotul* (1947), are adornments to science and to literature. In one of the delicious paradoxes in which the history of anthropology abounds, this former Oxford don became the best-known spokesman for the rights of the Indian Adivasi.

Elwin knew Mirabehn and did not always see eye-to-eye with her. He writes of a weekend they spent in a cottage in Juhu, owned by one of Gandhi's benefactors. It was a hot day, but as they were eating lunch Mira rose from the table to shut the windows. When Elwin complained he got this answer: 'The breeze is carrying salt particles. These may enter the food, and inflame your passions.' Elwin does not tell us of a sequel, long delayed, which is one of the most effectively suppressed secrets of Gandhiana. In the late nineteen-thirties, when she was in her late forties, Mirabehn fell passionately in love with the Sikh revolutionary Prithvi Singh Azad. The love was unrequited and a grieving Mira left Gandhi to find solace in the Himalaya.

Unlike Mira and Elwin, Spratt was never a Gandhi devotee, but living in India, at the time he did, he could hardly escape his influence. In March 1929 he was arrested and put in jail with several of his comrades in what came to be known as the Meerut Conspiracy Case. To his surprise, although the Communists had attacked the Congress as 'bourgeois nationalists' it was Congressmen such as Dewan Chamanlal and Dr Saifuddin Kitchlew who organised their defence. Convicted of 'conspiring to deprive the King Emperor of his sovereignty of British India', Spratt spent his time in jail reading a good deal of Gandhi. As he recalled in his fragmentary memoir, *Blowing up India* (1955), the Mahatma's 'ideas and personality strongly attracted the puritan in me and I was inclined to think that in internal Indian affairs he might be partly right.'

When he was released in June 1936 Spratt made the trek to Sevagram. A few pointed questions were asked, and answered, whereupon the Englishman settled down in Madras—he had fallen in love and was to soon marry a Tamil girl. In 1938 the now long-burnt-out Huxley Press (located at 114 Armenian Street, George Town) published his *Gandhism: An Analysis*, a tome of 515 pages, the most complete account of its subject to have appeared, and even now the most insightful work on Gandhi by a Marxist or quasi-Marxist. Earlier biographies, such as those by Joseph Doke and C.F. Andrews, had been highly reverential and totally authorised. Spratt's work was the first narrative account that sought to place incidents and campaigns in the context of contemporary history as well as the Mahatma's always developing personality. The renegade Leninist was deeply impressed by Gandhi's lack of dogma and his readiness to engage opponents in debate. Refusing to accept the class-reductionism of his peers, he maintained that the freedom movement was 'India's introduction to democracy', the first attempt to make of the people a political force. He acknowledged that Gandhi's non-violence was religiously inspired and not, as other Communists claimed, a 'class dodge' to tame the revolutionary instincts of the masses. In manner and choice of symbols the Mahatma sometimes seemed to be a backward-looking medievalist, but as Spratt most perceptively pointed out, 'Mr Gandhi's way may after all prove to be the true way to the modernisation of India . . . The contact of his mind is such as to promote in others the interest in practical matters and the empirical outlook which he himself possesses, the qualities which lead to scientific and technical advance.' All in all, concluded this Englishman and Marxist, 'Mr Gandhi is the Empire's most distinguished citizen.'

When Gandhi died in January 1948 Mira sent a message from her ashram in Rishikesh: 'For me God and Bapu have become one.' Spratt, who was by now an associate of M.N. Roy, wrote to Roy's wife that the assassination was

> certainly a blow to me. . . . I read his stuff quite a lot at one time, and went to Wardha and had long interviews with him. My feelings were distinctly of the filial order. One likes to criticise a person of that type, just as one likes to criticise any firmly established institutions—always subject to the proviso that one's critical suggestions are not carried out. That is the unspoken proviso attached to the fulminations of any British revolutionary.

Elwin, at the time, was in Benares, serving briefly as the deputy-director of the Anthropological Survey of India. He had stayed away from Gandhi in his last years, but now the old, proprietorial feelings of the disciple came back to him. As he wrote in his diary on the 31st of January, he was 'all day preoccupied with Bapu's funeral. Listened to broadcast, off and on, from 11 am to 5 pm.' A week later, he sat in a train compartment where a CID man and two merchants 'discussed, at the top of their voices, Gandhiji's assassination, but I do not think their hearts really bled for him.' Elwin's heart did, certainly, for as he wrote in his autobiography, he felt 'very sorry' about his isolation from the Mahatma 'in his last years [when] Gandhi reached his highest stature.'

The Mahatma was dead, but his country was free, and for these three critical admirers there was work to be done. Mirabehn, in the Himalaya, took it upon herself to issue warnings about the direction of economic development in post-Gandhian India. To Rajendra Prasad, now president, and to Jawaharlal Nehru, now prime minister, this former colleague in the jails addressed a stream of embarrassingly persistent letters. Why did the government promote large dams when irrigation needs could be more cheaply and efficiently met by small dams and tanks? Would not the chemicalisation of agriculture damage the soil and increase our foreign debt? Why did the Uttar Pradesh forest department plant the locally useless *chir* pine over the useful and ecologically more desirable *banj* oak?

Verrier Elwin had questions of his own, but was more lucky in the response. For Nehru, a kind of tribal lover himself, picked him up from his Mandla home and appointed him an adviser to the administration of the North East Frontier Agency. After twenty years of dogged work among the Madhya Pradesh and Orissa tribals, Elwin was despairing of their fate. Only the mosquito, he wrote bitterly, was the true protector of the aboriginals of central India: 'May it infect every pietist and reformer with cerebral malaria.' But in isolated NEFA, where the missionaries and moneylenders had not yet reached, there was hope. Touring among new and ever-more attractive tribes, training young officers with the mandate of the uncrowned King of Delhi, Elwin achieved much fame (and, it must be said, some notoriety) as the Philosopher of NEFA whose philosophy of tribal welfare was summed up in the phrase *festina lente*, 'make haste slowly'.

Philip Spratt, meanwhile, was leading an unglamorous existence in Bangalore, writing for and helping edit the weekly *Mysindia*, described by one who then read it as the '*Blitz* of the Right, only more intelligent'. For Spratt had moved from Communism to Capitalism, stopping for some time in the camp of M.N. Roy, another lapsed Marxist who had built, for himself and a few chosen others, the halfway house of 'radical humanism'. His marriage to an Indian helped Spratt see the fundamental incompatibility between patriotism and communism. 'The communist', he wrote in 1952, 'defends not his own motherland, but Russia. All his love is concentrated on Russia and its leaders: all his hatred on their opponents, especially the rulers of his own country.' He now dismissed communism, his old faith, as 'political dishonesty systematised'.

Spratt seems to have composed about half of each issue of *Mysindia*, writing in praise of Gandhi sometimes, and in criticism of Nehru all the time. He was active in such groups as the Indian Congress for Cultural Freedom, which asked that we take the American side in the Cold War, and the Forum for Free Enterprise, which, long before the International Monetary Fund was to do so, had urged that the Indian market be let loose for capitalists to exploit and for the people to prosper in. Kashmir was another of Spratt's obsessions. Give up the valley and keep Jammu and Ladakh, he recommended in an editorial of 1951, and in a succession of increasingly combative essays in coming years. He thought that the army would otherwise be in Kashmir forever, a drain on our exchequer and on the national morale. If only Nehru had listened to Spratt, then! Even now there is space for an anthology of Spratt's writings from the pages of a South Indian journal that is undeservedly forgotten.

Our three exemplars were joined in 1957 by a fourth British-born Indian. J.B.S. Haldane was born in 1892, into the intellectual aristocracy of Oxbridge. His father was a great physiologist, and the son cut his scientific teeth helping him conduct hazardous experiments on their own bodies. After graduating from Oxford the younger Haldane fought in the First World War. Wounded in Iraq, he was sent to India to recover and at this time 'determined to come back as soon as I could associate with Indians on a footing of equality'. That day was distant, so Haldane began an active and prodigious career in British science. He is recognised as one of the half-dozen top biologists of the century and as unquestionably the most versatile. He made fundamental contributions to evolutionary theory, biochemistry, and genetics. A committed Marxist, he also wrote a weekly column for the *Daily Worker* and, with J.D. Bernal and Lancelot Hogben, was a major figure in the popular science movement. A poem he wrote, 'Cancer's A Funny Thing', was anthologised in the *Oxford Book of Twentieth Century Verse*. Yet he once claimed disarmingly that 'the best and most important action of my life' was to find jobs in England for Jewish scientists fleeing Hitler.

All this may be found in *JBS*, Ronald Clark's biography of Haldane. But Clark guiltily skips past the last eight years of Haldane's life, when he renounced British citizenship to live and work in India. He was almost sixty-five when he came, his advanced age—as much as his great scientific distinction—marking him out from the others I have written about here. The conventional wisdom is that Haldane left England after the Suez crisis, not wishing to live any more in that 'imperialist' country. The French historian of science Francis Zimmerman has speculated that he wanted to take biology out of the laboratory and root it in the soil of the tropics. His sister, the novelist and travel-writer Naomi Mitchison, thinks he was attracted by the decency and moderation of the Indian leaders of the day who had been persecuted and put in jail by politicians who themselves fomented two great wars and numerous lesser ones. After the Lysenko fiasco Haldane was also disillusioned with the Soviet Union, and the figure of Nehru seemed more appealing than Stalin or Churchill ever could be.

Anway, when Haldane moved to Calcutta with his biologist wife he became totally Indian. He converted to vegetarianism and learnt adequate Sanskrit to shame his Brahmin students. He wore Indian dress, even on his visits back to Europe. For a Royal Society reception in London in 1961 he put on a saffron *dhoti*, with Naomi Mitchison inserting the safety pins. It is however recorded that he complained about the absence of a French typewriter at the Indian Statistical Institute (where he then worked)— how was he to carry on his controversy with Jean Paul Sartre? He gathered around him a bunch of devoted students whose recollections have appeared in a wonderful centenary album produced by the ISI in 1992. Space permits the reproduction here of only one Haldanism: his sharpness with a self-absorbed assistant: 'You are always telling me what is happening in your own mind, but science begins with an interest in things outside yourself.'

Within a few years Haldane had quarelled with Prasanta Chandra Mahalanobis, the ISI's founder-director. He took his wife, laboratory and assistants off to Bhubaneshwar, where the science-minded chief minister, Biju Patnaik, had given him land. In the time alloted to him

Haldane was not quite able to build a school of Indian biology, but he did put his finger on where its originality might lie. He had befriended the ornithologist Salim Ali, who preferred to study birds in the wild, rather than by shooting and stuffing them. This Muslim inspired the Christian to a series of suggestive essays on the possibilities of a Hindu biology. The greatest of modern Hindus, wrote Haldane, 'was quite clear that men have a duty of non-violence to animals. And there is no reason why biological research in India should not be conducted on Gandhian principles.' A non-violent genetics would study generations of ducks bred in tanks and observed with such simple instruments as a balance, a tape measure, and a chart of colours. The more courageous among the non-violent Indian biologists would experiment on themselves to perfect vaccines for immunising villagers against snake-bite. 'Two or three of them might die of snake bite before the process was fully worked out. If so they would not have died in vain.' Thus would India's greatest contribution to world culture, non-violence, be married to the scientific method, Europe's greatest contribution, with the hope that 'their offspring may raise mankind to a new level.'

Haldane died of cancer in Bhubaneshwar in December 1964, a verse from the Gita on his lips. Elwin died earlier that year, but not before finishing his memoirs, *The Tribal World of Verrier Elwin.* This is a crystal-clear summation of his work, which ranks with the self-testimonies of Gandhi, Nehru, Nirad Chaudhuri and Salim Ali as among the finest of Indian autobiographies. Spratt had almost a decade to live, which was spent for the most part in the service of C. Rajagopalachari's Madras-based journal *Swarajya.* In 1966 he published *Hindu Culture and Personality,* a densely written book that, at least to me, lacks the force and directness of his political writings. But Spratt himself regarded it as his opus, and I am told it has been industriously mined by later psychoanalysts.

Mirabehn left India in 1960, for Austria, and died only in 1982. In her new home she was visited (separately) by Ved Mehta and Sudhir Kakar. Both have since claimed, in print, that she had lost interest in Gandhi and India. The truth is otherwise. For, as her letters show,

Mirabehn never lost sight of her Master and their land. In the late 'sixties she came across a report in the *Hindustan Times* about the sufferings of the displaced and yet-to-be rehabilitated oustees of the Bhakra-Nangal project. Here was an injustice in search of a satyagraha; she wrote to Sarvodaya workers in India, and this was twenty years before Medha Patkar began her struggle for the victims of another dam. When the *International Herald Tribune* carried an article in praise of Lewis Mumford's ecological writings, she wrote in dryly that Gandhi had said much the same thing, albeit half a century earlier. And as Sir Richard Attenborough has written, Mirabehn provided 'unstinting encouragement' to him in the making of his film, 'relating anecdote after anecdote' and passing on the majority of Gandhi's letters to her. She also wrote to Morarji Desai, the prime minister, asking him to honour Nehru's original commitment to finance *Gandhi*. But when Attenborough sent her some early clips, she complained that Geraldine James, who played her, 'was so very much more beautiful than herself.'

The anthropologist Shiv Visvanathan has spoken of the 'Other Side of the Raj', the men and women who, despite their white skin, rejected colonialism to make their home in and take a stand on behalf of India. He has in mind people such as Annie Besant and Sister Nivedita, lovers of Hindus and Hinduism both, and B.G. Horniman, the great liberal journalist whose name, despite years of Shiv Sena rule, still adorns a major intersection in Mumbai. There are other names, now less well-known perhaps, and also one which, because of the saintliness of its bearer and his friendship with Gandhi and Tagore, towers above them all—Charles Freer Andrews.

Older histories of Indian nationalism generally allowed some space to these 'foreign friends of our freedom'. But the emerging histories of the Republic do not seem to remember the Britons who stayed on or—as in Haldane's case—came here after 1947; staying on, that is, not as boxwallahs and brown sahibs but as patriotic and public-spirited Indians. The four profiled here were all eminent Nehruvians, although two were more likely to oppose Jawaharlal Nehru's policies, while the other two not only supported them but also claimed a certain intimacy with their begetter—these two, Haldane and Elwin, died, poignantly, in the same year as Nehru.

All four furthered our understanding of Gandhi, taking his thought in directions the Mahatma might himself have hardly anticipated. In their wide-ranging careers they walked over or caressed most parts of the land: Mirabehn working in the west and far north, Elwin in the west, centre and north-east, Haldane in the east, and Spratt, splendidly and singularly, in the south. Two, Spratt and Mira, remained single-minded to the end, exchanging one set of certitudes for another. Two, Haldane and Elwin, had dazzlingly diverse interests, and also communicated them to diverse audiences, writing ferociously for the respectable and not-so-respectable press. Both were dogmatic in their youth, wedded to Marx and Christ respectively, but both came to embrace the Middle Way of the Buddha.

Elwin and Spratt married Indians and had Indian children. Mira wanted to but could not, while Haldane was already married when he came— significantly, his wife stayed on after his death, herself dying in 1978 of a jackal bite while on a field trip in the forests of Adilabad. But all four rejected bourgeois conventionality; they were emphatically, and all through, *risk-takers.*

Curiously, except for a brief acquaintance between Elwin and Mira, the four did not know each other. But we can see them together, a quartet of activists and scholars who ennobled and enriched the life of independent India.

Exiles in Their English Peace: Karl Marx and Nirad Chaudhuri

IN June 1994, briefly in London, I asked my host, Gopal Gandhi, to accompany me on a trip to Marx's grave in Highgate. We set off on a warm Saturday afternoon by tube to Highgate station. We came out of the station into the sun and proceeded to ask the first man we saw for directions to the cemetery. 'Climb the stairs onto the main road, and turn right', he said. 'It's about two hundred yards away, on your right—you can't miss it'. We did as we were told and started walking. A vista of houses and shops, street fronted, of stone, built in the early years of the century, was all we saw on both sides of the road. A park on the right-hand side briefly intervened but there was no sign of any graves within. We walked on, down a gently sloping road, talking, as two Indians would, of Marx and Mahatma Gandhi. I told Gopal the story of how Gandhi, in his seventy-fifth year, tried to read *Das Capital* while interred in the Aga Khan Palace in Poona in 1942–3, but found the going too difficult and gave up after the daunting first chapter on commodity fetishism. Gopal told me, in turn, the story of a press conference conducted by Gandhi's successor, Vinoba Bhave, at the height of the 'Bhoodan' movement. Vinoba was asked the difference between Gandhism and Communism, and he answered, 'Communism is Gandhism plus Violence'. This quickwitted reply pleased the reporters, but afterwards the sage *manqué* was brought down to earth by Jayaprakash Narayan, who challenged him: 'If Communism is Gandhism plus Violence, is Gandhism merely Communism *minus* Violence?'

We talked and walked till the two hundred yards became two thousand. The houses were now set further apart from the road, visibly newer and with well-kept lawns—we were in suburbia. We had been the victims, we realised, of an ill-informed 'know-all'. Then we spied a petrol pump, the equivalent in London of the *paanwallah,* so to speak, the station where everybody calls and where the employees make it their business to know every local landmark. '*Here* is where we'll find out', said both of us together, and walked in. An adorable old lady sitting behind the counter told us we would have to go all the way back to where we began. 'Just before you reach the tube station', she said, 'take the curving road to the right, climb Highgate hill, and there is the cemetery, on the left, as you go over the crest. You can't miss it.' And then, as we thanked her and went out, 'Give Marx my love.'

We retraced our steps. Highgate hill proved to be a hard and surprisingly steep climb. I had not realised that London could have slopes as steep as any in Shimla. The day was hot and I was overdressed, guided by my learned notions of an English summer day, as mistaken as my notions of the English landscape. The sweat dripped through my shirt on to my jacket and I began to feel desperately thirsty, almost dehydrated. I yearned for a cold drink but was too diffident to suggest it to Gopal, somehow feeling it would be contrary to the spirit of the ascetic Gandhi and the austere Marx.

At last we reached the top of the hill and began our descent. We passed older houses once again, with the odd sign marking the imminent redevelopment of some of them as apartment blocks. A post office and a bank, but still no cemetery. Suddenly my mind recalled an essay by the Oxford historian Richard Cobb about a walk through the streets of Paris in search of the grave of the French historian Albert Soboul. Cobb had as his companion a Chinese colleague who had never met Soboul but worshipped him as the great Marxist interpreter of the

French Revolution. The Englishman had known the historian well, as something of a charlatan in real life, a feckless husband and inventor of imaginary tales about his heroism in the Resistance—but he could not bring himself to tell his Chinese friend the truth.

We came down the slope to a busy road. Do we turn right, or left? Left, said the man we asked, 'then take the second turning right, walk to the church, and then left again down Swayne's lane. Down the hill, and it is to your left. You can't miss it.' These were precise directions, and they were correct. Ten minutes later we were at the gates of Highgate cemetery. We arrived at the very moment that they were being closed, with a lock being put through the latch. 'Sorry,' said the caretaker, 'but it is five minutes past five' (closing time). 'At home', remarked Gopal, 'we would have been able to ask him to "adjust".'

II

Six months later, on New Year's Day, I was back in London. We had taken the precaution of phoning the cemetery to find out the hours it was open to visitors. We left Gopal's house in Green Park after lunch but took the wrong connection at Euston. Service was erratic on the holiday and by the time we changed trains and reached Highgate it was half past three, but thirty minutes to closing time, put forward an hour in winter. As we came out of the station it was cold and windy, and I was grateful for the protection offered by the same jacket I had worn in June. A couple of hopeful enquiries and we found our way, somehow, to Highgate hill. We ran up and down, turned left and then right to Swayne's lane. We reached the cemetery at ten minutes to four, the last visitors of the day. Two minutes later we were at Marx's grave.

It was, in fact, a tombstone eight feet high with a polished brown bust of the great man on top. I had expected something smaller and older, from the time he was buried. What the original tombstone had been we had no way of knowing, but what we saw was not more than twenty years old, erected by some Communists perhaps, or even by the cemetery staff as their own Heritage Site (we had paid a one-pound admittance fee, marked for such preservation and enhancement). Finely scrubbed and polished, the stone had etched on it the slogan, 'Workers of the World Unite', followed by a series of names. These were, Jenny von Westphalen, Karl Marx, Helen Demuth and Eleanor Marx. At the foot of the stone was a bunch of fresh flowers from an earlier visitor of the day.

Gopal asked me to identify the other names. I jumped at the chance. The company Marx kept in death was pretty much the company he kept while he lived. Jenny Westphalen was the wife, four years older, aristocratic in background but devoted to her husband. Helen Demuth was Marx's housekeeper, and sometime mistress, who bore a son by him (adopted, to save everybody's face, by Engels). Eleanor was the beautiful and gifted daughter, a feminist and socialist who died by her own hand after discovering the truth about her father's relationship with Helen Demuth. It was a poignant listing, but one name would have made it complete— Friedrich Engels.

We turned away, heading back, I thought, for the entrance. 'There is something else I wanted to see' said Gopal, revealing for the first time why he had agreed so quickly to come with me on both occasions. To the left of Marx's tombstone was a sort of Comrade's corner, graves of exiled Communists from Iraq, Syria and other lands. The gravestone on the extreme right, which Gopal was looking for, was in the name of 'Dr Yusuf Dadoo, president of the South African Communist Party'. I now asked Gopal for details. 'He worked with Gandhi in India in the forties', he explained, 'and, back in South Africa was an early influence on Mandela.' An Indian and a Communist, the one direct link between Mahatma Gandhi and Nelson Mandela.*

III

A few days later, I was due to take my wife to Oxford. 'Come with me', said Gopal. 'I have to go anyway, to call on Nirad Chaudhuri.' Gopal,

*It struck me much later that Dadoo, like the Arab comrades who lay close to him, had been born a Muslim. Yet he chose to be buried in what was, in effect, a Christian cemetery, albeit in a corner of the field that would be forever Communist.

it is now time to reveal, was then the director of the Nehru Centre in London, and minister for culture in the Indian mission. Now Nirad Chaudhuri had been awfully neglected by the establishment in India; no honour had come his way, not even a Padma Shri. For a time even his works were blacklisted by his former employer, the All India Radio. He was, I suppose, deemed insufficiently patriotic for having dedicated the *Autobiography of an Unknown Indian* to the British Raj. Gopal, who knew this, had made it his business to call every six months on the greatest living Indian writer.

Nirad Chaudhuri lived alone in North Oxford, aged ninety-eight, and in total command of his phenomenal powers. He had lived in poverty in India and he now lived in poverty in England—poverty, that is, when judged by the standards of his class, the Bengali *bhadralok*, or by the life of other writers not a quarter as gifted but distinctly more saleable. His wife of sixty years had died three months previously. She had been an invalid for some time before that; like her husband, cared for by the British social security system. Their three sons were scattered around the world, and Gopal was worried about how he was coping with the loss.

Nirad Chaudhuri had been in England the past quarter of a century, but he remained a presence in Indian intellectual life. Newspapers—and not only Calcutta newspapers—carried interviews with him and articles by him. The essays and interviews spoke of his obsession with class, his love of English civilisation, and his despair at its decay. Like other leftists, I admired his style but not his politics. He was an icon—although I had spent three months in Oxford some years previously, I did not think then that I could visit him on my own. Gopal's offer to accompany him was one we could scarcely refuse.

We arrived at eleven, full of preconceptions, at a two-storey brick house with weeds running all over the garden. Decay outside, but not within. Nirad babu opened the door, clad in formal Bengali attire, an immaculate *dhoti panjabi.* He was tiny—less than five feet tall—but perfectly proportioned. For his age he was a 'physical and intellectual marvel', as described by Ramaswamy Venkataraman, the former president of India and Gopal's companion the last time around.

We were shown into the house. The sitting room of this English gentleman was like that of any Indian middle-class home: cluttered with sofas, stools, tables, serviceable rather than beautiful, the walls covered with framed prints and the shelves by books, china and bric–a–brac. We sat down and he talked, non-stop, for the next two and a half hours—in English mostly—with occasional dramatic recourse to Latin, Sanskrit, German, Bengali or Hindustani. At all times—whether handing out plates, showing us photographs, or speaking of his wife—his control was magnificent. He lost his patience only once, when Gopal got up, unasked, to help him open a briefcase. 'Sit down, sit down', he said, directing Gopal to his seat with one curved finger. '*Listen* to me.'

Some of what Nirad babu said was unsurprising. The bottle of port we brought with us was closely examined and deemed upper second-grade, fit to drink but not to serve. A passage was read from J.C. Squire's review of his *Autobiography*, published in the old *Illustrated London News*. He talked, at length, of the stately homes of England where he and his wife had been received as full equals. 'At the Duke of Blankshire's, I was admiring a gun on the turret, when the Duke remarked: "That was used at the Battle of Copenhagen". "Which one?" I asked. "Few Englishmen know there were two of them," replied the Duke, astonished.' This fascination for war had distinctively Bengali roots (in their designation by the British as a non-martial race) explained Nirad babu, as he reeled off the names of the guns used in the two World Wars.

Nirad Chaudhuri was pro British, and anti Muslim. He took exception to my wife's dress, a flowing *chooridar kurta*, saying, 'I would never wear a pyjama instead of my dhoti, because it is Islamic.' Then he turned to Gopal: 'I have just written a long article in Bengali on Subhas Bose and Mahatma Gandhi, and it is not too complimentary to your grandfather' (notorious for his love of Muslims).

I was drawn into the conversation, once. 'I believe you are working on a biography of Verrier Elwin. Whatever for?' 'Well, he was an unusual man', I cautiously replied, 'An Oxford scholar who lived with and wrote about Indian tribals.' 'I despise Indophile Englishmen', said Nirad babu. 'When Professor Hugh Tinker sent me his biography of C.F. Andrews, I told him: "What a hopeless waste of your time!" Do you know that Verrier Elwin reviewed my *Autobiography* for the Calcutta *Statesman*, most favourably, in 1952. Then when my *Passage to England* appeared in 1959 he dismissed it in the same columns. He said Nirad Chaudhuri took himself too seriously. Did he not know that already, from reading five–hundred–and–six pages of my autobiography?' I suggested that perhaps Elwin had criticised *Passage to England* to underline his loyalty to his adopted country—he was by then an Indian citizen, and an Indian government official. 'Nonsense', answered Nirad babu. 'The real reason was that he saw that I knew England better than he did. Anyway, after that I terminated my association with *The Statesman*.'*

Tea was then signalled by Nirad babu getting up and playing (on tape) a snatch of Mozart. The pot was brought in by a young Bengali woman scientist from the Institute of Virology, who came in on weekends to help in the house. The service was meticulously overseen by our host. He had asked for Darjeeling, not the inferior Assam blend. German Christmas Stollen was passed around, on plates of exquisite china ('Royal Derby—sixty pounds a piece—five pounds when I bought it.')

Afterwards we were taken upstairs to his bedroom. On one bed, his wife's, was laid out her wedding sari, and a Pashmina shawl, the first gift he had bought her. A Hindu wife, he told us, is 'like a gleaming marble bathtub with two golden taps: one hot, one cold.'

The room was a memorial to his wife, and also his study. By the side of his bed was a tiny table, smaller than a child's school desk, three

*Since renewed, for, as I dared not remind him, the 1993 Puja issue of *The Statesman* printed a long essay by Nirad babu on the incompatibility of Hindus and Muslims, in the past and in the present.

feet long and one-and-a-half feet across. It faced the wall and had a typewriter—this is where he wrote in English. A second table was set by a window, looking out into the back garden. It was bare. Here he wrote by hand in Bengali. Was there some deeper meaning in this, I wondered? The typewriter and the wall, the cold logic of English? The hand-held pen and the greenery, the emotions of his native Bengali?

Bengali and English were Nirad Chaudhuri's two tongues, and his two nationalities. Despite the title of his autobiography, his hostility to Indian nationalism had been unwavering. His personality, as his dress—*dhoti panjabi* at home, matched suit outside—held the two in balance. And yet, did the reversion to Bengali—his last books were in that language — signify a turning around from the image of an English writer and gentleman, crafted for the good part of a century? As we prepared to leave the phone rang. The scientist went to receive the call. 'Who is it?' asked the old man. '*Apner chele, desh theke*', she replied. It was his son, phoning from Calcutta, 'desh', *home.*

IV

Some time after this meeting, I came across, in the Verrier Elwin papers in Shillong, copies of his *Statesman* reviews of Nirad Chaudhuri's books. Of the *Autobiography of an Unknown Indian* (1951) Elwin remarked that it 'challenges comparison with Nehru's autobiography in its literary grace, its courageous outspokenness and the grand sweep of its historical vision.' The review was anonymous, so Chaudhuri wrote most disingenuously to the editor of *The Statesman*: 'I am writing this letter in the first instance to thank you for the appreciative review you have published of my book. Secondly, I should like to know if I may have the name and address of the reviewer. This is not in connexion with the review, but because the External Services of All India Radio, for which I work, wishes to get in touch with the writer for broadcasting an occasional talk by him.'

Evidently, if a man was wise enough to praise Mr Chaudhuri's book he was good enough to speak on the All India Radio. Eight years later,

Niradbabu's second book, *A Passage to England*, was sent to the same reviewer, who this time was distinctly less enthusiastic. 'Ever since the Geoffrey Gorers and Raymond Mortimers and even *The Statesman* placed his autobiography among the classics,' wrote Elwin (anonymously, again) 'Mr Chaudhuri has tended to regard himself as an institution. He is an oracle and everything that happens to him has a symbolic significance; his lightest word becomes a gnomic utterance. He is not pompous, not even specially dictatorial; he has just begun to take himself too seriously, to be too interested in himself.' Mr Chaudhuri, he continued, 'writes cleverly on the English weather, less cleverly on English religion, and very well in his chapter entitled "Adventures of a Brown Man in search of civilisation". Mr Chaudhuri's book, in short, would have been a notable one if it had contained less of Mr Chaudhuri. As it is, much of it is readable, entertaining and informative, and it should certainly be read.'

This seems a fair assessment, but it did not seem so to Mr Chaudhuri. We can be certain that he wrote once more to *The Statesman*, conveying more forcefully the views expressed to me some thirty-five years later. This exchange between author and reviewer, mediated through a once-great newspaper, merits a small footnote in the literary history of modern India. It was an encounter between two singular men, the Oxford scholar who became an Indian and the Bengali *bhadralok* who would be an Englishman.

Patriots

Ecological Patriot: M. Krishnan

I have before me a New Year's card for 1994. It has been made by an eighty-one-year-old man for his ninety-one-year-old sister. He lives in steamy Madras, she in Mysore, the town on the Carnatic Plateau which, he remembers, 'can be Arctic in December–January.' He is an artist, and so is she. To mark this, and the weather in Mysore, the card begins with his portrait of a bird in flight, its red beak and red legs and white-and-black wings etched against a blue sky. It is the White Stork, says the artist, helpfully providing its Latin and Tamil names too.

And why the White Stork? 'Can't you see the connection?' asks the artist of his sister. He reminds her of a poem addressed to the bird—some fourteen centuries previously by the poet Saththi-muth-thappulavar—as it passed Madurai en route to its winter grounds in Kanyakumari. One column then prints the ode in Tamil, the letters and words flawlessly formed; the other column offers a translation in English, in a typed draft scored over with handwritten corrections. The poet tells the stork 'with coral-red beak sharp-tapered like a split palmyra stalk' that, should it halt at the tank of his home village, Saththimuththam, on its return journey northwards, it should there seek out his wife in her 'wet-walled leaky' hut, listening 'to the gecko's whinnying voice for augury of my return'; and

> Tell her that you saw this abject being
> In Madurai, capital of the Pandya king,
> Grown thin with no clothes against the north wind's bite,
> Hugging his torso with his arms,
> Clasping his body with up-bent legs,
> Barely existing
> Like the snake within its basket.

Some family news follows, and then at the end of the card is a portrait in colour of the unhappy Saththi-muththap-pulavar. 'The stork is quite accurate', comments the artist, but 'I should not have attempted an impression of the poet—in my depiction, he looks more like a toad in a hole than a snake in a basket, though the foetal position must be correct.'

This New Year's card was sent by M. Krishnan to his sister Muthu. It is a period piece in the precise sense of the term—'an object or work whose main interest lies in its historical etc. associations' (*Concise Oxford Dictionary*)—an object or work that could only have been sent or received by one born before the First World War. The card continues a conversation conducted over decades between two old people of culture, learning, sensitivity, and *style*. It is also a handsome demonstration of the talents that made Krishnan the finest naturalist and nature writer in the land. In this private communication, as in his printed oeuvre, we find a distinctive combination of great skill, exceptional self-confidence, and obsessive perfectionism. We see at work the artist, scholar and writer, the man who would single-handedly annul the distinctions made by academics between nature and culture or literature and science. Even the showing off—the pedantic precision of the stork's Latin name, *Ciconia ciconia ciconia*—is in character.

Perhaps the most remarkable thing about this card, however, is that Krishnan made it in the knowledge that it might never reach Mysore. For there was a postal strike on in December 1993, and, as he told Muthu, 'only the good god knows when you will get it or, with unskilled replacements for the regular postal workers, if you will get it at all.' The card was produced out of affection for his sister, certainly, but also for the sheer joy of it. It was made by a man in love with his calling, a man with a supreme unconcern for what the world thought of him.

II

M. Krishnan was born in Tirunelveli on the 30th of June 1912, the youngest of the eight children of the Tamil writer and reformer A. Madhaviah (1872–1925). Madhaviah was employed in the Salt and Abkari Department of the Government of Madras. Posted in small towns, his work involved much riding on horseback, cross-country, in search of smugglers and drug peddlers. In his spare time he read and wrote. His vast output includes the first realistic novel published in Tamil (*Padmavathi Charithram*, 1898), an English novel published in London (*Thillai Govindan*, 1916), as well as essays, short stories, poems, and skits. In about the year 1920 he took premature retirement, commuted his pension, and with the proceeds built a house in the Madras locality of Mylapore. Adjoining the new family home was a shed where he installed a press to print his magazine, *Panchamirtham*. Madhaviah had resolved to devote the rest of his life to literature, but not much was left of it. He died at the age of fifty-five in the Madras Senate House, immediately after making an impassioned speech on the need to introduce Tamil or equivalent mother tongue as a compulsory subject for the B.A.

Madhaviah was a remarkable man, made more remarkable in the recollections of Krishnan. In a 'verified factual record' he compiled in 1990, the adoration is uncharacteristically unqualified, with a gloss and glow put on imperfect memory by a devoted son. The father, in this telling, was always at odds with authority, always ahead of the social and political currents of the time. In a more personal vein, Krishnan remembers early horse-rides with his father and the daily walks they took together before sunrise, to Marina Beach and back. He writes of how, in the last four years of his life, Madhaviah ate his meals with his last-born, and how at night his own cot was placed next to his.

When his father died the care and financial responsibility for the younger siblings was assumed by the second child, Lakshmi. Born in 1896, married in 1905, she had been cast away by her husband's family. Madhaviah took Lakshmi back and educated her. At the time of his death she was teaching at the prestigious Queen Mary's College, of which she was later to be principal. Krishnan was now studying at the Hindu High School; although not what we would term a 'prize' student, he read widely and had developed an interest in art: also in nature, for Mylapore in the twenties was something of a frontier settlement, stray houses with acres of shrub and pasture in between. The area was home to a teeming bird life and the odd jackal and blackbuck as well. The environment rubbed off: at the age of eleven this son of a scholarly Brahmin had as his pet a grown mongoose.

In 1927 Krishnan joined the Presidency College, an institution which, now decayed, was then in its pomp. He appeared for the Intermediate examination and, in 1931, for the B.A., one of his subjects the Tamil for which his father had so vigorously fought. The subject he most enjoyed was Botany, taught by Professor P.F. Fyson. Fyson was a fine field scientist who, judging from Krishnan's references to him in later life, deeply impressed the young student. He accompanied the Fysons on trips to the Nilgiri and Kodaikanal hills, learning science from the professor and discussing the techniques of water-colour painting with his wife.

Friendship with the Fysons did not come in the way of Krishnan getting a Third Class in his B.A. Job prospects were bleak, but an elder brother, M. Anantanarayanan, was in the Indian Civil Service,* and he had a father-in-law more eminent still. This was R. Narayana Aiyar, one of the first Tamilians to get into the I.C.S. Narayana Aiyar took Krishnan to an even bigger man, a knight no less, Sir T. Vijairaghavachari, who had among his many charges the Agricultural Research

*And later the author, in *his* spare time, of a well-regarded novel, *The Silver Pilgrimage,* originally published by Criterion Books, New York, in 1961, and reprinted in 1993 by Penguin India.

Institute in Pusa, a likely resting-place for a young fellow with an indifferent academic record but a serious interest in plants. When Sir T.V. was told of Krishnan's 'achievement' he advised him to do an M.A. and come back. Two years later the journey was repeated. In a letter written fifty-five years after this meeting the supplicant remembered the scene: 'The knight in an easy chair: me, next to him, in a bentwood chair; Mr R.N. in a sofa farther away.' 'Another Third Class', burst out the knight in a storm of protest. 'Now if you had only got a First Class in either the B.A. or the M.A. I could have done something for you.' 'If that were the case there would have been no need to come here at all,' remarked Narayana Aiyar and departed, taking Krishnan with him.

At the family's behest Krishnan then spent two years obtaining a law degree. He graduated in 1936 but there is no record of any subsequent briefs or court appearances. In those days the lack of an income was no bar to matrimony. Thus on the 26th of March 1937 Krishnan married Indumati Hasabnis from Bangalore. She was only fifteen, but in spirit and strength of will already a match for her husband.

The first 'verified factual record' I have of any paid employment dates to 1937, when Krishnan published some drawings and caricatures in the *Madras Mail.* The next year he was publishing essays on book-design in the low-circulation but high-prestige *Indian Affairs* and, more consequentially, nature notes in *The Statesman* and *The Hindu.* These early notes display the close observation and spare style that was to distinguish all his work. But as the aspirant novelist R.K. Narayan was finding out at about the same time, the concept of free-lancing was unknown to the moral and pecuniary universe of Tamil Brahminism. Thus in the early years of his marriage Krishnan irregularly held a 'regular' job—working initially with the Associated Printers, then with the Madras School of Art, and finally as the Publicity Officer of the local station of All India Radio.

In 1942, at his family's urging and with the help of what influence they could command, Krishnan was given employment by the

Maharaja of Sandur, who ruled over a small princely state in the northern parts of present-day Karnataka. Employment was, it seems, a somewhat incidental consideration—the main reason for the move was that his wife's doctor had advised them to relocate to a drier place. Krishnan was to spend eight years in the state—eight years under one paymaster but, true to form, in many jobs. In Sandur Krishnan served successively as schoolteacher, judge, publicity officer and political secretary to the maharaja. The work was dreary, but there was always the possibility of escape. For, in his tours through Sandur, the naturalist would come across the sambhur and the wild boar, jackals, jungle cats, porcupines and leopards. In this valley ringed by hills and forests, fields and shrub jungle within and the Tungabhadra flowing through them, and with the great ruined city of Hampi a day's bullock-cart journey away, Krishnan could nurture his love of nature and cultural history. He raised goats, occasionally grazing them himself; bred pigeons, running an experimental pigeon-post with the state's Boy Scouts; and he walked in the wild and among the Hampi temples, returning home to read by lantern-light the Tamil poets once patronised by the kings of Vijayanagara. He also developed an abiding fondness for *Mandalu-menasinakai*, chillies fried in oil, a culinary gem of the interior Deccan.

Krishnan was temperamentally well suited to the informal paternalism of the princely state. He could fit in here as he would never have in the rule-bound impartiality of British India. Sandur was Krishnan's finishing school or, to vary the metaphor slightly, the laboratory where he conducted the research for his unacknowledged doctoral degree. What he learnt there was communicated in the nature essays, cultural profiles, and short stories he published in the forties, under his own name in the *The Illustrated Weekly of India* and under the nom-de-plume 'Z' in *The Hindu*. For years afterwards he would embellish his articles with a fact or anecdote from his Sandur days. The state meant much to him, and he to it. Half-a-century after Krishnan left Sandur one of his students, M.Y. Ghorpade—in later life a well-known wildlife photographer himself—recalled

> one particular lecture on protective coloration, where the science and nature-study teacher, who was also a talented artist, drew a zebra and a donkey on a portable blackboard, which was moved farther and farther away from us, to demonstrate that, at a distance, the zebra with its broken pattern looked less prominent to the eye than the donkey in a block of single colour; though, at close quarters, it would be difficult to imagine how the vivid, black and white stripes of the zebra could ever look hazier than the dull, uniform brown of the donkey. My teacher was none other than M. Krishnan.

In 1949, when the state of Sandur disappeared along with 520 others into the Union of India, Krishnan returned to Madras, taking up residence in the tiled cottage his father had built for his press. He never took a job again, making a precarious but always honest living as a writer and photographer. In 1950 he began a fortnightly 'Country Notebook' for *The Statesman* of Calcutta; his last column was printed the day he died.

Alert and alive, at once scientific and speculative, peppered with allusions to literature and myth, opinionated, and acid in its wit, the column must rank as one of the remarkable achievements of English-language journalism in this country or any other. While *The Statesman* was his mainstay, Krishnan also wrote for *The Hindu, The Indian Express, The Illustrated Weekly of India, Shankar's Weekly*, and so on, and on a staggering variety of subjects. He is known above all as a great pioneering naturalist, as he should be. But in his day he had also served notice as art critic, writer of fiction, poet, translator, and literary historian. In January 1952 he even reported for *The Statesman* on the five days of the Madras Test of that year, the match in which Vinoo Mankad took twelve wickets as India beat England for the first time. These reports were said to be 'From a *Special* Cricket Correspondent', a seemingly curious description more true than the newspaper knew.

I once wrote of the opening batsman Krishnamachari Srikkanth that he was the only Tamil Brahmin who did not have security as his watchword. I had forgotten about Krishnan. His brother in the Indian Civil Service ended up as Chief Justice of Madras; his son in the Indian Forest Service had his final posting as the Principal Chief Conservator of Forests, Tamil Nadu; a nephew in the Indian Foreign Service was Ambassador to Germany and Japan. But Krishnan was always his own man, and not just in the matter of regular employment.

III

The library of natural history is dominated by spectacular habitats—oceans, mountains and deserts; and by charismatic megavertebrates—the whale, the lion, the tiger. Krishnan wrote, by choice, of the humdrum landscape of peninsular India, a countryside 'broken up with ridges and depressions, stones and burrows, wiry, much-branched shrubs and thorn and dessicated grasses, and an occasional patch of sand or rock or some succulent xerophyte.' It was his special gift to make this land come alive, to write about its apparent lack of colour in understated but wryly effective prose. While he knew the tiger and the elephant, he wrote as lovingly of the jackal, the *ghorpad*, and the spotted owlet, the small, homely, unglamorous denizens of the Indian countryside. That he wrote of the blackbuck in Ranibennur instead of the tiger in the Himalaya is one reason why he is not as well known as Jim Corbett, a state of affairs that does not properly reflect their respective skills as writers or naturalists. While we are in the business of comparison, let me also say that Krishnan had a sharply developed visual sense unmatched by other Indian nature writers.

Krishnan never talked down to his readers, assuming in them a knowledge and range of interests equal to his own. If they had not read Blake (and committed his poems to memory), or if they did not know who 'Eha' was, they could always go to the library and find out. In what I regard as his finest period—which ran, roughly, from 1948 to 1961—the learning was carried lightly, leavened by the more-than-occasional flash of humour, and this, in the best Anglophone fashion, generally directed at himself. But as he grew older the tone grew more sombre. The essays were still beautifully crafted and rich in detailed information. However, they were no longer so attentive to the human or cultural context, being natural history in a more straightforward sense. Krishnan changed, so to say, with the times: if from the nineteen-seventies we find an intensity of tone and even an impatient hectoring in his essays, this was not unrelated to the rapid disappearance of forests and wildlife all over India.

The ecologist Raman Sukumar has pointed out that Krishnan worked at a time when the 'environment' was not a glamorous subject attracting millions of dollars of research funding. This naturalist did most of his fieldwork and took all his photographs using his own funds. When Sukumar started research he went to Krishnan, who told him: 'When watching elephants for heaven's sake keep looking behind your back,' thus alerting the novice to the straggler in the herd who might come upon him suddenly, after his mates had passed by. Sukumar, who is now an international authority on the elephant, tells me that in a little-known note of 1972 the naturalist had anticipated high-tech science in two respects. First, Krishnan had observed that elephants communicated at sound frequencies not easily audible to humans, sounds he described as 'throaty, hardly audible, a throbbing purr'. Twelve years later, three scientists at Portland Zoo, working with fancy equipment among captive elephants, gave the phenomenon a name, 'infrasound', and a number, 14 hertz, a decibel-level way below the range of the human ear. Second, Krishnan speculated that female elephants sometimes chose their partners, a claim that, at the time, flew in the face of a consensus among scientists that elephant mating was determined by dominance hierarchies among males; but Krishnan's view is now seemingly confirmed by researches on the African elephant. It is not unlikely that other Krishnan theories, likewise based on sharp instinct and close field observation, will in time be certified by technology-driven research.

Krishnan had also told Sukumar the beginnner 'to study the elephant for its own sake. Don't expect anything to come of it.' Brave advice, even if Krishnan didn't always follow it himself. Working outside the system, he did occasionally try to manipulate it—as a member of the Indian Board for Wildlife (for more than three decades), and as part of the steering committee for Project Tiger. Now and then he sounded the tocsin, the chronicler of nature becoming the crusader for its protection. An essay dated 1970 on 'The Dwindling Animals of the Forest' complained that 'neither at the level of the illiterate poor nor among the educated people is there any popular feeling for wild life in India today.' He wondered why 'the centre cannot prevail upon the states to adopt a more conservationist attitude towards its wild life.' His last column, printed on the 18th of February 1996, provided part of the answer: the snag 'seems to lie in our Constitution, evolved by men with formidable knowledge of legal and political matters and hardly any of the unique biotic richness of India—they do not even seem to have realised that the identity of a country depended not so much on its mutable human culture as on its geomorphology, flora and fauna, its *natural* basis.'

Krishnan was an ecological patriot who believed—to quote from a 1974 piece—that only if 'we can save India and her magnificent heritage of nature for the generations of Indians to come, and safeguard the physical and organic integrity of our country, threatened today'—only then can we 'give them a country to be truly proud of'. This meant pushing back the forces that would destroy nature—dams, mines, commercial forestry, cattle, exotic species—to thus maintain 'the equipoise of nature and to do nothing to upset it'. It is time, he wrote, that 'we cultivated a narrow sort of patriotism in our floral preferences'. He could be ruthless in his opposition to species introduced from outside. He was once asked to speak at the Indian Institute of Science in Bangalore, by common consent the most beautiful of our university campuses. It was late February and the avenues were set alight by the *tabebuia*, whose spectacular yellow flowers were in blossom. The planting of this Central American tree, as of the other species that adorn the institute, was the handiwork of the director's wife. At a reception the lady asked Krishnan what he thought of the campus. 'Disgraceful', he answered, 'you should uproot all those foreign trees and plant some of our own.' On another occasion, when a kinsman wrote of the death by felling of a *gulmohar* tree near his house, Krishnan shot back: 'Anyway, why regret the demise of a gulmohar—an exotic that litters the ground beneath with fallen, faded flowers—a vermilion strumpet from Madagascar? If you want to see a truly impressive crown of red flowers, you should see the flame-of-the forest, *Butea monosperma*, entirely our own, early in summer—3 or 4 trees close together setting the horizon ablaze.'

Krishnan liked to contrast two authentically indigenous traditions of nature conservation, the traditions of Vedanthangal and of Ashoka. The first referred to a village near Chinglepet, where custom and religious tradition had for generations saved breeding birds from the hunter's arrow and the shikari's shotgun; the latter to the Mauryan emperor whose edicts commanded his people to protect rare animals and plants. Krishnan first visited Vedanthangal in the early nineteen-fifties, studying its avian life and history of protection and succeeding in having it designated as a formal 'sanctuary'. He knew that cultural traditions could be in harmony with nature. But he also sensed that in an altered modern context, with rapid economic growth and the increase in human population, traditional restraint had in many cases given way to greed. There would, he hoped, come a time when local traditions could once more contribute creatively to wildlife conservation. Meanwhile, the state had to take a proactive role in effectively protecting the habitats and species that remained.

Krishnan was a vegetarian who never held a rifle, a man who was exceptional in his generation for being a conservationist *qua* conservationist, not a shikari-turned-protector and member of a repentant butchers' club. The finest students of our natural history have either been Europeans, or Hindus and Christians of working-caste origin, or members of the Rajput and Muslim nobility. Europeans have been inspired to more serious study by their experience of the wild and their adherence to a post-Enlightenment scientific rationality; naturalists of plebeian background have been familiarised by an occupational tradition of working with animals or plants; *thakurs* and *nawabs* have been challenged by their aristocratic lineage to move from hunting to conservation. And yet it fell to a *rasam*-drinking, gun-loathing Tamil Brahmin to become the ablest naturalist of them all.

IV

What kind of man was Krishnan? His character is nicely revealed in the technical apparatus of his photography. He came to the craft late, when he was past forty, but brought to it a ferocity of commitment that was all his own. He strongly preferred black-and-white film to colour, and roll film to 35mm, for it enabled him to make large prints (36" by 24" or bigger still) that showed up animals in the wild in proper detail. However, these preferences ruled out the use of any of the makes of camera then available in the Indian market. This man, who in his lifetime was unquestionably the 'biggest name in India's wildlife photography', had more-or-less to manufacture a camera himself. This was, to quote his fellow naturalist E.P. Gee, 'a large, composite affair, with the body of one make and the tele lens of another, and other parts and accessories all ingeniously mounted together by himself. I cannot swear that I saw proverbial bootlace used to fix them all together, but I am sure there must have been some wire and hoop somewhere!'

This contraption was known, to master and acolyte alike, as the 'Super-Ponderosa'. In 1974 the body needed to be changed; the problem was that it was a German make, an *East* German make. If Krishnan wanted to import a Pentacon Six body without the accompanying lenses he had to overcome both the Iron Curtain and the swadeshi-minded Indian government. He wrote for a replacement to 120 suppliers of photo equipment in Europe, Asia and the Americas. Only one replied, Andrews and Company in Hong Kong. This, he thought, was actually a slice of luck, for his nephew had just been appointed to the Indian mission in that colony. This nephew could, when required, pay up, collect the box, and send it along to Madras. Krishnan now flew to Delhi and, 'after a specially unpleasant series of engagements with the bitter cold [it was December] and Sardul Singh, Deputy Chief Controller of Import and Export', succeeded in getting a licence allowing him to import two camera bodies alone.

Meanwhile, back behind the Iron Curtain, the East Germans had stopped production of the P-6. Andrews and Company, who had promised to supply Krishnan a box, now wrote to him saying they were 'temporarily out of stock', and would send the item later in the year. The truth was that, having heard of the brand's demise, the canny Chinamen had no wish to sell the box on its own—how then would they dispose of the lenses—which this particular customer had no use for? The story has a tame and typically Indian ending—a P-6 box was donated to the photographer by some friends in England.

Even when he could afford it, Krishnan never bought a car or a motor scooter. In the late sixties, his son Hari briefly contemplated buying a car, for as a forest officer he had much roaming to do. Father and son worked out the economics and decided each could afford a four-wheeler. No longer, it seemed, would the naturalist have to trust to his feet or a bicycle in negotiating the roaring Madras traffic. Days before the order was to be placed, recalls Hari, 'rescue arrived swiftly and unexpectedly from the Union Finance Minister in the form of an "upward revision" in the price of petrol'; for both of them the issue was put beyond doubt for good.

It is also in character that in 1995 Krishnan was still using the Swan Signature fountain pen with which he had written his B.A. examination. His attitude to the 'latest' in technology can be usefully contrasted to that of the poet Vladimir Mayakovsky. Born in a Georgian valley, Mayakovsky was unmoved by the glories of the Caucasus. He grew up in the woods, with a father who was a forest ranger. Accompanying his father on a round one night, the boy saw a factory on the far side of a river, gloriously illuminated. 'After seeing electricity', recalled Mayakovsky in his memoirs, 'I lost interest in Nature. Not up-to-date enough.'

Now Krishnan happened to be in the crowd that saw the display of India's first jet aircraft; he went away unimpressed—it was not natural enough. For these were 'just big, loud engines' whose power and speed was 'mechanical, chemical, inhuman'. What moved him was the 'living, muscular speed of animals', a quickness he could marvel at. 'If you like speed', he told his readers, 'and want to see something sustained in its effortless, rhythmic impetuosity, you should watch a herd of blackbuck going all out for a few miles—there is tangible, real speed for you.'

A younger friend who knew him well writes that while 'never guilty of underestimating his exceptional talent, Krishnan nonetheless lived a life of self-imposed obscurity. When not in the forests, he hibernated in the bush cover of his home-cum-studio in Madras.' There, when he was not developing film, painting a sketch or typing a column, Krishnan indulged in his *un*-natural interests—detective fiction, Carnatic music, and cricket. Of these I share only the last, but can certify here to a high degree of understanding. In a family history he once wrote titled 'The Descent of the P.H. ites', 1991, he entered this significant detail against the name of his brother P.M.Y. Narayanan (a medical doctor who died young)—'Was a lefthand batsman and bowler and could bowl the Chinaman'.*

'Krishnan's reclusion was notorious', remarks the same friend, and two stories testify to this. In the mid 'sixties, when Air India started a non-stop service to London, they offered to a select group of 'eminent Indians' free tickets for the inaugural flight, with a week of travel in the United Kingdom thrown in. A Tamil manager with Air India, devoted to Krishnan and his works, knew that the way things were ordered in India he would not be put on the list. Yet who could be more properly deserving than this scholar of English literature and this master of English prose? What could more become a *public*-sector airline than to pay for Krishnan to walk in the Lake District and examine the collections in the British Museum? After special pleading the manager got Krishnan's name put on the list and himself flew to Madras with the offer. It was refused, as was an all-expenses-paid invitation from the Smithsonian Institution soon afterwards—the money to come this time from the United States treasury. It was not that this Indian patriot could not

*On the field of play Krishnan was a fiery fast bowler, with a temper to match. My friend Anand Doraswami tells the story of a match in which Krishnan took two wickets in the opening over. Out came the next batsman, wearing a blue shirt and brown trousers, his leg-guards tied up with handkerchiefs. It was too much for the fastidious Krishnan. 'What is your name', he demanded of the batsman. 'Thirunavakkarasu', came the answer. 'I refuse to bowl to a man with that name', said Krishnan, and, tossing the ball to his captain, left the field.

cross the *Kala Paani*, but that the self-reliant, Thoreauvian individualist would not allow a mere government to pay for him.

Then, in the last months of 1969, when Krishnan was away in the forest, his wife Indu received a telegram from the Government of India, asking whether he would consent to being awarded the Padma Shri. Indu thought on her feet—who knew when her man would be back, and how he would respond to such a request. She wired his acceptance immediately. Once Krishnan returned he saw there could be no second thoughts and accepted the honour with grace.

V

Krishnan once told a friend that he was better known in West Bengal than his native Tamil Nadu. This was said with some regret, for he was, after all, Madhaviah's son. Copies of *The Statesman* rarely reach the city of Madras, but its Delhi edition found its way to the small sub-Himalayan town where I grew up. My father read *The Statesman* for much the same reason that Krishnan wrote for it: it had fewer misprints. The photograph that introduced his column did not hold me—newsprint could scarcely do justice to this master of the black-and-white art—but the writing did. In those days 'Country Notebook' alternated with a column by the politician Minoo Masani. Masani was a man of strong opinions too, but his opinions were not his own; they came from Milton Friedman and Margaret Thatcher. I read the *Sunday Statesman* closely one week and stamped on it the next.

While visiting Madras in the summer of 1979 I found that I was connected to Krishnan. The connection was tenuous—his brother, the chief justice, was married to my mother's cousin—and all I knew of his house was that it was 'somewhere near Rajeshwari Kalyana Mandapam'. That was enough, for the Tamil is the best short-distance cartographer in the world. Walking down Edward Elliots' Road, I was quickly directed to where Krishnan lived. His home was nondescript; a grey cement block tucked away behind an old Madras bungalow. It was late evening when I got there, catching the naturalist as he emerged from his dark-room, wearing a red checked *lungi,* a roll of film, dripping wet, in his hands.

On Christmas Day 1995, I was on Edward Elliots' Road once more. Except that it was now called Radhakrishnan Salai, and I was visiting another Madras institution—the son of the man who gave the road its new name. My visit ended, I walked out on to the pavement and saw, in the near distance, the board of the Rajeshwari Kalyana Mandapam. In minutes I was with Krishnan. He had forgotten our last meeting but took me into his study. Surrounded by books, a half-filled page scrolled into his typewriter, a cigarette in his hand, he talked for an hour. He still wore the red *lungi,* a dress which, in retrospect, seems to have mocked the pieties of Tamil Brahminism (the safe middle road of the white starched *veshti,* the white *banyan,* and the off-white *poonal*). Six weeks after this second meeting Krishnan was dead.

Krishnan could be savagely dismissive of those who failed by his own standards. Consider these three judgements, which I recall from our two conversations.

On a famous Tamil writer: 'That man was so unsure of his worth that he wrote under twelve pen names, using one to write a book and another to review it.'

On a well-known ornithologist: 'I told him when the Government appointed him to the high-powered committee on environmental protection, "Don't join, you'll make a fool of yourself. You may know something about birds, that does not make you an ecologist".'

On a respected editor who dared change one word in his copy: 'I had written of my father A. Madhaviah as "*the* Tamil scholar, poet and novelist"; it was changed to "*a* Tamil scholar, poet and novelist". My father was the most celebrated Tamil writer of his day, better known even than [Subramania] Bharati; this fellow in Delhi has made him an also-ran.'

And for Sarojini Naidu, whose verse was once much trumpeted but has now been described by the poet Arvind Krishna Mehrotra as 'mellifluous drivel', Krishnan saves his most caustic barb: 'According to

Sarojini Naidu the koel sings "Lira! liree! Lira! Liree!". I have not heard this call. Nor has anyone else.'

The contemporary meaning of 'civilised', writes Krishnan in one of his essays, is 'hypocritical and polite'. Here are some more delightfully uncivilised remarks gleaned from his letters:

> *Writing to the newly appointed Director of the India International Centre in New Delhi*: 'I remember the India International Centre as a rather heavily built boarding house with a large lecture hall attached, frequented by all sorts and conditions of culture-vultures and bores. I sincerely hope it has improved since.'
>
> *After reading a pamphlet, in Tamil, on the sayings of Mahatma Gandhi*: 'The rendering does not mask the dictatorial tone of the pronouncements.'
>
> *Commiserating with a friend posted to Japan*: 'I believe that Japanese English is a language even more difficult to follow than Jap Japanese.'
>
> *On an influential environmental organisation*: 'The World Wildlife Fund, that hotchpotch of truly fine and truly distinguished wildlifers and pretentious charlatans, to which both Peter Scott and Duleep Matthai belonged.'

VI

That Krishnan cared nothing for what the world thought of him must be a matter of regret. A Jawaharlal Nehru Fellowship (the first), a Padma Shri, a place in the Global 500 Roll of Honour of the United Nations Environment Programme—all these meant naught to him; but a dozen collections of his work could have meant a lot to us. As a chronicler of the natural world he was unequalled, yet his work is to be found for the most part only in his now inaccessible newspaper columns. He published only two slim collections: *Jungle and Backyard* (National Book Trust, 1963: reprinted in 1993 by Oxford University Press), and *Nights and Days* (Vikas, 1985), the text embellished in the first instance by his superb pen-and-ink drawings, in the second instance by his photographs. He also wrote a book on elephants for children, as well as an ecological survey of the mammals of peninsular India,

Indian Wildlife, 1959–70 (Bombay Natural History Society, 1975), the fruit of his Nehru fellowship. There were also some charming stories about a forest contractor named Dawood Khan, but the book where these appeared is not with me now. His last book, an original detective novel in Tamil, was published in 1995.

Where his natural allegiances lay with India as a whole, Krishnan's cultural affinities were more circumscribed. All his life he drew sustenance from what he once described as 'the meticulous traditions, the superb verve, the verbal pithiness and strength of eighteen centuries of Tamil poetry.' Fittingly, his last major essay was on the patronage of poetry in medieval south India. Krishnan himself felt of this essay (published in the second issue of the literary journal *Civil Lines*) that it was 'one of the best things I have written and wholly original.' The men and women he was writing about were, in fact, 'my personal literary ancestors'. Here Krishnan retold the story of Seethakkaathi Marakkaayar, a Muslim merchant more ready with his money than the wealthiest of Hindu kings. An indigent poet, hearing of his munificence, walked miles to meet him, but arrived the day the patron died. He reached the burial ground as Seethakkaathi's body, washed and bejewelled, was being lowered into the coffin. As he came near, the body's right hand flung out towards the poet. The helpers, recognising the significance of the act, took out the diamonds from the merchant's hand and handed them over.

There are few such patrons in our time, and Krishnan did not search them out anyway. His hero among Tamil poets appears to have been Kaallameghappulavar, an 'out-and-out freelancer' who seldom approached a patron, a man 'renowned for the spontaneity of his poetic verse', an 'acknowledged master of instant repartee [who] has written some foul-mouthed insults and curses in immaculate metres.' Krishnan's compliments and insults were offered in prose and by photograph, but otherwise the resemblances are striking. May his work live as long as that of his adored poets of the Tamil country.

Redeeming the Bharat Ratna: M.S. Subbulakshmi and Others

IT was at the Marwari Bhojanalaya in Amarkantak that I heard of M.S.'s Bharat Ratna. I was travelling with a friend in the Narmada country, in search of another musician around Subbulakshmi's age, a woman who had once sung Gond *dadarias* on All India Radio while being married to the anthropologist Verrier Elwin. Spending the day in Elwin's villages, we had returned to Amarkantak for the night. At the cash counter at our dinner-halt my companion spied a copy of a newspaper. It was the *Dainik Bhaskar*, published in Bilaspur. This announced the news of Subbulakshmi's award on the front page, while directing the reader to an explanatory editorial inside.

The Bhojanalaya's owner would not allow us to take the paper home that night. But he handed it over the next day, when we had one last *chotta thali* at his pilgrim eatery before proceeding to Anuppur, there to board the Delhi-bound Utkal Express. I allowed my friend to read the *Dainik Bhaskar* first, for his Hindi is better than mine, as is his understanding of Carnatic music. The Bharat Ratna was the theme of the lead editorial. The milestones in Subbulakshmi's career were marked, her indifference to glamour and fame praised, her religiosity and devotion commended. There was also an intelligent discussion of what separated and what united the Hindusthani and Carnatic styles.

Even the one error was revealing of the love the writer brought to his subject. This claimed that Jawaharlal Nehru's remark, that he was merely the prime minister of India while M.S. was the Queen of Song, was made after she performed at the silver jubilee of the founding of the United Nations (it was actually offered at a concert held in New Delhi for the Ramakrishna Mission, a small-scale national institution rather than an immoderately large international one).

Reading the *Dainik Bhaskar*, in an oddly bump-free jeep ride down the Maikal Hills, was to understand that there is more that unites India than the Bombay film and the game of cricket. It is in keeping with what we know of this land that a tribal in Bastar has an opinion on Rahul Dravid's forward defensive stroke, or that a Hindi-hating Tamil would hum and sometimes even sing the songs of Majrooh Sultanpuri. But here was an editorial writer in Bilaspur writing, and writing knowledgeably, about a performer he would never see and of a type of music it was not his everyday experience to hear. On the train we discussed the distance between his cultural world and Subbulakshmi's. Had the journalist ever attended a *cutcheri*? *Never*, I insisted, for not one has been organised in the history of his home town. Not in Bilaspur, replied my friend, but remember that the polyglot steel city of Bhilai is only eighty miles away. M.S. might not have sung there, but other musicians from the South have. Perhaps the journalist was in the habit of taking the bus down to Bhilai to hear them? Or is it simply that, as H.Y. Sharada Prasad once wrote, M.S. had long ago been anointed Bharat Ratna by the people of India, with her art recognised and cherished by anyone with a modicum of cultural intelligence?

II

Eighteen months before that meal in Amarkantak, I had undertaken a commission to publicise M.S.'s claim to be elevated to the Bharat Ratna. The commissioners, two in number, were high officials of the Government of India, outstanding public servants and patriots who were deeply worried about the debasement of standards in our land.

The senior among the sahibs was due to take up a new job, preparatory to which he wished to visit the ashram in Tirunavannamalai of the great sage Ramana. His colleague and I went along for the ride, to and fro from Chennai. Both ways, in the bus, we discussed how the Bharat Ratna had increasingly become the monopoly of dead or discredited politicians. Could not something be done about this? By the conditions of service, my friends could not express these views in public, but they suggested that I might.

Subsequent research into the history of the Ratna told a tale of decline. In 1954, the first year of the awards, three men were distinguished with the award: a statesman (C. Rajagopalachari), a philosopher (S. Radhakrishnan), and a scientist (C.V. Raman). The standard of values was biased against the political, a bias that sent signals down the pecking order as well (in the nineteen-fifties, dozens of scientists, scholars and musicians were also recognised by one of the lesser 'Padma' awards). True, Jawaharlal Nehru and G.B. Pant joined the ranks in 1955, as did B.C. Roy and P.D. Tandon a few years later. Before the decade was out, however, these gestures to Congressmen had been compensated by the award of the Bharat Ratna to the philosopher Bhagwan Das, the engineer M. Visvesvarayya, the Sanskritist P.V. Kane, and the educationists D.D. Karve and Zakir Hussain.

From the mid-sixties, however, the pendulum began to swing markedly in favour of politicians. Outgoing presidents (Rajendra Prasad in 1961, V.V. Giri in 1975) were honoured, as were serving prime ministers. Thus Lal Bahadur Shastri was made a Bharat Ratna after one war with Pakistan; Indira Gandhi after the next. These decisions were both relatively non-controversial, seen as rewards for able leadership in adversity. Later awards have been viewed more cynically, as being determined by partisan politics rather than performance. The government of Mrs Gandhi honoured K. Kamaraj, the government of Rajiv Gandhi honoured M.G. Ramachandran: both posthumous awards aimed at placating the Tamils. Then V.P. Singh, wishing to please the Dalits, advised the president to honour the long-dead B.R. Ambedkar. This opened up a Pandora's box, for till this time the awards had been restricted to the living or the freshly buried (thus also an award to Vinoba Bhave after his death in 1983). But now they increasingly fell prey to varieties of geographical and political correctness. The Gujaratis wanted a Bharat Ratna for Vallabhbhai Patel, the Bengalis one for Subhas Chandra Bose, the Muslims one for Maulana Azad. All three got it, although, as with Ambedkar, these post-posthumous awards, aimed solely at the next election, insulted the memory of outstanding statesmen. This was recognised by the family of Subhas Bose, which refused to accept the award. The list of gratified politicians was completed by Morarji Desai, made a Ratna shortly before he died, and Rajiv Gandhi, who joined the list after his assassination.

In 1996, when I came to disaggregate the Bharat Ratna awardees by profession, to the seventeen politicians listed above I could counterpose four scholars who advanced the frontiers of knowledge (Radhakrishnan, Raman, Das, Kane), four reformers who brought succour to the deprived (Karve, Hussain, Bhave and, most recently, Mother Teresa), and two technocrats who helped generate wealth for the nation (Visvesvarayya and J.R.D. Tata). The man unmentioned so far is the film-maker Satyajit Ray, who had to wait till he was dying to have his contributions to his country properly acknowledged.

By my figures, the *neta*/non-*neta* score in the first decade of the award was seven is to eight, whereas in the thirty years since Shastri's elevation only three non-political figures had been made a Bharat Ratna as against ten politicians. Nor were any of these honourable decisions, each being rather a guilty admission of failure. For Mother Teresa was made a Bharat Ratna after she obtained the Nobel Peace Prize, Satyajit Ray after he got an Oscar for lifetime achievement, J.R.D. Tata after the world had forced upon us the recognition that industrialists sometimes gave more to India than stewards of the public sector.

These facts provided decisive proof of a profound shift in the nation's honour system. But did these judgements, of who can be a Bharat Ratna and who will not, reflect the values of the country at large or only of its political class? To test the waters, I published an essay in

India Today (15 September 1996) suggesting that two of the most popular choices for the award of Bharat Ratna would be M.S. Subbulakshmi and Lata Mangeshkar. Both have been without equal in their chosen vocation, singing in voices of rare timbre and possessing a musical repertoire of dazzling virtuosity. As women both faced and overcame prejudice and hostility in a culture dominated by powerful men. Both have displayed a longevity that is remarkable in a profession that takes so much out of the voice and the mind. Throughout their careers, both have comported themselves with grace and dignity: not a note out of tune, but also never a word or gesture out of place. And both have been truly pan-Indian in their reach, each rooted in a rich regional tradition yet consciously and successfully reaching out to the rest of the land. We know them as 'M.S.' and 'Lata' not out of easy familiarity but because we love, cherish and honour them, because we cannot imagine life or India without them.

M.S. and Lata, I argued then, complemented each other exquisitely; the one the great torchbearer of a high classical tradition, the other the great innovator of a distinctively Indian popular art form. To make them Bharat Ratnas would help make up for a general neglect of the non-political in the life of the awards. 'It is by recognising M.S. and Lata, next January,' I wrote, that the president might 'help restore the dignity of the awards, and reassure the public that factors other than political preference and vote-banks count at the highest levels. The Nobel Committee is forever tainted by its failure to award Mahatma Gandhi the Peace Prize, this despite a public campaign initiated (interestingly enough by Americans) as early as 1931. The lustre of the Bharat Ratna has dimmed over the years, but it might yet be redeemed by a push and a nudge in the direction of the two great ladies of free India.'

My civil servant sponsors were still behind me, but by now I had made their cause my own anyway. *India Today* would not allow a 'freelancer' more than one crack, but fortunately other forums were available. In these I wrote obsessively of how the degradation of the Ratna showed that, as a nation, we had failed to nurture and develop our own autonomous standards of judgement and appreciation. Thus a presidential notification of January 1954 had made it clear that the Bharat Ratna was only for 'exceptional service towards the advancement of art, literature and science and in recognition of public service of the highest order', whereas the other Padma categories were merely for 'exceptional and distinguished service in any field including service rendered by government servants.' There were, I suggested, at least half-a-dozen living Indians qualified by these criteria, but whom past presidents and governments had ignored. Aside from M.S. and Lata these were Ravi Shankar, Bismillah Khan and K. Sivaram Karanth for the arts; A.P.J. Abdul Kalam and Amartya Sen for the sciences; and Baba Amte for 'public service of the highest order'.

My articles attracted some degree of attention. So did one of its subjects. Magazines which had quite forgotten about Subbulakshmi—she had not regularly performed in public for years—now sought to interview her. But when the time came, the president of the day used his prerogative to award the Ratna to two more politicians, Gulzarilal Nanda and Aruna Asaf Ali. Then he had to demit office, and a replacement moved into Rashtrapati Bhavan. This new fellow was a thinking man and he recruited into his staff other thinking men. And so it was that in January 1998 the great Subbulakshmi was finally given her due. Her case was helped by the fact that a person of intelligence and insight also then occupied the office of prime minister. It is almost certain that the proposal to make M.S. a Bharat Ratna was made, formally, by K.R. Narayanan, but it was made to I.K. Gujral, who had the decency to acquiesce. Earlier proposals in support of Subbulakshmi, one suspects, would have been shot down by one or the other of these pairs. This award could scarcely have been made with the combination of Mrs Indira Gandhi and Fakhruddin Ali Ahmed, Rajiv Gandhi and Zail Singh, V.P. Singh and R. Venkataraman.

A little before M.S., but after I had named him, Abdul Kalam was made a Bharat Ratna. Ravi Shankar followed, as did Amartya Sen, though only after he had been first awarded a Nobel Prize for Economics. My powers of prediction, it seemed, greatly exceeeded Bejan Daruwalla's. But the self-congratulation was tempered by the reaction to my original choice. While M.S.'s elevation pleased millions of Indians and an obscure Madhya Pradesh newspaper, others, in the capital naturally, were less generous. One Delhi columnist complained that the nation's highest award should not be bestowed on an artist, any artist, however gifted. Only generals and politicians, according to his reckoning, could be thus distinguished.

The political class thought this way too. The twin recognition within three months of a musician and a scientist (M.S. and Kalam) quickly led to claims being advanced in favour of N.T. Rama Rao by the Andhras, of Biju Patnaik by the Oriyas, and of Y.S. Parmar by the Himachalis. These claims were not granted—or at least not in the short term—but a living politician (admittedly a good one), C. Subramaniam, was made a Bharat Ratna, as—quite absurdly—was a man who has been dead more than forty years, Assam's first chief minister, Gopinath Bordoloi.

As depressing as the narrowness of vision is the amnesia, the forgetting among the intelligentsia about what the award means and who some of its great recipients were. When Abdul Kalam was made a Bharat Ratna, the *Indian Express* made the mistaken claim that Dr Homi Bhabha was the only previous scientist to be so honoured. The error was repeated in an editorial in the *Times of India*. Actually Bhabha was never made a Bharat Ratna. The *Times* and the *Express* probably reproduced the claim from a *Press Trust of India* release that made the mistake in the first place. But why did the newspapers not check? Sheer laziness, or perhaps the assumption that if a scientist is made a Bharat Ratna he is bound to be close to state power, as Kalam is and Bhabha once was? What else can explain the obliteration from their record of C.V. Raman, made a Bharat Ratna in the first batch, 1954, and a scientist of such towering achievement that all other Indians are also-rans by comparison? Also forgotten, incidentally, was the engineer M. Visvesvarayya, not a 'pure' scientist but an applied one, like Kalam.

The Hindu, a newspaper which prides itself on being slow but truthful, seems to have cross-checked, and did not make this mistake. But it made other ones. It complimented Kalam on being the 'second

Tamil' to be made a Bharat Ratna, the first being C.V. Raman. Raman was, admittedly, of Tamil blood, but he made his home and did much of his scientific work in Bangalore. If the Tamils want to claim Raman they could also claim Sarvepalli Radhakrishnan, a Tamil-speaking Andhra who lived in Madras. But why did *The Hindu* forget the name of the long-serving chief minister of Tamil Nadu? Because they privately agreed that MGR didn't deserve the Bharat Ratna, or since he was, by blood, not a Tamil but a Malayali? And why did *The Hindu* forget an earlier chief minister of Madras State (as Tamil Nadu was then known), K. Kamaraj? And how could *The Hindu* forget a Bharat Ratna who was a Tamil by blood and chief minister of Madras as well as a writer and scholar of distinction? How did this Iyengar-owned paper forget the name of Chakravarti Rajagopalachari?

Andrea, a character in Bertolt Brecht's *Galileo*, remarks that 'Unhappy is the land that has no heroes.' To this Galileo responds: 'No, unhappy the land that needs heroes'. I must admit that I am with the unsung Andrea here. All nations need heroes, the question is the criteria by which they reward or remember them. The Bharat Ratna is our preeminent national honour, to be bestowed with care and discernment. But it has been so polluted by politicians that we have forgotten a time when the award matched the awardee, when, by making C.V. Raman or Jawaharlal Nehru Bharat Ratnas, India was doing little more than honouring herself.

To restore our sense of cultural pride and dignity, to get rid of the corrosive cynicism that now dominates our public life and public discourse, the citizens of India need once more to believe that the nation will reward the truly deserving. Were one to start at the top, with our highest honour, then the principle of just and fair recognition might come also to permeate more mundane spheres of our national life. To put the Bharat Ratna beyond the divisive and sectional interests of the Indian politician, it is imperative that posthumous awards be completely forbidden. One precedent here is the Nobel Prize, never granted to the dead. Another precedent is the Companion of Honour, Britian's highest civil award. This too is handed out only to the living, with the futher caveat that there cannot be more than a fixed number (twenty, I believe) of C.H.'s at any time.

A third precedent, and closest at hand, is the title of Sangita Kalanidhi bestowed annually by the Music Academy in Chennai. On one wall of the Academy hang portraits of all the Kalanidhis. But the facing wall keeps room for singers or musicians who died young, before they could be so dignified. This is where we find portraits of M.D. Ramanathan and T.R. Mahalingam, who would certainly have been made Sangita Kalanidhi had they lived ten or twenty years longer.

Following this principle would bar men like N.T. Rama Rao or Biju Patnaik from being made Bharat Ratnas, while encouraging their followers and admirers to remember them in other ways, by attaching their names to schools, hospitals, film studios or cricket stadiums. It would free the award from considerations of creed and political affiliation in favour of real, long-lasting and trans-personal achievement.

If the ban on posthumous recognition tends to reward musicians and scientists, scholars and social workers, then so be it. For the applause over Amartya Sen's Bharat Ratna was scarcely confined to economists or Bengalis, or for Ravi Shankar's to musicians and Bengalis. Meanwhile, within my original list there are men (and a woman) who wait to be made Bharat Ratnas. Sivaram Karanth, alas, is dead, but Bismillah Khan and Lata Mangeshkar still actively perform, and Baba Amte still actively serves. As with Bilaspur's *Dainik Bhaskar* and M.S. Subbulakshmi, their elevation will be acclaimed by Indians who do not speak their language or always understand the subtleties of their craft.

RECIPIENTS OF THE BHARAT RATNA, 1954–99
(with primary professional affiliation)

C.V. Raman (scientist)	1954
S. Radhakrishnan (philosopher)	1954
C. Rajagopalachari (politician)	1954
Jawaharlal Nehru (politician)	1955
M. Visvesvarayya (technologist)	1955

Bhagwan Das (philosopher)	1955
G.B. Pant (politician)	1957
D.K. Karve (social reformer)	1958
B.C. Roy (politician)	1961
P.D. Tandon (politician)	1962
Rajendra Prasad (politician)	1962
Zakir Hussain (educationist)	1963
P.V. Kane (Sanskritist)	1963
Lal Bahadur Shastri (politician)*	1966
Indira Gandhi (politician)	1971
V.V. Giri (politician)	1975
K. Kamaraj (politician)*	1976
Mother Teresa (social worker)	1980
Vinoba Bhave (social worker)*	1983
M.G. Ramachandran (politician)	1988
B.R. Ambedkar (politician)*	1990
Morarji Desai (politician)	1991
Rajiv Gandhi (politician)*	1991
Vallabhbhai Patel (politician)*	1991
Maulana Azad (politician)*	1992
Subhas Chandra Bose (politician)*#	1992
J.R.D. Tata (industrialist)	1992
Satyajit Ray (film-maker)	1992
Gulzarilal Nanda (politician)	1997
Aruna Asaf Ali (politician)*	1997
Abdul Kalam (technologist)	1997
M.S. Subbulakshmi (musician)	1998
Ravi Shankar (musician)	1999
C. Subramaniam (politician)	1999
Gopinath Bordoloi (politician)*	1999

*Award made posthumously. *#Award returned by family.

(Note: this list excludes the two foreign citizens made Bharat Ratnas, Khan Abdul Ghaffar Khan and Nelson Mandela.)

Afterword: The hardcover edition of this book was released in the second week of December 2000. The next month, on the occasion of Republic Day, Lata Mangeshkar and Bismillah Khan were awarded the Bharat Ratna. A friend in *India Today*, marvelling at my predictive powers, wrote suggesting that I publish an article recommending a raise for him. The consequences of our campaign have indeed been gratifying: it seems that politicians, or their advisers, sometimes read lowly hacks who presume to reflect the popular mood. Will they now complete the job and honour Baba Amte?

Our Once But Not Future King: Jawaharlal Nehru

'HE was India's once—and we may hope—future King.' So runs the last line of the third and final volume of Sarvepalli Gopal's authoritative biography of Jawaharlal Nehru, published in 1984. Nine years previously Gopal had written in the Preface to his first volume: 'This has not been an easy book to write.' For 'Jawaharlal was the hero of my youth, . . . to me his image still glows.'

By the time Gopal had finished his study, his hero was no longer a hero to others. Thus the wistful ending of the third volume, the hope that Nehru might yet regain the lustrous place he once held in India's political and intellectual life. As it happens, Nehru's reputation has slipped still further, at any rate among the thinking and chattering classes. Thirty-six years after his death, it is at its very nadir.

To gauge just how low Nehru's stock has fallen, let us consider an essay published in July 1964 by Rajni Kothari in the *Economic Weekly* of Bombay. Kothari was then, as he is now, one of the most influential Indian intellectuals: those who know his work would not call him an admirer of Nehru. However, in the essay, written with Nehru's memory still fresh in his mind, he wrote of the late prime minister's 'great unifying role' in a difficult period of transition, his shaping of the institutions and procedures of democracy in a large, diverse, and newly independent country. Nehru, wrote Kothari, 'gave rise to a pragmatic orientation to politics, taught Indian leaders the art of managing men and institutions and based political solidarity on the complex mechanics of secular relationships rather than on neat notions of sacrifice and transcendental nationalism.' Moreover, he created an ideological consensus on the need to wed socialism with democracy, a consensus Kothari clearly believed would last and render obsolete 'the wholly artificial left–right dichotomy in our politics.' Dismissing talk of the 'end of an era' with Nehru's demise, the political scientist commented: 'Nothing has ended with the passing away of Nehru: everything of value he left behind is going to last.' There could be 'no better memorial' to the recently deceased leader, he concluded, 'than a continuous search for building further on the foundations he left behind and wherever necessary, improving upon them.'

Reading this essay today, one is struck by the extent to which Nehru once dominated the moral, intellectual and political landscape of India. But thirty-six years is a long time in the life of a nation, and Kothari's assessment can now be seen to have been wide off the mark. The ideological consensus Nehru nurtured has broken down as tendencies of left and right, far from being rendered obsolete, have emphatically reasserted themselves. No longer are political alliances built on the 'complex mechanics of secular relationships'. Rather, caste, religion and ethnicity, 'primordial' ties as it were, are what increasingly bind political parties and movements. Again, the values and procedures of democracy, which Nehru deeply cherished and upheld, have been cast by the waywide. No one has worked on 'building upon or improving' the foundations he laid, though a good many have tried to destroy them.

A future historian, assessing the decline and fall of Nehru in the Indian imagination, might reckon 1977 to be the watershed, the year in which the delegitimation of Nehru began gathering pace. That was when the Janata Government came to power, after long years of Congress rule (or misrule). The Janata Party brought together three disparate political groupings, united in the first instance by their opposition to the Emergency and to Indira Gandhi. These were the

Jana Sangh, the Socialists (both PSP and SSP), and the old style—so to speak 'Gandhian'—Congressmen.

The Janata Party is long dead, and its constituents have each gone their separate ways. Yet an examination of their political styles, in the years since, reveals that aside from the Emergency and Mrs Gandhi, these three political groupings—as well as the intellectuals who supported them—were, and are, also united by their hatred of Jawaharlal Nehru.

Each of the fragments of the Janata experiment has had its own reasons for opposing Nehru and his legacy. The Jana Sangh, now metamorphosed into the Bharatiya Janata Party, chooses to attack Nehru's philosophy of secularism, which in their view has rested on the 'appeasement' of minorities. The claim here is that Nehruvian 'pseudo-secularism', apart from showing grave disrespect to Hindu sentiments, is in the end responsible for all instances of communal and ethnic conflict, most obviously in Kashmir.

By contrast, the Lohiaite Socialists see Nehru as the symbol of the upper-caste, upper-class, English-speaking intelligentsia that has held sway since independence. This elite, they contend, has manipulated both political and economic power to its advantage. In the process, it has denied the aspirations—political, economic and cultural—of the low- and middle-caste, non-English-speaking majority, whom they themselves seek to represent.

If for the BJP Nehru could not represent the 'spirit of India' because he did not subscribe to the right religion—indeed he subscribed to no religion at all—for the Lohiaite his being unfit to rule was proven by the fact that he stood apart, in class, culture and language, from those he ruled over. The Gandhian critique takes a different line of argument altogether. It contends that Nehru, despite being the Mahatma's acknowledged heir, ultimately betrayed his legacy. Where Gandhi fought for a country based on agriculture, a confederation of self-sufficient village republics, they see Nehru as having imposed a model of industrial development that centralised power in the cities by devastating the countryside. Those who attack Nehru in the Mahatma's name have argued forcefully that planned industrialisation has fuelled both environmental degradation and social conflict, outcomes that could have been avoided if India had instead followed a 'Gandhian' approach to economic development.

To the Hindutva, Lohiaite and Gandhian critiques has now been added a fourth. This comes from supporters of economic liberalisation who point an accusatory finger at Nehru for pushing the state up the commanding heights of the economy. Without Nehru's folly, they say, India would long since have become a Tiger to beat all the other Asian Tigers. As a passionate free-marketeer remarked recently, Raj Krishna's derisive phrase, the 'Hindu rate of growth', should be renamed the 'Nehru rate of growth'.

This is a change of name that would be welcomed by the BJP, and perhaps tacitly by the Congress as well. For Nehru's own party has most emphatically turned its back on his legacy. It was the Congress that first committed itself to freeing the economy from the constraints of state and domestic market. It has responded to the Lohiaites by adopting Mandal—to which creed Nehru would certainly have been opposed. No one can accuse the Congress of being secular, or even 'pseudo-secular', for it has cultivated religious sensibilities as assiduously as anybody else. Indeed, it is remarkable how little use is made any more by the Congress, in rhetoric or in practice, of Nehru's name and legacy.

It is a curious irony that almost the only defenders of Nehru today are to be found among the Marxists. So long as he lived, Marxists were unsparing in their criticisms of Nehru. They saw him as a well meaning but fatally indecisive man, unable or unwilling to expropriate the propertied and bring about real socialism. Immediately following Rajni Kothari's essay in the *Economic Weekly* of 1964 was a Marxist plaint bemoaning India's ill-fortune in that its long-time leader was not made of the same fibre as Lenin and Stalin. But now, with Eastern Europe gone, Indian public-sector companies have become the flagship of socialism, to be defended to the last. In this scenario Nehru has at last become, for the Indian Marxist, an ideological ally rather than foe.

In this defence of Nehru the Marxists stand isolated. As I have argued here, his intellectual and political legacy has been attacked, sometimes devastatingly, from a variety of vantage points. To me, Nehru's posthumous reputation brings to mind a remark of the nineteenth-century British radical, Edward Carpenter. Carpenter claimed that 'the Outcast of one Age is the Hero of another'. He obviously had himself in mind—an environmentalist and prophet of sexual liberation well ahead of his time. But the case of Jawaharlal Nehru shows that the opposite is equally true. That is, the Hero of one age can very well become the Outcast of another. For no man was so greatly adored during his lifetime, yet so insistently villified since his death.

This transformation is made all the more poignant when we consider that Nehru himself was serenely confident of his place in the heart of India's posterity. This comes out in his Last Will and Testament, where he asserts that the Indian people have loved him as they loved no one else before or since. It is also illustrated by a tale I was once told by the old I.C.S. officer C.S. Venkatachar. One day in the mid nineteen-fifties, shortly before he achieved superannuation, Venkatachar passed the prime minister in the corridors of the secratariat. 'I say Venkatachar', said Nehru. 'I believe you are retiring soon. Have I given you a photograph of myself?' The reply was in the negative, so Nehru at once sent round a framed and inscribed photograph.

That photo, the famous Karl Karsch portrait of the philosopher-king in contemplative mood, thereafter dominated Venkatachar's drawing-room. The civilian died in 1999; but in deference to his memory the family has not disturbed the arrangement of artefacts in his room. In a house in Bangalore's Jayamahal Extension, thus, there stands a small memorial to Nehru. Thousands of other Indian homes have meanwhile discarded their own lovingly framed photographs of our once but not future King.

The Dictator's Defence: Indira Gandhi and the Indian 'Emergency'

'I had always believed that Mrs Gandhi had no faith in democracy, that she was by inclination and conviction a dictator. This belief has tragically turned out to be true.'

—Jayaprakash Narayan, prison diary, entry of 22 July 1975

'I have no more powers than I had before.'

—Indira Gandhi, in an interview with NBC, 24 August 1975

'Today's papers also publish a Mrs Gandhi-Karanjia interview. Most of it is the usual stuff: self-righteousness, smugness, and the pose of being the country's saviour.'

—Jayaprakash Narayan, prison diary, entry of 22 August 1975

'I am a very humble person.'

—Indira Gandhi, in an interview with the Mauritius Broadcasting Corporation, 4 October 1975

'Today the only thing the people are allowed to do is to sing the praises of Mrs Gandhi.'

—Jayaprakash Narayan, prison diary, entry of 7 September 1975

'I do not think there is anyone who is less authoritarian than I am.'

—Indira Gandhi, in an interview with American journalist Mary Carras, July 1978

BETWEEN June 1975 and January 1977 Indian democracy took an extended leave of absence. Under directions from the prime minister, Mrs Indira Gandhi, political opponents were jailed, human rights extinguished, news censored, and a personality cult of the Leader promoted. The 'Emergency', as it is known, was once regarded as a defining moment in the history of independent India. After it was lifted, and Mrs Gandhi dethroned, the Emergency experience was viewed as a 'near miss' so to say, whereby this country had narrowly failed to permanently join the well-subscribed ranks of the world's dictatorships. Political commentators alerted the citizenry to its lessons—not to allow bureaucrats and judges to ally with political parties, never to justify curbs on freedom of expression, above all to always put faith in process rather than personality.

June 2000 marks the twenty-fifth anniversary of the declaration of Emergency. One might have expected solemn and cautionary remembrance. Instead, recent events suggest that the Indian political class may be revising its views of the Emergency. The ruling coalition in Delhi is dominated by men who were once jailed by Mrs Indira Gandhi. Yet, this past January, the Government of India awarded the Padma Vibhushan—the country's second highest honour—to one man who was cabinet secretary during the Emergency, and to another who, as high commissioner to the United Kingdom between 1975 and 1977, enthusiastically spread false information about the situation at home. Then, in March, the person who had been Indira Gandhi's ambassador in the United States died. His obituarists respectfully marked the important milestones in his career without so much as mentioning his time justifying the Emergency in Washington. Service to the state, it seems, shall be rewarded regardless of the kind of service or, indeed, the kind of state.

Perhaps the most daring re-interpretation of the Emergency comes in a recent book by Mrs Indira Gandhi's long-serving Principal Secretary, P.N. Dhar.* The Emergency, we may recall, was promulgated after a High Court judge in Allahabad found the prime minister guilty of 'electoral malpractices'. An appeal to the Supreme Court could be made, although the prime minister would, in the interim, have to vacate her post in favour of some other Member of Parliament from the Congress party. The thought was abhorrent to Mrs Gandhi's family and advisers—and to herself too. Hence the declaration of Emergency.

In P.N. Dhar's account, the Emergency was not really a consequence of Mrs Gandhi's fear of losing her personal position. It was, rather, the outcome of the year-long agitation against corruption and maladministration led by the veteran Gandhian Jayaprakash Narayan. This agitation, in his interpretation, had undermined law and order, caused anarchy, and spread violence. Were one to reduce his argument to numbers, then it would appear that the responsibility for the declaration of Emergency was 90% Narayan's, 10% Mrs Gandhi's. Dhar does not deny the violations of human rights and the state violence during Emergency rule, but he determinedly draws the reader's attention to the simultaneous decline in prices. If Narayan was principally responsible for the Emergency, then, suggests Dhar, the prime minister's second son, Sanjay Gandhi, was principally responsible for what went wrong during the Emergency. The harassment of slum dwellers and the forced sterilisations were the work of the son—who held no official position—but the rise in foodgrain production and the checks on inflation were, one supposes, exclusively the work of the mother.

For a dictator, Indira Gandhi had a remarkably long training in the school of democracy. On her thirteenth birthday, her father, then in prison, began writing her a series of letters, later published as *Glimpses of World History*. Starting with the Greeks, this wide-ranging tour took in the old Indian village republics, ancient Chinese kingdoms, the rise

*P.N. Dhar, *Indira Gandhi, the 'Emergency' and Indian Democracy* (New Delhi: Oxford University Press, 2000).

of monotheism and its associated political formations, Buddhism, the Mughals, and the Industrial Revolution, and much else besides. Jawaharlal Nehru was both an Indian patriot and a Western-trained socialist-democrat for whom history unfolded as the oft-interrupted progress of the human animal towards greater sociability and freedom. The latter chapters explored how 'democracy, which was for a century and more the ideal and inspiration of countless people, and which can count its martyrs by the thousands', was now 'losing ground everywhere'. The last letter, sent to Indira on 9th August 1933—three years after the first—ended with this excerpt from Rabindranath Tagore's great poem, *Gitanjali*:

> Where the mind is without fear and the head is held high;
> Where knowledge is free;
> Where the world has not been broken up into fragments by narrow domestic walls;
> Where words come out from the depth of truth;
> Where tireless striving stretches its arms towards perfection;
> Where the clear stream of reason has not lost its way into the dreary desert sand of dead habit;
> Where the mind is led forward by thee into ever-widening thought and action—
> Into that heaven of freedom, my Father, let my country awake.

Glimpses of World History sold briskly, and in time the author was persuaded by his publisher to bring out an expanded edition. A freshly writen postscript, dated 14th November 1938, outlined the major political developments of the nineteen-thirties. 'The growth of fascism during the last five years and its attack on every democratic principle and conception of freedom and civilisation,' wrote Jawaharlal to Indira, 'have made the defence of democracy the vital question today.' Unfortunately, 'democracy and freedom are in grave peril today, and the peril is all the greater because their so-called friends stab them in the back.'

Later, as she came to adulthood, Mrs Gandhi voted, with hundreds of millions of others, in five general elections in free India. All were won by the Congress party—three times under Jawaharlal Nehru's leadership, twice under hers. The evidence suggests that, even while he was alive, she did not completely share her father's faith in the democratic process. In December 1949 she protested his non-interference at the take-over by lesser Congressmen of the *National Herald*, a newspaper started by Jawaharlal and regarded by some as Nehru family property. 'You tolerate a lot of things', she told her father, sarcastically: 'It makes one's heart bleed to hear everyone say that it is no use bringing anything to your notice since you don't do anything about righting things.' In 1956 she protested his allowing autonomy in dealing with their states to regionally powerful and respected Congressmen: 'You are tending more and more to accept without question, the opinions of certain people with regard to certain parts of the country.' Most famously, as Congress president in 1959 she prevailed upon Nehru to use a previously unused provision of the Indian Constitution to dismiss the democratically elected Communist government of Kerala.

Also in 1959, while on a visit to Kenya, Mrs Gandhi had spoken approvingly in public of one-party regimes. The Chinese invasion of October 1962 and the criticisms it spawned of Nehru and his policies appeared to have consolidated these feelings. In January 1963 she wrote to a friend, complainingly, of 'the price we pay for democracy [which] not only throws up the mediocre person but gives strength to the most vocal howsoever they may lack knowledge and understanding.'

These reservations were to find full expression in the Emergency of 1975–7. One might damage the revisionist views now current by a careful social history of those years, by a documentation of democracy's destruction and the spread of terror, intimidation and violence. By contrast, this essay seeks to set the record straight in the words of Mrs Gandhi herself. My aim is to demonstrate that the Indian prime minister was an actively willing dictator, not a reluctant one pushed by malevolent opponents and an unruly son into extinguishing democracy. My main sources are her own words, as articulated in print as well as in some private correspondence that has never before been made public.

II

Mrs Gandhi's singular contribution to Indian political discourse was the idea of the 'foreign hand'. The nationality of this hand is hard to establish, although one presumes it was coloured white. A week after the declaration of Emergency, the prime minister gave an interview to M. Shamim of the *Times of India.* 'The aim of the opposition parties was obvious', she remarked; it was 'to paralyse the Government and indeed all national activity and thus walk to power over the "body" of the nation. The situation had come to such a pass that a few more steps would have led to disintegration, which would have exposed us to foreign danger.' She returned to the theme in a speech of 11th November, broadcast over what was now routinely referred to, if in private, as All Indira Radio. Here, the prime minister told the nation that 'there are many people outside the country who are not our well-wishers and who do not like to see India being strong and united and carrying forward its economic programmes. This was their desire and their efforts and our countrymen also got entrapped in the process.'

Then, and afterwards, it was difficult to reliably identify these foreign ill-wishers. In 1975 India's otherwise most dangerous neighbour, Pakistan, had recently been defeated on the battlefield, and was still to come to terms with the loss of its eastern wing. With Mao on his deathbed, China was not in an adventurist mood either. As for the Russians, there was in place an Indo-Soviet Friendship Treaty. No European country had much of a stake, political or economic, in India. Was it the United States of America that Mrs Gandhi had in mind? She would never clearly say, although her advisers and followers would occasionally speak of the dark doings of the Central Intelligence Agency.

This paranoid talk of interfering foreigners is best understood, perhaps, in the light of internal politics, in view of the rapid fall in Mrs Gandhi's own popularity. The decline had been dramatic. The year 1971, let's remember, had begun with the sweeping victory of her Congress party in the general elections, and had ended with the decisive triumph over Pakistan in the Bangladesh war, a win in which more credit was seen to accrue to the prime minister than to her generals. She was now the elected Empress of India. Opposition politicians began comparing her to the all-powerful Hindu goddess Durga, a comparison made permanent in a series of murals painted by the famous artist M.F. Husain. No one dared predict how long her lawful reign might last. But then two bad monsoons supervened, and OPEC raised the price of crude oil. The scarcity of water and fuel was made more deadly by nepotism and graft. The prime minister's son Sanjay, a half-trained mechanic with no proper qualifications for the task, started building a car factory with land and loans alloted at preferential rates by public institutions. Two crucial Congress-ruled states, Gujarat and Bihar, saw the unprecedented spread of official corruption.

The response to all this was the movement led by Jayaprakash Narayan, which quickly spread from his native Bihar to other parts of the country. Suddenly, the empress began to look vulnerable. Mrs Gandhi's predicament, *circa* 1974–5, is comparable to the situation of the Zimbabwean president, Robert Mugabe. Mugabe too started on high, and at first climbed higher. The early years in power of the former freedom fighter were marked by racial reconciliation and all-round economic growth. Here too, drought and graft and nepotism combined to raise the hopes of the opposition. Mugabe's initial response to criticism was to concentrate power in his hands by marginalising and persecuting erstwhile comrades such as Joshua Nkomo. This was, if inadvertent, a leaf out of Mrs Gandhi's book, for she had swiftly cut to size Congressmen who enjoyed an independent source of moral or political authority. When the criticisms of his increasingly dictatorial rule intensified, Mugabe answered with talk of conspiracies aided by homosexual-friendly Western powers. Like the Zimbabwean, Mrs Gandhi found it hard to understand, for herself, how a previously adoring citizenry had begun to make noises of protest. It was altogether more convenient to blame foreigners than to look for signs of flawed governance within.

During the Emergency the Congress president, D.K. Barooah, coined the slogan 'Indira is India, India is Indira'. Equating herself with the nation—or at any rate with the nation's best interests—was often Mrs Gandhi's own endeavour too. The Emergency was declared, she claimed in that broadcast of 11 November 1975, because

> we felt that the country has developed a disease and, if is to be cured soon, it has to be given a dose of medicine, even if it is a bitter dose. However dear a child may be, if the doctor has prescribed bitter pills for him, they have to be adminstered for his cure. The child may sometimes cry and we may have to say, "Take the medicine, otherwise you will not get cured". So, we gave this bitter medicine to the nation.

'Now when a child suffers', continued the doctor-matriarch, 'the mother suffers too. Thus, we were not very pleased to take this step. We were also sad. We were also concerned. But we saw that it worked just as the dose of the doctor works.'

The Indian dictator's mentality is also revealed in some previously unpublished correspondence with her English friends. The art historian and ex-Indian Civil Service officer W.G. Archer had written to Mrs Gandhi in December 1975 to congratulate her on her 'bold action'. She 'must have been bitterly aggrieved', wrote Archer, 'that many supposed "friends of India" in this country had patently failed to understand or approve your action in declaring the Emergency.' Now the prime minister was indeed cognisant of the general and well-merited opposition of the British intelligentsia to what she had done. While some English politicians—such as Michael Foot—had offered unconditional support, the press was not so obliging. *The Times* carried a series of hostile reports, prompting the Indian high commissioner B.K. Nehru (now a Padma Vibhushan awardee) to write a letter to the newspaper describing conditions in Indian jails: 'The care and concern showered by the state authorities upon the welfare of the detenus who are well housed, well fed and well treated, is almost maternal.' But the criticisms persisted. The December 1975 issue of the respected *Encounter* magazine printed a long essay sympathetic to Jayaprakash Narayan under the tell-all title 'Indira Gandhi's Prisoner'.

Jawaharlal Nehru's daughter could live more easily with American or Soviet disapproval. So she wrote back to W.G. Archer saying she was 'touched' by 'the understanding you show of the complex situation in our country'. She continued:

> India is not an easy country to know. Perhaps that is the reason why we irritate the Western world so much. The struggle here is not merely one of economic growth or even of social justice but of retaining our individuality and developing in our own way. Unfortunately most educated Indians are taken in by the glitter of the affluent countries and by their propaganda that theirs is the best of all possible worlds.

One is struck by the resemblance here to sentiments expressed by the likes of Mobutu Sese Seko, Fidel Castro and Lee Kuan Yew, that is, by authoritarians of military or communist or any other provenance. These would reject human rights as a Western imposition, and home-grown defenders of those rights as Western agents. To that presumed universalism is offered the Singaporean or Cuban or Indian alternative of 'retaining our individuality and developing in our own way', a way that does not admit of such irritants as freedom of speech and freedom of association.

In March 1976 W.G. Archer visited India and met Mrs Gandhi. His notes of the interview reveal a ruler whose resolve was mixed with a dangerous dose of paranoia. 'I have to keep India together', she said to him: 'that is an absolute must.' 'Total freedom' (of the press and public opinion) 'will be fatal to India.' Likewise, 'total devolution [will] be fatal to India'. And, notably, 'The Emergency had made the State Ministers shake in their shoes. This was long overdue . . .'.

So far as this historian can judge, neither before nor during the Emergency was there any serious threat to the unity and integrity of India. Would freedom of the press and public opinion be fatal to India, or to Indira? The question was raised in October 1976 by the British columnist Bernard Levin. Levin wrote a two-part essay in *The Times* which focused principally on press censorship and interference with the judiciary in India. 'After studying a substantial amount of material on the subject,' Levin concluded that 'Mrs Gandhi's shabby little regime' definitely qualified for that definitive epithet, 'totalitarian'.

He ended his essay by quoting the farewell editorial of the Bombay journal *Opinion*: 'The current Indira regime, founded on 25 June 1975, was born through lies, nurtured by lies, and flourishes by lies. The essential ingredient of its being is the lie.'

The Emergency lasted for twenty months. In January 1977, to everyone's surprise, elections were called. There are competing explanations as to why this decision was taken. Within India at the time, as I myself recall, it was widely believed that Mrs Gandhi's own trusted spies from the Government's Research and Analysis Wing had predicted a comfortable victory for her. In his book, P.N. Dhar speculates that she wanted once more to hear the accolade of the people, to seek through the campaign trail the admiration and reverence that had so readily come her way in 1971. A third possibility is that Mrs Gandhi was shamed by the example of Pakistan, then enjoying one of its all-too-rare periods of democratic rule.

When general elections were due in early 1976 Mrs Gandhi amended the Constitution to extend, by a year, the life of the Lok Sabha. Later, the Lok Sabha's life was extended by a further year, until early 1978. Her advisers, and especially her son Sanjay, thought this process could continue forever. One still does not know, for certain, why in 1977 she decided to hold elections after all. Anyway, her party was comprehensively defeated, and the prime minister and Sanjay lost in their constituencies. Others saw her defeat as a commentary on authoritarianism and abuse of power. But for Mrs Gandhi it was time to unwrap, once more, the theory of the foreign hand. Thus the unseated dictator wrote to a relative that 'people have always thought that I was imagining things or overreacting but there has been a deep conspiracy and it was bound to overtake us.' Or, as she helpfully explained to a foreign interviewer, 'they had a lot of money to spend . . . Some sections in the Janata party had the support of the Western press, Amnesty International and other Western organisations. Another section was supported by the Soviets.'

Mrs Gandhi was now out of power, but the condemnation of the

Emergency persisted. In *The Guardian* of 16 November 1978, a British radical of the left, E.P. Thompson, recalled a visit to New Delhi in the winter of 1976–7. The prime minister personally received the gift Thompson was carrying—copies of letters written by her father to his—but meetings elsewhere and with other people convinced him that Mrs Gandhi and her son Sanjay had unfairly confiscated and abused the good name of Jawaharlal Nehru. In his essay, Thompson wrote with feeling of how, despite spending years in British jails, Nehru could still befriend Englishmen: 'One would have to go rather far back in British history to find an article of that quality: to find persons willing to undergo years of imprisonment, and to emerge with unflagging intellectual vitality and with so little bitterness.' This was a civilised human being and, as his years in office showed, a democrat besides. During the Emergency Mrs Gandhi and her son were teaching the Indian people to turn their backs on 'the best traditions of Congress and of Nehru.'

III

Mrs Gandhi had certainly read Bernard Levin in October 1976, and it is likely that, two years later, she read E.P. Thompson too. Like other Indians of her class and generation, she respected both *The Times* and *The Guardian*, the one the voice of the British establishment, the other the vehicle of progressive, anti-imperial, and generally pro-Indian sentiment. But their barbs were nothing to one that came her way in October 1981. The Emergency was now a distant memory, and the person who brought it about was now back in office, after being two-and-a-half years out of power. Mrs Gandhi saw, or was perhaps alerted to, an item in the British press which claimed that Lord Louis Mountbatten, the viceroy who had so gracefully brought down the Union Jack back in August 1947, refused to visit India between 1975 and 1977 as it was then a 'police state'. Mountbatten was dead, so the Indian prime minister instead addressed her complaint to his son-in-law, Lord Brabourne. 'During the emergency', wrote Mrs Gandhi to the English family whose approval she most sought,

> some people were arrested, some were politicians but the larger number were what we call anti-social elements—smugglers, dacoits, hoarders, black-marketeers, etc., whose activities had been pushing up our prices, creating shortages and were generally harmful to the people as a whole. Not once during [the] emergency was there any show of police strength. We ourselves released all political prisoners some time before the 1977 elections. When the Janata Party came to power, it released the criminals, with dire consequences from which we have not yet recovered.

This is an illustration of what George Orwell called 'newspeak', the language of euphemistic lying characteristic of dictators and dictatorial regimes. It was a language that came naturally to Indira Gandhi. In a broadcast of 27th June 1975 that first justified the Emergency to the nation, she said 'the purpose of censorship is to restore a climate of trust'. In August of that year, with all her political opponents locked up in jail, fundamental rights extinguished and the media censored, she informed the American journalist Norman Cousins on a visit to his country that 'what has been done is not an abrogation of democracy but an effort to safeguard it'. In a televised discussion on this trip to the U.S.A., she magisterially announced that 'people are already being released almost every day'. A little later, she told a Bombay weekly that 'there is no use of force and . . . there is no show of force anywhere in the country. The truth is that the police have had less work since the Emergency than ever before.' In the last week of 1975, alerting a conference of lawyers to some impending amendments to the Constitution, Mrs Gandhi remarked that 'if any change is required, it will be not to lessen democracy but to give more meaning to democracy, to keep democracy, to make it a more living democracy'. Such gems, carefully culled from their boss's speeches by a craven high commissioner and his staff, were printed on art paper by an expensive London studio and presented to the world in a pamphlet with the wonderful title: *Democracy Preserved: Facts about the Emergency in India.*

More notable than Mrs Gandhi's attitudes while the Emergency was on was her retrospective defence of it. This, as the comments to Lord Brabourne suggest, is total. Consider also Volume III of Indira

Gandhi's *Selected Speeches and Writings*, issued by the Publications Division of the Government of India in October 1984, the very month she fell to assassins' bullets. At the heart of the book is the reproduction of a series of speeches delivered and interviews undertaken during and in defence of the Emergency. Their re-publication in 1984, we may be assured, was approved by Mrs Gandhi herself.

Consider, finally, an excerpt from an interview given in July 1978 to the American writer Mary Carras. During the Emergency, said Mrs Gandhi, 'We built our foreign-exchange reserves, and we were beginning to make a go of the public sector. Production had gone up and corruption had come down, and everything was going much more smoothly . . . During the first year of the emergency, everyone (except the smugglers) asked why we hadn't done it earlier.'

An awful lot of smugglers must have been granted the vote in the elections of March 1977. Or perhaps we should set against the dictator's defence the pithy remark of an Indian jurist that the Emergency was a 'fraud on the president, a fraud on the Council of Ministers and a fraud on the people.' In my view the fairest comment on Indira Gandhi's Emergency was reported by the distinguished American journalist A.M. Rosenthal. Rosenthal, like E.P. Thompson, would underline the contrast between the democratic Nehru and his dictatorial daughter. Visiting New Delhi in late 1975 he was told of a grim joke doing the rounds within which it was assumed that the father still lived while his daughter reigned. Thus 'Indira is in the Prime Minister's house, and Jawaharlal is back to writing letters to her from jail again'.

No amount of whitewash can remove the stain upon Indian democracy caused by the naked self-interest of the illiberal daughter of a quintessentially liberal father.

The Editor and the Son: Khushwant Singh and Sanjay Gandhi

IN the summer of 1970 Khushwant Singh took a month's leave from editing the *Illustrated Weekly of India*. He had been awarded a fellowship by the Rockefeller Foundation, to be spent in the estate they owned on a hill overlooking Lake Como in northern Italy. The Villa Serbelloni, as those who have been there know, is a sensuously beautiful place to live a month in. Or a week, or a day. The food is good, the wine better, the views out of this world. Between meals, one might walk through the pines or admire the garden, or drink coffee in a cafe by the waterfront. When the Foundation invites a writer here he is not even expected to write.

The one thing the estate lacks is a tennis court. For Khushwant, who had played two sets in a colonial club every morning of his life, this was a real and unanticipated hassle. Reluctantly, he decided to make do with a daily swim. After an early breakfast he would walk down the hill and breast his way across the lake. Then, his abundant hair hung out to dry, clad only in the mandatory *kaccha*, but with his *kada* glistening in the mid-morning sun, he would climb the hill on the other side. In time he would return, get into the water once more, and swim back to the Villa Serbelloni.

This daily ritual was followed, with increasingly awed fascination, by residents on the far shore. Back in the nineteen-seventies the north of Italy had some peasants, real peasants, who cultivated fields and reared sheep on the slopes of the mountains that ring Lake Como. Nothing in their culture or folklore had prepared them for the sight of a Sardar after his Swim. The lord who once lived in the manor house had been seen, if at all, only atop a horse. Of the Americans who later patronised the place, the odd fellow might have entered the water, sometimes, but then he was coloured white, had close cropped hair, and was clean shaven besides.

A week passed, and still the Sardar came, every morning. Another week and the peasants had convinced themselves that this was a saint, *il santo.* By the end of his stay he had been elevated further still, to the rank of 'great saint', or *il santo grande.* So epochal was Khushwant's holiday in the Como hills that to this day local history is marked by reference to it. Do you not remember the murder of that inn-keeper, an old man will say, it happened the winter following the visit of *il santo grande.*

II

The story of Khushwant Singh's beatification was told to me by the philosopher Ninian Smart, whose wife is Italian, and who owns a little cottage in the hills abutting Lake Como. The Sardar does not, I believe, know of his elevation at all. Were he to be told the tale he would have a hearty chuckle. Heartier still would be the chuckles of the hundreds of thousands of Indians who read him. For these have been brought up to understand that the Sardar is an authentic anti-saint who has malice towards all and whose wordly ways would make Mahatma Gandhi weep. Was not one of his books called *Not a Nice Man to Know*? And another advertised as *Sex, Scotch and Scholarship*, the order indicating that the third item would be seriously contaminated by the first two?

Khushwant has indeed drunk much Scotch in his time. True, only a *chotta* peg or two every evening, but then he started early and has, bless him, lived long. The sex, or at any rate much of it, has probably taken place mostly in the mind. But contrary to what he says, and contrary to what his readers think, his claims to sainthood shall not be seriously challenged by his personal habits. Certainly the peasants of Lake Como would make light of them. Their holy men, like the fictional Don Camillo, have liked their wine and their illegally shot game, and their women too. This is well known to and easily forgiven by their lay followers.

In Italy and in India, Khushwant Singh's claims to sainthood shall be challenged not by Sex or Scotch, but by Sanjay. It is that other 'S' that lies like a dark shadow behind his reputation as writer and citizen. I recall a conversation in 1978 with a mutual friend who had had a book dedicated to her by Khushwant Singh. When I reminded her of this, she quickly explained: 'It was in his pre-Sanjay days.' (The lady was herself a brave opponent of the Emergency.) But time heals, and ordinary Indians are amnesiac anyway. The Sardar has written a great deal after Sanjay Gandhi's death, some of it hackwork, but much of it good, wise and generous. His literary reputation stays high. His recent fiction may be ordinary, but his fine early novels and stories and the outstanding *History of the Sikhs* remain in print. His reach and readership are greater, by far, than that of any other Indian writer. Meanwhile, his political reputation has steadily climbed. He has associated with no would-be dictator since. He came out against Jarnail Singh Bhindrawale, which was brave, because he could so easily have been bumped off. He has come out against the Hindu fundamentalists, which is braver still, because some of those fellows are now in power.

But he did support—and more than enthusiastically—an ill-educated and despicably despotic lumpen named Sanjay Gandhi. Why?

III

June 2000 marked the twenty-fifth anniversary of the declaration of the Emergency. Back issues of the *Illustrated Weekly of India* provide an indispensable window to the events of that time. Let's begin with the issue of 6th April 1975 and its cover story entitled 'Total Revolution'. This eight-page illustrated article examines the movement against the ruling Congress led by Jayaprakash Narayan. The editor, whose byline accompanied the piece, made clear his personal admiration for Narayan. Jayaprakash, he wrote, was 'a great and good man', a 'man of courage who has often championed unpopular causes', the 'most spectacular figure in the 1942 "Quit India" movement', who 'more than any other person or voluntary organisation staved off death from hunger in the Bihar famine of 1967'. JP's current ideology, of 'Total Revolution', was, however, a bundle of contradictions—'he has been talking and acting as if he is Garibaldi, Lenin and Mahatma Gandhi all rolled in one.' Moreover, the JP movement had gathered around it a band of opportunistic followers united only by their hatred of the prime minister, Mrs Indira Gandhi. Their agitation sought to undermine established procedures and elected governments. 'Once a person is fairly elected', wrote Khushwant,

> no pressure must be brought on him to prevent him from discharging his duties as the representative of his people till the people themselves decide at the end of his term to replace him. This is fundamental to the working of democracy. This is what JP's movement seeks to destroy.

The balance with which the essay on JP was written is not visible in a laudatory article published, a month later, on Sanjay Gandhi. This focused on his Maruti car project, then under attack for violating established procedures and for being granted government favours out of turn. Khushwant presented a vigorous brief on behalf of Sanjay Gandhi as an entrepreneur who was yet to enter politics. The project, he wrote, was wholly indigenous. Its cars would cost Rs 5000–6000 less than other cars in the Indian market and would run 18 kilometres to the litre. The peasants whose land had been acquired, said the editor, were paid in excess of the market price. Indeed, 'far from causing hardship, Maruti has opened up avenues of employment to hundreds of families of unemployed Punjabi refugees who live in and around

Gurgaon.' The journalist's defence of Sanjay Gandhi was unqualified. He made the scarcely credible claim that, far from being helped by government officials, Sanjay's project was 'overscrutinised', with permissions 'grudgingly given' because he was the prime minister's son. Anyway, the criticisms would be answered by deeds, for in four years' time Sanjay's factory would roll out 50,000 cars a year. 'Soon little Marutis should be seen on the roads of Haryana and Delhi, and a month or two later they will be running between Kalimpong and Kanyakumari.'

The little Marutis that *now* run on Indian roads have nothing at all to do with Sanjay Gandhi's project. After his death his family, then in power, appropriated the name Maruti and attached it to the Japanese design and production of a standard Suzuki vehicle. Sanjay's own factory did not produce a single roadworthy car.

Khushwant's essay on Maruti marks the beginning of his professional interest in Sanjay Gandhi. The Emergency was declared in the last week of June 1975, and at first the son stayed with his prototypes. In a few months he had begun moving into politics, his moves marked by the increasing regularity of his appearance in the *Illustrated Weekly of India*. The issue of 25th January 1976 carried an 'exclusive interview' with Sanjay (the interviewer's name is not mentioned), where he defended censorship, and where in answer to the question 'What has the country gained in the six months of the Emergency? And what has it lost?' he remarked: 'The greatest gain is a sense of discipline and the speeding up of work. I could give a long list of figures of the achievements on all points—from the lowering of prices to increase in production. This rate of progress was unimaginable a year ago.' Sanjay continued: 'What has the country lost? Smuggling, blackmarketing, hoarding, bus-burning and the habit of coming late to office.'

Once more, we must remind ourselves of some too-easily forgotten facts—namely, that Sanjay Gandhi was not a Member of Parliament, nor of the civil service, nor an office-bearer of the ruling Congress. He was simply the younger son of a prime minister who had locked up opposition politicians and concentrated various powers in her hands. These powers were taken away from institutions such as Parliament and the cabinet and were being shared with Sanjay, who had become an illegitimate second-in-command, more important now than any other minister of the Government of India.

The *Weekly*'s approval of the risen son was wholehearted. The Independence Day issue of the magazine carried a cover story on 'The Man who Gets Thing Done', with its centrepiece an essay-interview by the editor. The interview itself was odd, as these things go, for Khushwant appears to have done most of the talking. A list of leading questions were met by unhelpful answers. Asked of his grandfather's impact on him, Sanjay answered: 'I cannot recall any specific way in which he influenced me.' 'What about books?' the editor persisted: 'Any book influenced you particularly?' 'I cannot think of any' was the response. The words were slightly more forthcoming when it came to politics. 'Why don't you stand for the Presidentship of the Congress?' asked the editor. Sanjay answered that the thought had not entered his head, but added that the Congress did need vitalising. When asked whether he had seen the article in the *Weekly* on changes in the Constitution, Sanjay answered: 'Yes, I saw it but I didn't read it.' He did, however, express his preference for a presidential system of government. And he did support compulsory sterilisation.

The interview was accompanied by a long biographical sketch. The editor had talked to Sanjay's friends, to officials who had worked in the prime minister's household, and to other interested parties. One interviewee remarked that 'all my other friends are dull compared to Sanjay.' Another said 'Sanjay has a real spirit of adventure.' A third added: 'Sanjay does not know the meaning of the word "fear".' Others spoke of his 'sense of justice.' Interestingly, the editor was now on the defensive as regards the Maruti project: 'The only valid criticism that could be made against Maruti', he wrote, 'is that the production is well behind schedule and although considerably cheaper than other makes, it will not be a people's car.' Sanjay Gandhi could not run a factory but, it appears, he might yet successfully run a country. Consider then the article's conclusion:

> Sanjay Gandhi has many more critics than his mother. 'On whose authority is Sanjay doing what he is doing?' they ask. I would like to put to them a lot of questions in return. 'Do you agree that what Sanjay is doing is for the good of the common people and therefore of the nation? Didn't our slums need clearing? Didn't our population need to be controlled? Didn't our forests need to be saved? Wasn't corruption to be rooted out? Why cavil about someone who is at long last getting all this done?'
>
> Sanjay has taken a heavy load on his young shoulders. He has a long and arduous road ahead of him. Do not strew banana skins on his path. Help him to reach his goal of a prosperous and happy India. We, of the older generation, can only dream dreams. Let our young men see visions and make those visions a reality.

This last paragraph was set in bold black type. Any further reservations about his ascendancy to power were, one supposes, quelled by the invocation of Sanjay's horoscope:

> For you, sporty, flighty, frank but philosophical Sagittarius, top-notch achievements will be registered in 1976. At the same time wagging tongues could land you in a legal case, or slander. However, you can take it in your stride (*Bejan Daruwalla—Orient Paperback*).

Three months later, in its issue of 14th October 1976, the *Weekly* ran two pages of photographs under the overall caption: 'Sanjay, Maneka Conquer Maharashtra'. Sanjay Gandhi had joined the Congress' youth wing, a veneer of legitimacy to cloak what was already so evidently a family affair. The photos showed him addressing Congress workers, visiting slums, and having his marriage freshly solemnised by Sikh rites at the great *gurudwara* in Nanded. The head-text said: 'Sanjay won over Maharashtra with his candour and his forthright and down-to-earth talk. Maneka did so with her quiet charm and pleasing personality.' In his 'Editor's Page', Khushwant wrote admiringly of the couple's visit. Sanjay Gandhi had 'added a new dimension to political leadership', for

> he has no truck with shady characters or sycophants; he is a teetotaller, he lives a simple life, he speaks little, he speaks in an honest and forthright manner, his words are not hot air but charged with action. He has done excellent work in Delhi. He has electrified the country's young people and channelised their energies into constructive work. He has awakened all Congressmen everywhere and put them into action. His Youth Congress has done more work in these two years than the main Congress could do in the last five years. Above all he is the first Congress leader who has taken on himself the unpleasant task of cleaning and purging the party of its ills. More power to Sanjay!

Soon, the editor could test how widely his sentiments were shared. In January 1977 Mrs Gandhi announced elections. Her now-freed opponents came together to form the Janata Party. The 23rd January issue of the *Illustrated Weekly of India*, meanwhile, carried the news that Sanjay Gandhi had been voted by its readers as the Indian of the Year '76. But as the campaigning got under way, it became clear that the *Weekly's* readership was not a reliable cross-section of the people of India. In Delhi, the slum-clearance programmes initiated by Sanjay Gandhi had caused much resentment. Across northern India, the Sanjay-inspired campaign of compulsory sterilisation became the key election issue. Democrats and civil libertarians everywhere targeted the son as being responsible, in the main, for the spread of fear and the absence of freedom.

In its issue of 20th February 1977, the *Weekly* ran a long story on 'Youth Congress Power'. The pictures showed Sanjay in various appealing poses: riding in an open jeep doing 'namastes' to cheering crowds, being formally introduced to his mother at a Youth Congress meeting, speaking from a podium himself. The accompanying article was by the editor. 'Since Sanjay is one of the main issues over which the elections will be fought', he remarked, 'it is best to clear the cobwebs of prejudice created by wholly unsubstantiated gossip of his style of functioning and ask ourselves honestly: do we or do we not need Sanjay Gandhi?'

Khushwant's answer was to outline what he believed Sanjay Gandhi had accomplished. To begin with, Sanjay had taken in hand the most critical of all India's problems—population control. The case, it must be admitted, was made with eloquence and skill:

> We've had Health Ministers like the spinster Rajkumari Amrit Kaur peddling coloured bead rosaries, Chandrasekhar with his cafeteria approach, transistor radios and prizes and statistics to bamboozle us; we have Karan Singh with his stale witticisms and more statistics. Precious little did all this add up to. The spiral of births continued in its dizzy climb upwards. And suddenly, last year, it was checked; family planning was converted from a plan into an actuality. It was done by Sanjay Gandhi. He may not have had any authority to do it, but he did it.

The editor rejected all talk of wrongdoing:

> You will have heard a lot of stories about how it was done. Old women's tales of how men and women too old to procreate were sterilised; how boys and girls too young to copulate were deprived of their legitimate right to raise a small family. Check on them carefully and you will discover that there is no truth in them; they gained currency because it is human nature to circulate tales without checking their veracity. Pressure there certainly was but no violence or intimidation. Pressure there must be; in fact it should be increased: no licenses for driving, no ration cards, no jobs or promotions or cheap housing for those who refuse to fulfil their duty to society.

Khushwant then offered his opinion of Sanjay Gandhi's other programmes. 'There was a lot of claptrap about the use of bulldozers', he claimed. In any case the cities had been beautified, the slums removed and the stench cleared. 'All this was done by Sanjay Gandhi. He may not have had any authority to do it, but he did it.' Smugglers and tax evaders had been brought to book or put in gaol. 'Sanjay Gandhi had a big hand in clearing out these people. He may not have had any authority to do it, but he did it.'

Alas, there were people who had seen the bulldozers and even made way for them, people who could certify to the truth of the sterilisation horror stories, people who would less impatiently ask questions about means and ends and about authority and responsibility. The elections were, as Khushwant Singh recognised, to be a verdict on Sanjay Gandhi. As it turned out it was not the verdict he wanted.

IV

We have now seen how a popular and respected editor made of himself and his journal a mouthpiece for Sanjay Gandhi. Why did he? I can offer six possible non-competing explanations.

Consider, first, the influence of culture. The fact of Sanjay Gandhi having married a Sikh would have mattered somewhat to a man who has been deeply loyal to his community, and been its historian too. To the man whose father, Sir Sobha Singh, built much of New Delhi, and who had spent much of his own life there, the fact of Sanjay working to clean up the capital would have mattered deeply.

Second, there is the affinity of ideology. Khushwant is a lover of nature, knowledgeable about trees and about birds. That 'point' on Sanjay's programme, a point so grossly neglected by other politicians, appealed to him. So did the focus on population control, which like many other Indians he thought the most pressing question of all.

Third, there is the personal element. Sanjay and Maneka cultivated the editor, and like most men out of power he was prone to flattery from those in it. Khushwant, moreover, is a man of spontaneous generosity, always willing to believe the best, to trust and publicise the work of those he likes. The aspect of his character which once led him to gift his typewriter to the impecunious Nirad Chaudhuri, and to protect Chaudhuri against hostile critics, also explains why, once Sanjay befriended him, he would back him to the end.

Fourth, there is the psychological attraction of the young for the middle-aged. For what one cannot, by reason of circumstance or temperament, achieve oneself might yet be accomplised by the young: 'Despite the receding hairline he is an incredibly handsome young man', wrote the editor about the Man who Gets Things Done: 'he has dark, fiercely intense and honest eyes.' I might, just a little fancifully, suggest that Khushwant saw himself as a father-figure, with Sanjay the substitute son, the 'doer' who would efficiently execute the wishes of the parent who merely wrote.

Closely allied to the foregoing were the honest patriot's worries about the future of India. His own late-life crisis had merged with the mid-life crisis of the nation. Khushwant had witnessed the partition of his beloved Punjab, then worked with zest to help build Jawaharlal Nehru's India: to begin with, as a diplomat and, later, as editor of the Planning Commission's journal *Yojana.* After Nehru's death he had, with other decent folks of his generation, seen a collective dream disintegrate due to corruption, sectarianism and the erosion of public institutions. With every passing year, the ageing patriot grew evermore desperate about the fate of his land: 'We, of the older generation, can only dream dreams. Let our young men see visions and make those visions a reality.'

A final explanation invokes the peculiar frailties of the professional writer, the all-too-striking similarities between Khushwant's defence of Sanjay Gandhi and the submission to authoritarian rulers of other wordsmiths down the ages. Consider thus Graham Greene's admiration for the Panamanian dictator General Omar Trujillo. Or Gabriel Garcia Marquez's support for the Cuban dictator Fidel Castro. How does one reconcile these with the writer's own intelligence and his otherwise well-established love of liberty? By underlining, perhaps, the writer's susceptibility to flattery from above, and the writer's fascinated envy of the man of action.

In the early nineteen-eighties, Salman Rushdie wrote a public relations tract on behalf of the ruling Sandinistas of Nicaragua called *The Jaguar Smile.* Like Khushwant with Sanjay, Rushdie took momentary leave of his senses and his values and placed his great gifts at the service of an authoritarian state. This, in his view, was justified by the Cold War, and the threat to the Sandinistas from the even uglier men supported by the Americans. But then the Cold War ended and the book was withdrawn. It no longer forms part of the novelist's up-to-date curriculum vitae. But one day a nasty historian will dig out the book and do to Rushdie what I have done here to Khushwant Singh.

Finally, and in fairness to Khushwant, it must be said that sycophancy comes easily to Indians. We submit totally to people in power and reject them totally when they are out of power. A Secretary to Government does not have to check the calendar to know when he is to retire: he can monitor the time remaining in office by the ever-less-extended bows from the *chaprassi*, the *babu*, the chauffeur and of course the additional secretary. So long as Sanjay Gandhi was in power, the deference towards him, of millions of people, was unquestioned. Narayan Dutt Tewari, the chief minister of India's most populous state, once carried his slippers. The seniormost of Congress cabinet ministers, Jagjivan Ram, sucked up to Sanjay Gandhi till the day elections were announced, but defected from the Congress when his spies told him that the opposition would win.

As for Khushwant, with his old-fashioned sense of loyalty, he stayed with the ship until it sank. After the Congress and Sanjay lost, the owners of the *Illustrated Weekly of India* sought to curry favour with the new rulers by sacking the most successful editor the journal had ever had. But Khushwant did not abandon his friend, and lived to see him win a seat in Parliament in January 1980, when the Congress returned to power in New Delhi. Six months later, Sanjay died in an air crash. Khushwant, who was now editor of *The Hindustan Times*, wrote an emotional tribute. 'The only possible inheritor of the Sanjay cult who will figure', he remarked, 'is Maneka. She is like her late husband, utterly fearless when aroused, the very incarnation of Durga astride a tiger.' In light of what Sanjay and Maneka were known to have done during the Emergency, this was both colossally stupid and touchingly loyal.

V

Khushwant Singh's support to Sanjay Gandhi was somewhat redeemed by his simultaneous support to free speech. To the extent allowed by the censor, he allowed dissident voices to speak in the *Illustrated Weekly of India*. In October 1975 he printed an article by his assistant editor, R. Gopalkrishnan, entitled 'Sakti or Woman Power', which artfully and allusively pleaded for a restoration of democracy. 'There is today a great demonstration of woman power in India', wrote 'RGK'.

> Some people believe that, astride on her lion, the Goddess Durga is riding again in our midst. But all are not agreed about who the demons are that she should destroy. Also, most of us wish that the Devi will shed her awesome form and appear again as the loving Ambika or the Mother Goddess.

When, in May 1976, Vinoba Bhave expressed his support to the Emergency, Khushwant published an essay of dissent by an old Gandhian, Sriman Narayan. Inspired by Bhave, Indira Gandhi had spoken, in a public forum in Nagpur, of how 'all talk of satyagraha has no place in the new India we are trying to build.' Gandhi's satyagrahas, she said, were aimed at an external, colonial power—but now India had a government of its own. Sriman Narayan, who had a rather more extensive knowledge of the Mahatma, then provided chapter and verse to show that Gandhi believed that satyagraha was the 'inherent right of the citizen', and that one should certainly protest against an unjust state run by one's own countrymen.

In August 1976 Khushwant used his editor's page to complain of the continuing censorship. He had heard Indira Gandhi's customary Red Fort speech, he said, in the hope that 'the 30th Independence Day celebrations would be ushered in with a proclamation that the Emergency was being lifted, the members of the Opposition having realised the folly of trying to subvert democratic institutions were being released, freedom was being restored to the press and a date set for the General Elections.' Indira Gandhi spoke, alas, of other things. The editor, an 'incorrigible optimist', now hoped that the list of freedoms he had prayed for would be announced on 'Bapu's next birthday anniversary, failing that, Nehru's, Indira Gandhi's and the next Republic Day.'

Above all, Khushwant Singh used the correspondence columns of his journal—the columns read least attentively by the censor—to express the diversity of Indian opinion. Thus on 22nd February 1976 the

Weekly printed an article by S.N. Agarwal called 'Make Sterilisation Compulsory—Now!' Subsequent issues carried letters explaining precisely what that might mean. M. Iyengar, writing from Madhupur, described a vasectomy camp he had attended: 'Razor blades straight from the market were being used while doctors smoked and chewed *paan.* Nor surprisingly, a near fatal accident took place. And how many infected wounds will have to be nursed in the days to come is anyone's guess.' Dr Jagjit, writing from Bombay, accepted the importance of birth control, but asked 'how, in a democracy, a man can be dragged out of his house against his will and have a part of him cut off—which is what compulsory sterilisation amounts to.'

Of course Sanjay Gandhi did not read these letters, and perhaps the editor thought them to be old wives' tales himself. But to his credit he printed them. Later in 1976, after the publication of his own celebratory tribute to 'The Man who Gets Things Done', some readers wrote in to cautiously praise the editor and his hero. Others wrote to criticise and condemn. S.C. Suri of Poona suggested changing the name of the journal to 'The Illustrated Weekly of Indi(r)a and Sanjay'. Saeed Muhammad of Madras remarked that he had previously heard of 'journalists being *chamchas* of the power-that-be. But you have taken a step further and gone in for projecting the powers-to-be—a new dimension to sycophantic journalism.' Best of all was a communication from Satyanarain Singh of Bombay, printed as the lead letter in the issue of 12th September 1976. 'Since your homily to Sanjay Gandhi', wrote this reader, 'butter has become scarce and its price has gone up.'

The editor of the *Illustrated Weekly of India* had lost his ability to reason and his sense of proportion but not, thank goodness, his sense of humour.

Stalinist and Indian: E.M.S. Namboodiripad

THE paradox of Indian Marxism is that its practice has always been more appealing than its theory. The Naxalite theoreticians dismiss swidden or shifting cultivation as a 'primitive economic practice', bound to disappear with modernity, yet their cadres organise tribals to protect their traditional forest rights, in most cases the right to cut swidden in land usurped by the government. The Communist Party of India (Marxist) swears by Soviet-style central planning, but in West Bengal they have taken the process of political and economic decentralisation further than has any other party anywhere else in India.

Communists used to speak of 'socialist internationalism', that is, the right to take their orders from Moscow or Peking, yet they are now, and have been for some time, the most patriotic of Indians. Certainly it is only in the Communist Party of India and the CPI(M) that one finds politicians who have enjoyed power for long stretches but are not known to take bribes or maintain Swiss bank accounts.

E.M.S. Namboodiripad, who died in March 1998, was a fundamentally decent and public-spirited man whose mind was messed up by reading too much of J.V. Stalin and V.I. Lenin. In his tribute to EMS, published in *The Telegraph*, Ashok Mitra called him a 'great Marxist theoretician whose thoughts had a pure classical grandeur'.

With due respect, this is one party man talking about another. While Namboodiripad wrote many works of history and political theory, none rose above the second rate. Even if one allows the qualifier '*Marxist* theoretician', EMS does not begin to compare with men such as D.D. Kosambi and Ranajit Guha, who stretched Marxism to its limits, going beyond economic determinism through the incorporation of insights from archaeology, linguistics, numismatics and, above all, anthropology.

As a historian, Namboodiripad interpreted everything through the lens of class struggle and the inevitable victory of revolutionary communism. As an ideologue he followed a man greatly inferior to Karl Marx, and even Lenin, namely Stalin. I have before me a booklet called *On Organisation*, published by the undivided CPI in 1954, and based on a series of lectures delivered by its leading theoretician to the Central Party School in Delhi. Stalin has just died, but Nikita Khrushchev's famous speech repudiating him lies a safe two years in the future. EMS thus begins his talks with the obligatory salutation: 'As Comrade Stalin explained in his *Dialectical and Historical Materialism* . . .' Some pages later we find a worshipful reference to Stalin's 'last work on the *Economic Problems of Socialism* in the USSR', followed again by a long quote. Deeper into the tract are excerpted some gems from Stalin's *Foundations of Leninism*, another book that quickly and deservedly fell into oblivion.

In his writings, Namboodiripad was a craven follower of a crude despot, but as a practising politician EMS was one of the finest in the land. He was, for most of his life, a leading light of the most progressive party in the most progressive state in India.

Much has been written about the Kerala miracle: the strides in health, education and land reform and the quality of governance that has made this possible. As a column of the left and twice chief minister of the state, EMS was a key player in all this. His work for his people was repaid by a deep and genuine affection. On one of his last birthdays, 10,000 Malayalis contributed voluntary labour to desilt a long stretch of an irrigation canal, the patriarch looking on. It was a remarkable tribute, when compared especially with how the birthdays of politicians in other parties are remembered by their followers.

The moral distance between men like EMS and those who now rule India was underlined some years ago by an incident little noticed at the time. In January 1992, P.V. Narasimha Rao's government decided to award the second highest national honour, the Padma Vibhushan, to EMS and to Atal Behari Vajpayee.

It was a noble gesture, recognising contributions to national life by people other than Congressmen—one cannot see governments headed by Indira Gandhi, Rajiv Gandhi or Sonia Gandhi displaying such generosity of spirit. Now while Vajpayee accepted the award, EMS declined, for his personality would not allow attention to be drawn to his achievements. Some weeks later, his home in Kerala was robbed. The police caught the burglar, repossessing for the original owner the stolen goods amounting to one gold sovereign and Rs 800. This after fifty years in public life.

Mitra speaks of the 'purity' of EMS's thought, but we might speak with more justice of the purity of the lived life. In her novel, *The God of Small Things*, Arundhati Roy makes the unfortunate claim that EMS transformed his family home into a luxury hotel. As everyone in Kerala knows, this was another Namboodiripad with similar initials: the Communist EMS had in fact donated his property to the party, an early example of a lifelong and always unselfconscious asceticism.

When one considers what kind of man EMS was, one must also consider it a great pity that he mortgaged his mind to Stalinism. Namboodiripad, of course, did not regret this. He liked to write of how he left his landlord family to join the Congress, then helped start the Congress Socialist Party, then broke away altogether to become a communist, the last constituting, in his view, the decisive step towards the promised land. Both Mahatma Gandhi and Jawaharlal Nehru he criticised as 'bourgeois' leaders who could not transcend the ideology of their class.

There is a most revealing moment in his book, *The Mahatma and the Ism*, where he complains of the poverty of Gandhi's intellect. This man, he says, came as a student to London in 1889, when *Das Kapital* had just appeared in its first English edition, when the Fabian Society of the great Bernard Shaw and the greater Sidney Webb was taking its first bold steps. And yet, writes a non-comprehending EMS, Gandhi chose to join Henry Salt's Vegetarian Society.

The Marxist was bewildered, but bourgeois thinkers like myself see Mahatma Gandhi's vegetarianism as a prelude to his mature political philosophy. For his later attitude to compatriots and adversaries was steeped likewise in *ahimsa* and *karuna*, the ideas of non-violence and compassion. Namboodiripad could not understand this, which is why, in the late 'thirties, he left the Congress for the CPI.

In the next decade his new party committed a series of colossal errors: the support to the British during the war, the support to the Pakistan movement, the ridiculous Russian-inspired attempt to foment an armed revolution immediately after India gained independence. But what if EMS and other like-minded patriots had followed Gandhi instead of Stalin? And what if socialists like Acharya Kripalani and Jayaprakash Narayan had also chosen to stay within the Congress? Might not the party that came to power in 1947 have then had a first-rate set of organisers providing the support that Nehru so desperately lacked to challenge the bunch of conservatives and reactionaries he was instead left with?

This did not happen and EMS and his comrades went on to lead a double life of bankrupt ideology and meaningful practice. Totalitarian thinker and practising democrat, subservient Stalinist and proudly patriotic Indian: this was the tragedy as well as the achievement of E.M.S. Namboodiripad.

Jai Vigyan, Jai Vinash: Bombast, Bomb-blasts, and Certain Indian Scientists

He who invented the atom bomb has committed the greatest sin known to science.

—Mahatma Gandhi, after Hiroshima

I extend my felicitations to all scientists and technologists who have made this possible, and say to them, 'India is proud of you'.

—The President of India,
after the nuclear tests of May 1998

THERE were once two aspiring scientists growing up in the Bangalore of the 1940s. One was a physicist, the other a chemist. Both were fired by the quest for new knowledge, both were inspired by the movement of national regeneration promised by the leaders of a soon-to-be-free India. The institutes of higher education at home were not developed enough, so despite their patriotism both thought it wise to hone their skills in the United Kingdom. Both obtained their Ph.D.s from the Imperial College of Science and Technology and returned home immediately after being awarded their degrees. While both were ambitious, and each possessed intelligence of a high order, neither sought to market his talent in the bazaars of the West.

The physicist wished above all to be a theorist, but thought that to pursue that ambition would be an abdication of social responsibility in a country eager to change, grow, develop. He joined India's atomic energy programme, which was personally overseen by the prime minister. Like Gandhi, Jawaharlal Nehru had been appalled by the bombs dropped on Japanese civilians. If anything, he was more deeply wounded by the act, for his faith in modern science had been all the greater.

I have always believed that the extraordinary support provided by Nehru to India's atomic programme was a product principally of his need to restore faith. For this science-worshipper and erstwhile student of science, the generation of atoms for peace could redeem the promise of science and rid it of the ugly stain of Hiroshima. Not long after the bombs were dropped on the Japanese, Nehru befriended Homi Bhabha, a man with a first-class physics degree from Cambridge and an artist and painter besides. The men were brought together by a shared intellectual pedigree and cultural orientation but one suspects that his own, indifferent second-class degree made Nehru trust Bhabha all the more; certainly he supported his friend's Atomic Energy Commission to the hilt. No government department has been so generously funded or so completely insulated from bureaucratic and political interference. The conditions of work within it were most conducive for scientists of merit, as for instance our young physicist from Bangalore.

Meanwhile his fellow townsman, the chemist, trained also at the great Imperial College, returned to Bangalore to join the faculty of the Indian Institute of Science (IISc). If the AEC (with its component elements such as the Bhabha Atomic Research Centre) constitute one of the few world-class Indian technical research programmes, the IISc is the only Indian institution that, in quality and commitment of faculty, equals a top-flight Western university. Our chemist fitted easily into this place, guiding students and writing an acclaimed book on electrochemistry. But like the physicist he came to believe that 'pure' research was an unpardonable luxury in a country as poor as ours. With some colleagues he established a group that would promote the 'Application of Science and Technology for Rural Areas', ASTRA for short. The tasks ASTRA set itself were the generation and dissemination of technologies that would be low-cost, non-polluting, and of benefit to the poorest of the poor. These included biogas plants, energy-saving and smokeless *chulas*, and sturdy and economical houses made of mud blocks: all were promoted by ASTRA with some success in the villages and towns of Karnataka.

ASTRA was established in 1974. For all his work in the more conventional fields of science, the chemist came to regard the creation of ASTRA as his most lasting achievement. Oddly enough, it was also in 1974 that the physicist from Bangalore oversaw what is considered to be his most decisive contribution to Indian science. This was the nuclear test carried out in the Rajasthan desert in the summer of that year, the necessary precursor to the tests of May 1998.

As the 'Father of the Indian Bomb,' the physicist was much in the news in the summer of 1998, his opinions on the newest explosions respectfully conveyed to the public. Raja Ramanna needs no introduction, but most readers will, I think, be unfamiliar with the name of A.K.N. Reddy, the chemist whose career bears so many parallels with Ramanna's. They share a home town, a London alma mater, a deep and enduring commitment to their land. Where they differ is in the choices they have made, the rather different ends that have dictated what they have done with their minds and with their time. Where one has devoted his science and his life to the greater glory of the Indian state, the other has tried to bend it to the service of the Indian villager.

II

The careers of A.K.N. Reddy and Raja Ramanna illustrate the two rather different trajectories of Indian science. For some considerable time now, only one of these paths has been noticed and praised, funded and promoted. The process culminated in the drama surrounding Pokharan II, but in truth the bias had been visible for some time previously.

The vulgar cheerleaders for the science of destruction go by the euphemism 'defence experts'. These experts do not don uniforms, nor are they generally seen with revolvers at their hip or rifles at their shoulder. They do not design weapons either. Yet they devote their days and probably their dreams to devising ever-more complicated ways of using science to eliminate 'hostile' targets and, by extension, hostile populations.

In this herd of consenting adults there is one man who stands out. His name is K. Subrahmanyam. He is the most fanatically persistent and most persistently fanatic advocate of India's nuclear option. He used to be in government, then in semi-government, and now rests in the folds of a New Delhi newspaper. His arguments were once compressed in file notings and semi-secret reports; they now reach the public domain in great profusion through the editorial and signed column. Perhaps one should withdraw the plural, for his argument is singular, albeit expressed in different ways: Indian scientists must help India make the bomb, more bombs, better bombs, bigger bombs, newer bombs.

The pathetic single-mindedness of K. Subrahmanyam was manifest most starkly in an editorial he wrote when Abdul Kalam was awarded the Bharat Ratna. This praised the scientist, but then offered extraordinary speculation as to why he had been chosen for the award. Was it, the editorial wondered, that the Indian government was thus buying Kalam's compliance—that by means of the Bharat Ratna the government would cap his desire to build more deadly weapon carriers?

In a nation rich in conspiracy theories, this one must take the *barfi*. Tragically, the influence of Subrahmanyam and his ilk is far-reaching. Super-patriots seeking superpower status willingly worship the bomb-makers and missile designers who, they hope, may yet succeed where the Indian economy and the Indian cricket team has failed. The deference paid to a certain kind of science is truly extraordinary. I have quoted at the head of this essay the tribute offered by President K.R. Narayanan to the bomb-makers, and it was Prime Minister Atal

Behari Vajpayee, no less, who declared that from now 'Jai Vigyan' would be appended to the old patriotic slogan 'Jai Jawan, Jai Kisan'. These cues from the top were eagerly taken up by the media. After the Pokharan blasts, the widely circulating newsmagazine *India Today* put on its cover the scientists who supervised and managed the tests—Abdul Kalam, of course, but also AEC men such as Anil Kakodkar and R. Chidambaram. The scientists happily posed for the camera—posed, that is, in *military uniforms.*

Those uniforms have much to hide. For the main beneficiary of the militarisation of Indian science has been our nuclear energy programme. It was originally designed for 'peaceful uses', that is, for generating electricity. But in that endeavour it has lamentably failed. Independent studies have demonstrated that the nuclear energy industry is environmentally disastrous and economically unviable. Anywhere else the discipline of the market and a concern for the health of the ordinary citizen would have made the industry shut down. Instead, and by virtue of its association with the science of destruction, its grants are increased every year.

Speaking in Bangalore a year after the blasts of May 1998, the chairman of the Atomic Energy Commission, R. Chidambaram, claimed that the AEC would generate 20,000 megawatts of power by the year 2020. He could make this statement only because no one in the audience remembered the promises made by previous AEC chairmen. Back in the 1950s, when nuclear energy was all the rage and scientists the world over were claiming that it would soon be 'too cheap to meter', Homi Bhabha predicted that by 1980 the AEC would supply 10,000 megawatts of power. By 1983, roughly ten per cent of the target had been achieved. Undaunted, Raja Ramanna, then in supreme charge of the nuclear programme, promised that by the year 2000 the AEC would generate 10,000 megawatts.

When Chidambaram made his tall claims in Bangalore, he did not, of course, refer to the unfulfilled promises made by his predecessors; Indian technocrats, like Indian politicians, depend much on the forgetfulness of the Indian public. He could be certain that those listening to him did not recall what Bhabha and Ramanna had said, or, even if the odd person did, that he would be too polite to remind him of it. The AEC chairman knew too that with Pokharan II, his tribe of scientists had achieved cult-like status For them, as for Keats's nightingale, 'now more than ever seems it rich to die': now, more than ever, were they immune from any kind of criticism.

Thus far, the nuclear estate in India has been protected by its close links with the bomb-makers. It is very much the spoilt child of the state: 60% of the total science budget of the country is diverted to the AEC. What has it done to justify this most favoured status? If its budget is reduced in half, and the money reallocated to solar energy and the construction of small dams, would this not be more beneficial to the poor and to the environment? It is well past time that these questions were asked and clear answers demanded. For many years now I have been a student of India's nuclear estate, reading and digesting the scarce information that brave critics manage to uncover. Two books I would recommend are *Nuclear Energy and Public Safety,* edited by Vinod Gaur and published by the Indian National Trust for Art and Cultural Heritage; and Jeremey Hall's evocative *Real Lives, Half Lives: Tales from the Atomic Wasteland* (Penguin Books), a brilliant exposé of the harm done by nuclear energy worldwide. Also worth reading is the journal *Anumukti,* edited by the physicist Surendra Gadekar from Vedchi in Gujarat.

From these studies and other such documents it seems conclusive that nuclear energy is uneconomic. The AEC currently survives only because of the huge subsidies provided by the state. But how much longer can a poor country afford such subsidies? For the 1870 megawatts of power the AEC does generate, the people of India have, over a period of fifty years, spent thousands of crores. The economic inefficiences apart, nuclear power is also a major threat to democracy and environmental sustainability.

Alas, nuclear energy is also the only public- or private-sector industry that is never asked to account for its ways. And the patriotic support provided by Pokharan II will allow the AEC to escape scrutiny for some more time yet. There is perhaps a case to be made for the bomb: I will not make it. There is no case whatsoever for us to divert so much money for the production of so little of this dangerous form of energy. The AEC must be held accountable to market norms and democratic scrutiny. A commission of experts should be appointed by the Government of India, consisting of an economist, a legal expert, a couple of doctors, and an energy scientist familiar with alternatives. This commission should examine the promises made by the AEC, and judge them by actual performance. Perhaps we will then discover that in the name of science and patriotism we have created a financial and moral scandal that will put Bofors and our nefarious politician-criminals in the shade.

III

The countenance of A.P.J. Abdul Kalam is known to almost all literate Indians, but who can recognise the name of Pushkaran Sethi, the inventor of the Jaipur foot, the scientist who has helped make less sorrowful the lives of thousands of victims of road accidents and land mines? Or of Laurie Baker, the Kerala architect who has saved crores of rupees for individuals and governments through artfully designed, eco-friendly, and cost-effective dwellings?

There are indeed two paths for Indian science, one of which was most visible in the certificates so handsomely dished out after the nuclear tests of 1998. But should we shout 'Jai Vigyan' only when science makes a terrific noise, when it announces to the world that India yields to no one in the manufacture of weapons of mass destruction?

I think that aspiring scientists need to know that their contributions to India's future do not necessarily lie in the Atomic Energy Commission or the Defence Research and Development Organisation. They must learn as much about Laurie Baker as of Abdul Kalam, of A.K.N. Reddy as well as Raja Ramanna. They should certainly be acquainted with what Mahatma Gandhi told students of the Science College in Trivandrum in 1925:

> Unfortunately we, who learn in colleges, forget that India lives in her villages and not in her towns. India has 700,000 villages and you, who receive a liberal education, are expected to take that education or the fruits of that education to the villages. How will you infect the people of the villages with your scientific knowledge? Are you then learning science in terms of the villages and will you be so handy and so practical that the knowledge you derive in a college so magnificently built—and I believe equally magnificently equipped—you will be able to use for the benefit of the villagers?

These words, spoken more than seventy years ago, cannot be considered out of date. For India is still a land of villages. Villages where the work of modern science has scarcely penetrated, villages for the most part bereft of clean energy, safe water, effective heath-care, reliable housing. Here lie the real challenges for Indian science. But who is to confront them when makers of missiles and blasters of bombs are the only scientists held aloft as icons and role models?

Players

The First Great Indian Cricketer: C.K. Nayudu

WHO was the first great Indian cricketer? The name that would come to most people's lips is K.S. Ranjitsinhji, the immortal 'Ranji'. But Ranji learnt and played his cricket in England, and he was himself quite clear that he was an 'English cricketer'. A more plausible candidate is Palwankar Baloo, a slow bowler who was a prodigious success in the Bombay Quadrangular, in his time India's premier tournament. For my money, however, the first great cricketer produced in India, for India, was the all-rounder Cottari Kankaiya Nayudu.

When reckoned in purely statistical terms, C.K. Nayudu's playing record is modest. He had a highest score of 81 in seven Tests, and a first-class batting average of just under 36, which is some twenty points behind Gavaskar's and nearly forty points behind Vijay Merchant's. But as John Arlott once remarked, cricket historians should be concerned 'with greatness, not damn dots'. Nayudu's own claims to cricketing greatness rest on the explosive quality of his batsmanship, the variety of his all-round skills, the longevity of his career (he played his last Ranji Trophy match at the age of sixty-one, scoring 84), and above all on the sheer strength of his personality.

Nayudu made his first-class debut in the 1916 Quadrangular. Over the years, he built a formidable record in the tournament, holding the

Hindu side together by his batting, by his complementary skills as an off-spinner and close fielder, and in time by his leadership. In 1925 he hit a brilliant 153 for the Hindus against a visiting M.C.C. side, an innings which first established him as a cricketer of more than provincial interest. This was a ferocious innings against a high-class attack, studded with 11 sixes and 13 fours. A victim of this assault, the medium-pacer Bob Wyatt, wrote thirty years later of Nayudu's ability to 'drive good length balls back over the bowler's head'. But Nayudu, remembered Wyatt, was no mere slogger, for 'his perfect poise, high backlift in a long pendulum swing brought beauty to his strokes'.

When India toured England in 1932, the team's captain, the Maharaja of Porbandar, generously stood down for Nayudu to lead India in its first official Test. Already, on his first appearance at Lord's, against the MCC, 'C.K.' had struck a fine 118. One of his drives left the Home of Cricket, being last seen, in the words of an eyewitness, 'sailing in an easterly direction'. Wisden was sufficiently impressed to choose Nayudu one of its Five Cricketers of the Year. Some called him the Don Bradman of India. But the critic Neville Cardus would have none of this. As he pointed out in a suggestive comparison, 'Nayudu is lithe, wristy and volatile. Bradman is sturdy and concentrated, his play never suggests that elusive and poetic quality which is best called sensibility'. Nayudu was 'a very sensitive batsman, from each of his strokes you get the impression of a newborn energy, of a sudden improvisation of superb technique'. Bradman was machine-like, Nayudu greatly gifted yet fallible. This made him, in comparison to Bradman, more attractive to the bowler and spectator alike, for 'the glorious uncertainty of cricket is not endangered by Nayudu'.

Nayudu was also chosen to captain India in her first series at home, against Douglas Jardine's M.C.C. side of 1933–4. He toured England again in 1936, scoring a brave 81 in the Oval Test, after being hit in the chest by a bouncer. At the age of 41, his Test career was effectively over. However, the Ranji Trophy had now replaced the Quadrangular as the chief domestic competition. Nayudu, based in Indore, was to forge a highly successful team for the state of Holkar, winning four championships in eight years. Perhaps the most notable of these was the campaign of 1945, when C.K., aged fifty, scored an immaculate, match-winning double hundred in the final, played against Baroda.

An aunt of mine, who grew up in Indore and knew C.K. well, years ago gifted me a picture of the great man. This captured Nayudu outside the London Zoo, lissom and upright, a lion cub in his arms: I tucked it away for safety in the pages of a book, George Woodcock's *Anarchism.* I never saw the picture again, for which I blame my choice of book. For a volume on anarchism would not contain C.K., a leader of extraordinary forcefulness known with reason as Holkar's Hitler. He set impossibly high standards for his Holkar men, who included such fun-loving cricketers as S. Mushtaq Ali and his own younger brother, C.S. Nayudu. While in the field Nayudu would not allow his players to take a break, imperiously waving away the drinks trolley before it could enter the field of play. The one exception he made was for the great English cricketer, Denis Compton, who played for Holkar during the war. Even C.K. did not expect an Englishman to go out unassisted in the tropical sun, so Compton alone would be allowed at the appropriate time to steal a glass of lime juice off the drinks wagon.

In the popular imagination Nayudu is remembered most of all as a legendary hitter of sixes. With Kapil Dev and Krishnamachari Srikkanth, he was one of the very few Indian batsmen who never had to face the barracker's insistent cry, 'Hit Out or Get Out!' In Hyderabad they will tell you of a six he hit out of the Secunderabad Gymkhana into the Plaza Cinema. In Madras they still speak of a straight drive that sailed out of Chepauk, clearing the tall trees that then ringed the ground to land beyond the canal outside. I even know a man in Bangalore who claims he saw C.K., when batting at the old Central College ground, hit a six that landed in the Swastik Cinema, a carry, when last measured, of a mile-and-a-half.

Urban Indians of an older generation are wont to remember two things: where they were when Mahatma Gandhi was assassinated, and their first sight of C.K. at bat. When Nayudu turned sixty, in 1955, the vice-president, Sarvepalli Radhakrishnan, was asked to present him with a purse. Radhakrishnan recalled going 'all the way from Oxford to London' to see C.K. bat in 1932 (no doubt playing truant from the lectures he was paid to deliver as the Spalding Professor of Eastern Religions). From the other side of the political spectrum the Communist MP, Hiren Mukherjee, spoke of his first view of C.K. at the Eden Gardens. Nayudu made only 9, but, as Mukherjee remembered it, 'he had, in his short stay, made a glance to leg which gleamed for a fraction of a second and has been treasured in my memory ever since.'

More pertinent than either of these appreciations was this tribute by an anonymous critic, which captures both the virtuosity of Nayudu's strokeplay and the power of his personality:

> In many a pavilion and clubhouse in India there hangs a photograph of a cricketer, standing erect with bat raised, glaring defiantly from under the peak of his cap as though daring the bowler to do his worst. It depicts C.K.'s outlook. Nayudu was a genius who brooked no opposition. There was no bowler to whom he would pay deference . . . he would drive a half-volley and then flick the next ball off the middle stump to the fine-leg fence. When he cover-drove it was as though someone had wound him up with a key and suddenly released the spring. He would stand on his back foot, crash the ball past the bowler and back-cut the ball between first and second slip, a stroke that can be described as being almost posthumous.

There is little question that the public responded to Nayudu as to no other cricketer before or since, the only possible exception being Kapil Dev. In 1937, when a M.C.C. side visited India, a popular campaign failed to stop the selectors from dropping Nayudu for the Bombay Test. When C.K. next played in Bombay, in a Festival Match bringing together the top Indian cricketers, he hit a stirring hundred. He was eighty not out overnight. As one journalist wrote, the next morning 'a number of flower sellers with a cute sense of trade paid for admittance and got to the crowded stands with loads of garlands'. When Nayudu reached his century, it was 'the signal for general turmoil as almost simultaneously there was a rush from all sides towards

India's cricket idol and he was almost smothered with flowers'—not to speak of sheafs of hundred-rupee notes, thrown reverentially at his feet.

Public acclaim of C.K.'s powers, always out of the ordinary, was in this case heightened by the injustice he had just suffered at the hands of our ever-whimsical selectors. Thus, as the *Bombay Chronicle* reported, 'Whether C.K. played a ball, sent down a delivery or did some fielding, everything was cheered.' When he came off the field, 'he was literally mobbed by his youthful admirers, each wanting to tap their hero on his back.' C.K. somehow made it to the pavilion, but still the crowd 'refused to disperse unless Nayudu came out. C.K. had to appear three times on the Club House deck before the thousands, who called for Nayudu decided to tread their way back home.'

A more surprising tribute was offered by the great movie director, V. Shantaram. *Duniya na Mane* was released in Bombay while Nayudu was being humiliated by the selectors. After C.K. had answered them with his bat, the director began advertising his film with the heading 'Nayudu was surprised'. The hoarding went on to compare C.K.'s shock at being dropped with the state of the film's heroine, Nirmala, at being made to marry a man she did not love. As the ad ran on, Nirmala, like Nayudu, 'declared open war against those responsible for the mean trick. . . .' Now has Mahesh Bhatt ever used an innings of Tendulkar's to promote his new film?

India's All-Star Cricket Eleven

In the history of Indian cricket there have been many great players but only a handful of stars. Greatness is a product of technical genius, judged by statistics and the verdicts of other cricketers. Stardom is a more complicated thing, for it takes one out of the field of play into the heart of a society. Statisticians and critics might deem a cricketer great, but he will be a star only if his play and personality resonate with what his culture most deeply values. Graham Gooch had a higher Test average than David Gower, but Englishmen, by and large, never warmed to him as they did to his left-handed counterpart. In that class-conscious society. Gower was celebrated as an elegant throwback to the 'Golden Age' of cricket, the ranking officer to the worthy Gooch's sergeant major. Likewise, as an all-wicket batsman Gordon Greenidge was greater than Vivian Richards, but it was given to the Antiguan to embody the political as much as the cricketing hopes of the Caribbean people.

The curious thing about the first Indian cricketing celebrity was that he played for England and was a shameless apologist for colonialism to boot. But as Alan Ross once remarked, it 'was the idea of Ranji, the awareness that it was an Indian who had become the greatest batsman in the world, that contributed more than anything else to the Indian cricketer's realisation of his own possibilities.' And to his sense of loss, for K.S. Ranjitsinhji, the Jam Saheb of Nawanagar, played no more than three or four times on Indian soil. In September 1914—fat, forty, balding and half blind (as a consequence of a shooting accident)—he turned out for his native Kathiawar against the Bombay Gymkhana. It was a working day, and a friendly match, yet thousands came (to quote the next day's *Bombay Chronicle*) 'in expectation of seeing His Highness the Jam Saheb play one of his masterly innings.' They gave him a rousing welcome when he came out to bat. Alas, Ranji was bowled for a duck, and the crowd 'rapidly thinned' thereafter.

But they were back the next day, for decent cricket allows one another chance. When Kathiawar batted again, the crowd were 'keenly disappointed' that Ranji was not going to open, 'their disappointment growing into almost positive despair' when the openers refused to get out. When a wicket fell a 'yell went up', followed by a 'prolonged burst of cheering as H.H. the Jam Saheb emerged from the Gymkhana Pavilion.' Kathiawar required only 31 runs to win, and these did not take long in coming. The players were leaving the ground when the spectators, 'apparently not satisfied with the limited opportunity they had of seeing Ranji bat, shouted out "Play on." Bowing to the wishes of the crowd, the Bombay Gymkhana skipper . . . sportingly allowed the game to be continued and stumps were drawn only when the Jam Saheb had been bowled.'

Had Ranji played more often in India such scenes would have been more frequent. Had he played in another age he would have been obliged, his wealth and notorious fear of the camera notwithstanding, to advertise drinks he never drank and shirts he never wore. One who did both was the incomparable C.K. Nayudu, in whose career the Jam Saheb himself had a little-known but, perhaps, not insubstantial role. C.K.'s uncle had been a contemporary of Ranji's at Cambridge: told of the nephew's cricketing interest, the prince passed on three items of advice: '*Balla seedha rakho. Ghabrao mat. Aur jor se maro.*' It was the last injunction that the young man took to heart, for Nayudu became famous as a hitter of sixes. A full thirteen of these came one afternoon at the ground Ranji once graced, the Bombay Gymkhana, if in a rather more serious match, for the Hindus versus the visiting M.C.C. side of 1926–7.

That innings of Nayudu's has been lovingly recreated by E.L. Docker in his *History of Indian Cricket.* He tells us of a cartoon in the next day's paper, depicting a group of spectators watching the match from the top of the Rajabhai Tower. 'Don't hit us, C.K.,' they are saying, 'we're not playing.' Docker makes manifest the larger meaning of Nayudu's achievement, the ways in which his thrashing of the English bowling came to symbolise a rising nationalist sentiment. When, on the first day, C.F. Earle scored 130 with eight sixes in a 'hurricane of hitting,' this seemed in the order of things, for white was made to vanquish black and brown. It was Nayudu's extraordinary reply, 153 with 13 sixes, that made people believe, almost for the first time, that Indians could play cricket on equal terms with the British. If cricket, then why not politics too? The importance of the match, writes Docker, 'lay in the emotional scene at the finish when outside the pavilion in the quickening dusk people began to gather in little groups craning their necks, straining every muscle to catch a glimpse of their hero, touch him, garland him with flowers, press gifts into his hand. How he had raised them up! What glories had he shown them!'

Nayudu was the first Indian cricketer to possess a truly national and all-class appeal. Following his 153 the textile workers of Parel hosted a reception at which they presented him with a cheque. Twelve years later, after another great innings in Bombay, the director V. Shantaram used Nayudu's name to advertise his new film. In between, C.K. had hit hundreds of sixes, captained India in its first Test, and in 1933 been chosen one of *Wisden*'s Cricketers of the Year. By standing up to officious Englishmen and authoritarian Maharajahs, he had also proved himself a man of principle. Nayudu had little interest in politics, but his achievements on the field, as much as its character off it, make him Indian cricket's Learie Constantine, the man whose cricketing feats presaged national freedom.

In the West Indies, Constantine's work was carried on by the great trio of Frank Worrell, Everton Weekes and Clyde Walcott. Nayudu's shoes were, likewise, too spacious for one man to step into. To their three W's we have our Four Musketeers, the generation of stars whose playing career coincided with the transition from colonialism to Independence.

The eldest of this quartet, Lala Amarnath was an all-rounder of prodigious skill, a leader of imagination, and a rebel with a cause. Lala was the first Indian to score a hundred in a Test match, that too on his debut. (The opposition and venue were the same as in the case of Nayudu's first great hundred, but of course there had been nothing official about that one.) After migrating from his native Lahore, Lala became captain of the first Indian team sent out under the *Tiranga Jhanda*, to Australia in 1947. Thereafter he was in and out of office more often than M. Karunanidhi. Well into his retirement, he remained a considerable figure in the world of cricket. Till about ten years ago, he was to be occasionally seen at the Ferozeshah Kotla, pipe in hand. The first man to spot him would tell his neighbour, and within minutes a buzz would go around the crowd: *Lala aa gaye hain.*

Junior to Lala by one Test was Vijay Merchant, the man who inaugurated the Bombay School of Batsmanship. There are men who have since watched Gavaskar and Tendulkar yet insist that neither can hold a candle to Merchant. A member of a high industrial family, Merchant was a patriot who withdrew from the 1932 team of England because of the ongoing Civil Disobedience Movement. Fourteen years later, he was in England, playing for India, when his friend John Arlott asked him whether, in light of the Hindu-Muslim feud, Independence would be worth it. The batsman drew himself up to his full height (an inch above Gavaskar's) and stiffly answered: 'Excuse me, John, but was it not the case that Englishmen had to fight a civil war before being granted their freedom.'

In later life, Merchant liked to employ cricketers down on their luck: he also gave generously to public causes.

The other Vijay, Hazare, came from a model social background to achieve equal renown with an equally straight bat. Democratic India would honour Merchant for placing patriotism above privilege, and honour Hazare for the dignity and good grace with which he met success. It fell to Hazare to be the first Indian to hit hundreds in each innings of a Test match, in Adelaide, against one of the strongest attacks in cricketing history (Lindwall, Miller, Johnston and others). Five years later, in steamy Madras, he led India to its first victory in a Test match, over England. Forty-four years later, I was allowed a taste of the reverence he commanded in an older generation. I was watching a World Cup match on television, in the company of the Bangalore critic, T.G. Vaidyanathan, when the camera cut to a man in the stands, immaculately attired in tie and blazer. Tony Greig now informed us that this was 'the former India batsman, Vee-Jaye Has-a-ri.' Vaidyanathan's response was altogether more interesting. Suddenly confronted with Vishnu in the flesh, this devout Tamil prostrated himself before the screen.

As a student of Presidency College, Vaidyanathan had cut class to watch parts of that epic 1952 victory. He cheered Hazare and Amarnath, but most of all the man of the match—the Indian bowler who took eight wickets in the first innings and four in the second. His last name was Mankad, his first name Mulvantrai, but he was known by neither. He bowled left-arm orthodox, and batted right hand, mostly unorthodox. He played professional cricket in England and advertised Brylcream in India: years later another dasher, Farokh Engineer, followed him in both respects. He broke many records but like all stars he is known both by his (numerous) feats and his (odd) failures. An uncle of mine, who batted right hand and bowled left arm, had worshipped Vinoo for years, from afar, before he finally saw his hero play. Alas, this was a match when an ageing bowler was put to the sword by two young panthers, Garfield Sobers and Rohan Kanhai. To hear my uncle tell the story, in trembling voice, is to feel the terror and torment that, as much as pleasure and potency, shall always accompany the veneration of heroes.

Move on quickly through the fifties, a decade barren of stars, a time when the nation's energies and imagination poured into the concrete that built dams and the fire that made steel. Fast forward, then, to the early 'sixties, and the return of the One-Eyed Prince. Ranji lost an eye at the end of his career, 'Tiger' Pataudi at the start of his. Otherwise he would have been as good as Bradman. He remained a fine attacking stroke player and an outstanding field. Pataudi led India to its first victory overseas, but he was a star in any case. Only Imran Khan of all the subcontinent's cricketers has had anything like the same charisma. Tiger had Imran's stylishness without his conceit, plus a beautiful wife from a famous Bengali family. That he was a hereditary Nawab also helped, as did the ease with which he gave up his title after privy purses were abolished in 1969. Where his fellow princes went to court or joined the Swantantra Party, Tiger remained captain of India, merely changing his name in the scorebook from 'the Nawab of Pataudi, Jr' to plain M.A.K. Pataudi.

The next of our stars, Bishan Bedi, was to Pataudi in social terms what Hazare had once been to Merchant. The sardar's foreign car and (for a time) foreign wife, not to speak of his Nangal-Northampton accent, were the signs that cricket could help one 'make it'. But this was one achiever who looked below him, for it was Bedi who first fought to ensure a fair deal, commercially speaking, for Indian cricketers. It was also Bedi who, well before Jaggubhai Dalmiya, first challenged England's claims to run world cricket according to its lights.

As a bowler Bedi was without equal, a unique combination of poetry (for the spectator) and poison (for the batsman). To watch him bowl I once queued up all night, with some 60,000 others, to get a ticket for a Delhi Test. Above the cold pavement where we stood now stands the office of *The Pioneer*: a not incidental connection, for next to me in line was the paper's present editor. For the match itself we sat on hard seats, huddled up, to watch Bedi bowl.

Bedi was the Sardar of Spin, leader of a great quarter whose art and achievement definitively marked India as the home of slow bowling. In what must be the most solemnly scientific book ever written on cricket, Ashis Nandy explained the civilisational context which produced a Bedi and a Chandrasekhar. Spin bowling, explained the sociologist, personified the androgynous, non-violent, quintessentially anti-as-well-as-post-modern essence of Indian culture.

Two men who appear not to have read Dr Nandy's book were Kapil

Dev and Sunil Gavaskar, for one bowled fast and the other not at all. Almost nobody has taken more Test wickets then the first, no one has scored more Test hundreds than the second, yet only a Bill Frindall or a B.B. Mama will count their stature in numbers. Sunil and Kapil carried Indian cricket from Tests to *tamasha*, from a game played in whites and with clean-shaven bats to the epoch of the coloured pyjama and the bat with words and symbols all over it. When cricket made its marriage with consumer capitalism these two were the Union's legitimate children. They dined with industrialists and judged fashion shows, their faces peeped out of magazines and television advertisements. Together they made possible the marketing success of Indian cricket's latest star, S.R. Tendulkar.

In 1993, fresh from back-to-back double hundreds, Vinod Kambli observed, 'Sachin took the lift to the top floor, I walked up the stairs.' Kambli then took the elevator back to the bottom, and began climbing once more. But his mate stayed on the top storey, where he has since constructed a penthouse. In a culture steeped in envy, this is one success story that none of us will carp at. A notoriously censorious press allows him to get away with blue murder. When asked why he married a woman older than him, Sachin answered that Mahatma Gandhi had done likewise. What in another man would be colossal immodesty was in this one merely a sweet soundbyte.

All stars are or once were great cricketers, but to be great is not necessarily to be a star. The list offered here will not satisfy everyone; indeed, it leaves out two of my own all-time favourites. One is Palwankar Baloo, a slow left armer as deadly as Bedi or Mankad, and also a Dalit hero before Ambedkar. The other is Mohammed Azharuddin, who batted like Ranji sometimes, and fielded like the Tiger all the time. I have omitted them, as I have omitted other worthies, on the grounds that in their case cricketing genius doesn't seem to have translated into stardom, defined as an appeal that is countrywide and persists beyond retirement. But my list will, I think, please the politically correct, for in its ranks one finds princes and commoners, northerners and southerers, some Hindus as well as a Muslim, a Sikh, and a Christian. Best of all, it adds up to the number without which good cricket is inconceivable.

Here then, in batting order, is my All-Star Eleven:

Vijay Merchant
Sunil Gavaskar
K.S Ranjitsinhji
Sachin Tendulkar
Vijay Hazare
M.A.K. Pataudi
C.K. Nayudu
Vinoo Mankad
Lala Amarnath
Kapil Dev
Bishan Bedi

Who will keep wickets? The Lala, as he once effectively did in a Test. But who will lead the team, when all eleven did so in their time? My own choice would be that imperious commoner, C.K. Nayudu.

Raj Karega Khalsa: Bishan Bedi and Company

ALMOST my first cricketing memory is of a Sikh opening batsman hitting a six over the beech trees that ringed the cricket ground of the Forest Research Institute, Dehra Dun. It was, as I recall, a pull shot, and that fearful stroke out of the ground and into the sky was my first acquaintance with cricket as a man's game, as distinct from the stuff I played at home with plastic bat and plastic ball. Looking back, it stands to reason that it was a Sikh who did it. For my home town was founded by Sikhs in the seventeenth century, its economy and social life boosted by Sikh refugees in the twentieth century. And one would expect a Sardar to *hit* a cricket ball.

The community of Sikhs has made a staggering contribution to Indian sport. Think of our great hockey sides of the 'fifties and 'sixties, of Balbir and Udham, Gentle and Gurbux, Harbinder and Prithipal, and those stalwarts of the 1975 World Cup winning team, Ajitpal and Surjit. One village, Sansarpur in Jullundur district, has produced seventeen hockey internationals. Turn now to athletics, and the records broken and medals won by the quarter-milers Milkha Singh and Paramjit Singh, and the high-hurdler Gurbachan Singh Randhawa. Some of India's finest footballers have been unshorn, such as little Inder Singh of JCT Mills, Phagwara, greased lightning in his boots, and Jarnail Singh of Mohun Bagan, who despite a head injury played and scored the winning goal in the 1962 Asian Games final.

The Sikhs have given Chiranjeev Milkha Singh to the world of golf, Randhir Singh to the world of rifle-shooting. There has even been a highclass Sardar tennis player. This was Jasjit or, more familiarly, Jaz Singh, a fellow from Texas who briefly came home to help India beat Australia in an epic Davis Cup semi-final, played in Calcutta's South Club in 1974. Then there is the Sikh sailor M.S. Kohli, and the polo-playing Sikh brothers Billy and Pickles Sodhi. In the sport of mountain-climbing too the Sikhs have been on top, not least Gurdial Singh, doyen of Indian climbers (and, I am proud to say, an old teacher and birdwatching companion of mine), and H.S. Ahluwalia, hero of the successful Everest expedition of 1965. And let us not forget Indian sport's best-loved voice, Jasdev Singh of All India Radio, who commentated with zest on all the above games—and then some.

The Khalsa has also made an immense contribution to Indian cricket. It was a Sikh, Maharaja Bhupender Singh of Patiala, who captained the first All India team to tour England, in 1911. True, he helped pay for the team, but then he could hit a cricket ball a long way too. Patiala's secretary was that famous Parsi left-hand batsman Keki Mistry. Mistry's eye and his boss's cash brought a stream of English and Australian cricket coaches to India at a time when they were most needed, to catch and train *desi* lads with a good eye but no knowledge of technique. The patronage was wholly secular; one of the wards who made good was that salty Hindu, Lala Amarnath. Nor was it confined to the land of the five rivers, for Patiala's last gift to Indian cricket was the Ranji Trophy.

Fittingly, it was a Sikh who dominated the first-ever Ranji Trophy match. This was the Tamil-speaking Sardar, A.G. Ram Singh, who took 11 wickets for 35 runs as Madras beat Mysore in a day, on November 4th, 1934. Ram Singh was a high-class left-hand all-rounder who, but for the presence of the peerless Vinoo Mankad and the onset of the Second World War, should have played many times for India, whereas all he got was two unofficial Tests. He was a singular cricketer with, for a man of his religion, a singular name. The story goes that when he first moved to Madras, his neighbours asked him where he came from. 'Amritsar', he replied. And what is your caste, they persisted. 'None', replied Ram, 'for I am a follower of the last Guru, who did not believe in that touch-me-not, taste-me-not nonsense.' And so he became, in the Tamil style, Amritsar Gurugobind Ram Singh, the first Sikh to have two initials *before* his name.

But not the last. For A.G. was the obligatory prefix worn by all his cricket-playing sons. The eldest, Kripal, was a cultured right-hander who scored 73 and 91 when Madras beat Holkar in 1954–5 to win the Ranji Trophy for the first time. The next winter Kripal scored a hundred on his Test debut—against New Zealand, at Hyderabad's Fateh Maidan. He was dropped soon thereafter, but some years later made a comeback to the Indian side as an off-spinning all-rounder. His brother Milkha was a strokeful left-handed batsman who was blooded into Test cricket far too early. He did, however, have a prodigious Ranji Trophy record, especially against the old enemy, Mysore. Ram's youngest son, Satwinder, played with distinction for Indian Schoolboys and Tamil Nadu, but a knee injury prohibited further advance.

All the A.G.'s spoke Tamil rather than Punjabi, and cared more for *sambaar saadam* than their ancestral *sarson ka saag*. Kripal Singh, however, fell in love with a Christian girl and converted. The beard was now shaved off, but the initials stayed (although it was rumoured that they now read, 'Arnold George'). Kripal is certainly the only man to have played Test cricket under two different religious affiliations. His son Arjan, always clean shaven, and coached by grandfather Ram, once scored a triple hundred for Tamil Nadu in the Ranji Trophy.

The world of cricket has been enriched by Sikh commoner and noble alike. The Malaysian-born Sardar, Lall Singh, played in India's first Test, at Lord's in 1932. There he brilliantly ran out Frank Woolley in the first hour of a low-scoring match in which he himself scored 15 and 29, batting at number eight. The next Sikh to be capped for India was Patiala's son, Yadavindra. He was a tall and upright hitter who scored 24 and 60 in his sole Test. In an age where religious identities were less rigidly defined, both Lall and Yadavindra played for the Hindu Eleven in the Bombay Quadrangular.

A cousin of the younger Patiala, Rai Singh, toured Australia with Amarnath's side in 1947, playing one Test, in Melbourne. He hit a rapid 24, including a pulled six out of the stadium. Thirty-seven years later I played club cricket with him in Dehra Dun. He was pushing sixty and had a glass eye. He still bowled outswingers with a high, classical action and fine control. By this time some other Sardars had also been capped for India. They included Maninder Singh, who all too infrequently reminded one of his mentor, Bishan Bedi. One such occasion was the Lord's Test of 1986, where his second innings' figures were 20.4-12-9-3. Three years previously, another Sardar had contributed materially to another Indian victory on the same ground. This was Balwinder Singh Sandhu, the slightly built medium pacer from Bombay who bowled Gordon Greenidge in the 1983 World Cup final. No Sikh stumper has played Test cricket, although Daljit Singh—once TISCO's public relations officer and now coach of the Punjab Ranji team—came close.

In cricket as elsewhere, the Sikhs have shown themselves to be a greatly talented and much travelled community. Consider then this All-time Eleven:

1. N.S. Sidhu (Punjab and India)
2. Yadavindra Singh (Southern Punjab, the Hindus and India)
3. A.G. Milkha Singh (Madras, Tamil Nadu and India)
4. Lall Singh (Kuala Lumpur Cricket Club, the Hindus, and India)
5. A.G. Kripal Singh (Madras and India)
6. A.G. Ram Singh (Madras and India)
7. Rai Singh (Southern Punjab, the Services, and India)
8. B.S. Sandhu (Bombay and India)
9. Daljit Singh (wicket-keeper—Bihar, Services, and Punjab)
10. B.S. Bedi (captain—Southern Punjab, Delhi, Northamptonshire, Rest of the World and India)
11. Maninder Singh (Delhi and India)
    Manager and Patron: Maharaja Bhupinder Singh of Patiala

With Sidhu and Milkha to bat, and Bedi and Ram to bowl, this side should, at least on a turning track, be a match for a side picked from among the other communities of India.

II

It is three hundred years since the founding of the Panth, and a quarter-of-a-century since I first made the acquaintance of the greatest of Sikh cricketers, Bishan Bedi.

When Karnataka met Delhi in a Ranji Trophy quarter-final in 1974, I was between school and college, spending the six-month vacation playing cricket in Bangalore. My landlord knew the manager of the Delhi side, who, one evening, brought his skipper along. The host had kept on ice a full, unopened bottle of Chivas Regal. In those insular, swadeshi-dominated days, this was a possession of which the value could not be reckoned in rupees, even thousands of these. In a matter of hours that bottle of whisky was polished off by the chief guest. The talk, of course, was all cricket, with only about half-a-dozen words addressed to me. 'Spin the ball', '*Spin* the ball', said Bedi, 'at your age I would not worry about control. Spin the ball.'

The next morning, a good breakfast and shower and jog having worked the booze out of his system, Bedi proceeded to spin the home team out. These included the wickets of Brijesh Patel, caught at slip by one that turned and bounced, and G.R. Viswanath, bowled middle stump trying to cut the arm ball. But the Delhi batsmen were worse at playing spin, and the Karnataka side had within its ranks the other members of the holy trinity—Prasanna and Chandrasekhar. The satisfaction experienced by this sixteen-year-old was thus complete—I had met Bishan Singh Bedi, but my side had won the match.

I moved to St Stephen's College later in 1974, yet in five years in the same city, and playing cricket all the time, I did not manage to speak to Bedi. But his footprints were everywhere. The streets of India are now awash with foreign cars, but at that time, at least in Delhi, all such had CD (for Corps Diplomatique) on their number-plates. Among the very few exceptions were two Volkswagen Beetles: one, pale-yellow, owned by Professor Mrinal Datta Chaudhuri of the Delhi School of Economics; the other, turquoise blue, driven by the captain of the Delhi Ranji Trophy team. By the presence or absence of that blue Beetle one knew whether the great man was at the Ferozeshah Kotla or not.

When Bedi moved from Punjab to Delhi in 1968, he had worked out a ten-year plan to make the city the capital of Indian cricket. His strategy had two main aspects. First, he imported into Delhi other experienced cricketers, such as the Amarnath brothers and Madan Lal from Punjab, and Chetan Chauhan from Maharashtra. Second, he sought out and brought to wider exposure the talent in the colleges of Delhi University. I thus played with and against several cricketers chosen for higher honours by Bedi. These boys worshipped him, the admiration tinged always by fear. We freshers in the St Stephen's College Eleven also lived in dread of Rajinder Vats, a huge fast bowler and hitter of sixes who made us bowl to him for hours in the nets. But then Arun Lal told us of how, during fielding practice at the Kotla, Vats dropped three catches in a row. Bedi told the 'pahalwan' to circumnavigate the field, only once, but holding a brick in each hand.

That Arun Lal was himself capped sixteen times for India was owed, in good part, to Bedi. The Sardar picked him up from university cricket and sent him to bat at number three for Delhi, ahead of the Amarnaths. Bedi liked Lal for his application, his big-match temperament, and above all for his sharp fielding close to the wicket. Nurtured by Bedi, these skills helped Lal go further than his close contemporary, Hari Gidwani of Hindu College. Gidwani was a silken timer of the ball with a prodigious range of shots. Yet he sadly lacked self-belief. I recall a match at the Kotla, Delhi versus the Services, where Gidwani was about 80 not out at the first drinks interval. Bedi sent him a message, saying he wanted to close the innings but would wait till he got his hundred. Gidwani crawled along, and was 99 not out at lunch. His captain, thinking always of the team, declared.

With Bedi's brilliant motivational skills and his own genius with the ball, Delhi won the Ranji Trophy in 1978–9 and 1979–80. The Delhi and Districts Cricket Association responded by stripping him of the captaincy and throwing him out of the playing eleven. Some years later he was invited back to Punjab, to coach and manage its Ranji

Trophy team. This time the raw talent was provided by the boys of the Guru Nanak Dev University, the experience by the much-capped Navjyot Singh Sidhu, and by Gursharan Singh, a capable middle-order batsman who had originally played for Delhi.

In 1992–3, as the Punjab team worked its way through the knock-out phase of the Ranji Trophy, I heard, once more, stories of what Bedi would do to young men who strayed out of line. When the opener Sapan Chopra disputed an umpire's decision, his manager made him run ten penitential rounds after close of play and also dropped him for the next match. Punjab eventually reached the finals, where they were to play Maharashtra, in Jullundur. The visitors had left Pune with the good wishes of the centenarian D.B. Deodhar, who, like Bedi, knew what it was to captain a Ranji Trophy winning side.

The Punjabis versus the Marathas, a battle of the two most combative peoples of India. It was a close match, won eventually by the home side. When the last Maharashtrian wicket fell, the Punjab captain, Gursharan Singh, grabbed a stump and ran off the field, followed by his men. They made straight for Bedi, at whose feet they laid the spoils of war, the stumps, and prostrated themselves. The Sardar himself then turned and touched the feet of an old man beside him. This was his coach, Gyan Prakash, whom he had brought along that morning from Amritsar. That, so to say, was where it all began, the original inspiration for the 267 Test wickets and the Ranji Trophy victories of Delhi and Punjab.

Bedi then quarrelled with the Punjab Cricket Association, or perhaps they with him. He now runs a cricket clinic in Delhi, but is, formally speaking, unattached. It must be admitted that he is not one of nature's diplomats. He speaks too soon and too often for comfort. But he is also, of all Indian cricketers, born or unborn, the most generous and selfless of men. And he has forgotten more about this lovely game than the rest of us will ever know.

Once, in print, I made the mistake of referring to Bedi's 'whisky-waistline'. Not longer afterwards I bumped into the Sardar at the Chinnaswamy Stadium in Bangalore during an India–Australia Test match. He contested the accuracy of my description. True, the accumulated kilogrammes showed, but my diagnosis was flawed, for he had been for years on the wagon. I offered him a conciliatory cup of Mysore coffee, and together we watched Shane Warne trying to bowl out the Indians. When the leg-spinner went round-the-wicket to Navjyot Sidhu, Bedi was deeply upset. 'Why doesn't the lad go back over the wicket', he said, 'he should bowl in the orthodox fashion, flight the ball and let his art and the wicket do the rest. Why this round the wicket nonsense? The Indians will pad him away till the cows come home. I shall talk to him this evening.'

Speak to him he did, for when I had dinner with Bedi that night Shane Warne had already called, leaving two empty tins of baked beans behind. I was not, alas, privy to their conversation, but I shall not easily forget the pain and worry in Bedi's words that day. The slow bowler was speaking over the Indian, the claims of the craft-guild winning out over the claims of nationality.

The Road to Vijay Hazare

I know a man who knows a man who knows a man who once batted for four hours in a Test match with Vijay Hazare.

Actually, the links that bind me to God are even closer than that. My first cricketing mentor was my uncle, N. Duraiswami, a skilled left-arm slow bowler, captain for many years of Friends Union Cricket Club, one of Bangalore's top teams. Now, for a brief while, Durai had the uncommon privilege of having a Test cricketer play *under* him. This was the off-spinner V.M. Muddiah, who turned out for the F.U.C.C. when posted with the Air Force station in Bangalore. Of all the people he played with or against, my uncle most respected Muddiah's cricketing acumen. 'Mudi once told me', became a handy way to start a conversation or end an argument. To be sure, there must have been times when my uncle was making it up. But if he wanted to convince us of the merits of any particular view, say that an off-spinner should bowl only to a two-seven field or that fast bowlers made poor captains, it was enough for him to mutter those four words. 'Whatever you say, *Mudi once told me* . . .'. The authority cited here had, after all, played for India, and at Lord's too.

The player V.M. Muddiah acknowledged as *his* mentor was Hemu Adhikari. Adhikari is known to my generation as the man who successfully managed the Indian team which defeated England in 1971 and 1972–3. But in his youth he was a Test cricketer himself, a capable middle-order bat and a brilliant fielder capped twenty-one times for his country. Now Muddiah had appeared in only two Tests for India; moreover, he played under Adhikari for the Services in the Ranji Trophy. Whereas with Durai and company Mudi could monopolise the conversation, if Hemu were around, and opened his mouth, the off-break bowler would, I suppose, have shut his.

There was, in consequence, an occasional variation in my uncle Durai's cricket talk. 'Mudi once told me' was sometimes substituted, to devastating effect, by 'Mudi says Hemu once told him'. I have little doubt that when Muddiah talked and Durai listened, the words that were *most* decisive in concluding a cricketing lesson were: 'Hemu says that Hazare once told him.'

For Adhikari was born and raised in Baroda, whose Maharaja had acquired Vijay Hazare for his Ranji Trophy team. As a schoolboy Hemu spent hours at the Polo Ground watching his hero bat. As a college student he played under him for Baroda. As a young army lieutenant he played with him for India, the two adding 132 runs in the Adelaide Test of January 1948. After he was promoted to the rank of Captain, Adhikari was invited to play for India against England under Vijay Hazare, himself a former Captain in the Baroda State Army who had cheerfully exchanged that capital 'C' for the honour of leading his country on the cricket field. Through all this Adhikari revered Hazare. There must certainly have been occasions in the Services dressing room when a debate was definitively concluded by Hemu quietly insisting, 'But Vijay *bhai* once told me.'

It is time to rephrase that first sentence. My cricketing guru's guru's guru's guru was Vijay Samuel Hazare. As a boy learning the game in school and college, I was always a mere three handshakes away from that cricketing immortal. As I grew older, however, I began climbing up the hierarchy of hero worship: I met V.M. Muddiah and befriended him. Muddiah tried and failed to teach me the straighter one, which he bowled much as Saqlain Mushtaq does. Over cups of coffee in his Bangalore home he told me a heap of cricket stories. Most of these, at my prodding, were about the original holy trinity of Indian slow bowlers, Mankad, Gupte and Ghulam Ahmed. But there was also one about Hazare.

In the winter of 1958–9, the Services met Baroda in the Ranji Trophy final. Hemu Adhikari knew that the match hinged on how many runs his mentor would make. Hazare was now forty-two, and still batting well, his marvellous technique compensating for slowness of eye. Now Hemu remembered that, ever since the England fast bowler Frank Ridgway had hit him on the head, Hazare was somewhat uncertain against the bumper, at least early in his innings. So Services won the toss, and put Baroda in. The India fast bowler Surendranath knocked over a couple, and Hazare came in at 10 for 2. As his captain had instructed him, Surendranath bounced the old man first ball. An intended hook shot flew high into the hair, dropping in, and then out, of the hands of fine-leg. 'Now he'll score a hundred', shouted Hemu in exasperation. Actually Hazare made a double hundred, and Baroda won in a canter.

Years after Muddiah told me this story I met Adhikari himself. He was the chief guest at a cricket party in New Delhi, where one of the accredited invitees, Sujit Mukherjee, had taken me along. As readers of his marvellous *Autobiography of an Unknown Cricketer* will know, Sujit played Ranji Trophy cricket for Bihar and was on the faculty of the National Defence Academy, one of his colleagues there being the aforementioned Adhikari. There is a passage in the book which tells of how Sujit took the N.D.A. students to the Bombay Test of 1956, where each of them also played, in their mind, every one of the defensive strokes with which Hemu helped save the match for India.

The party was at the home of an old Services cricketer, the other invitees also old Services cricketers. Stories of how Adhikari had turfed Salim Durrani out of the Indian team for returning late to the hotel had prepared me for a martinet. But Adhikari turned out to be surprisingly gentle, and, for the most part, silent. Seizing the opportunity to prod his memory, I asked him about Bradman and Lindwall and Miller, then about his teacher: 'What was Hazare like as a fielder?' was my question. When Adhikari did not answer I put the question once more. 'Why do you ask', he said, 'All you had to do was put a bat in his hands and glory in the result.'

Glorying in the result meant watching Hazare bat; I was born too late for that. But glory of another kind was mine some years later, when Vijay Hazare entertained me in his Baroda home.

II

Vijay Hazare lives in a modest apartment overlooking the Polo Ground in Baroda, the scene of his world record partnership of 577 with Gul Mahommed back in 1946–7. On the door is an exquisite nameplate, the letters lovingly engraved in gold, the work of a craftsman of long ago whose skill must have disappeared with him. As we climb the stairs we are unexpectedly greeted by loud barking, the work of two dogs of indeterminate breed but savage countenance. The dogs are quietly whisked away and the daughter-in-law of the house takes us into the living room. Cups and shields are displayed on shelf and table, these won by the lady's husband and son, both Ranji Trophy cricketers. There is but one memento inscribed to the original sportsman of the family. It was presented to Hazare on his eightieth birthday, by the Western Railway Workers' Union. Other and more substantial trophies must, one thinks, be hidden away in an inner room, safe from an inquisitorial public.

In a minute or three the great man walks in, erect, his eyes alert. He says at once that he might not be able to talk long or talk coherently, for the previous day he had been taken to witness (and bless) a schoolboy tournament, walking more than a hundred yards in the sun, from road-head to pavilion. My escort, a kindly Gujarati journalist named Vyas, had already warned me that the eighty-four-year-old had good days and bad, clear-eyed remembrances as well as unconscionable lapses of memory.

In the event we spoke for a hour, my questions always answered crisply and directly. Which was his greatest innings, I asked? The triple hundred in the Pentangular against the Hindus, 309 not out out, of a total of 387, in statistical and other terms the finest single-handed show by any batsman in cricket history? The double hundred in the Ranji Trophy final of 1958–9, a knock which effectively ensured that one of his pupils, the Baroda captain D.K. Gaekwad, would be appointed captain for the 1959 England tour (instead of his other pupil, the losing Services captain, Hemu Adhikari)? Or the two hundreds in the Adelaide Test of 1948?

The Adelaide knocks, of course, answered Hazare. The Indians had been two days in the field, while Bradman and company scored 674. When they batted in reply, Hazare scored 116 and Phadkar 123. At one point Hazare hooked Miller for three consecutive boundaries early in the over. The fast bowler asked Bradman for an additional fielder on the on side, which was refused. Miller then bowled three lollipops, which the batsman politely patted back down the wicket. Bradman did not give the fast bowler another over.

India eventually reached the respectable score of 381. But they still had to follow on. In the first over of their second knock Ray Lindwall had Mankad caught behind and then bowled Amarnath. Hazare went in at 0 for 2, and batted for the next six hours, before he was ninth out, for 145. India ended with 277, with the only other serious contribution being Hemu Adhikari's 51. Hazare's second innings was marked by some magnificent cover drives off the spinners Johnson and McCool. Both knocks were chanceless, the hundreds scored against one of the finest bowling and fielding sides in the history of the game. It is safe to say that no Indian, before or since, has batted so well in adversity.

On the evening of his second hundred Hazare was taken out for dinner by the great slow bowler Clarrie Grimmett. Years before, in 1937, Grimmett had visited the state of Jath in western India, on a coaching assignment. Hazare was then employed by the Maharaja of Dewas, the Raja of Jath's brother-in-law. With his boss's permission he joined Grimmett's camp. The Australian bowled Hazare some balls, and came to the sensible conclusion that there was little he could teach him in that department. Will you not then teach me the googly, asked the pupil. No, answered the master, for you will not be able to control it. But I will teach you the finger-spun leg-break. This ball then became a key weapon in the armoury of this medium pacer. I took 578 wickets in first-class cricket, said Hazare, a figure remembered with the delight of the batsman who would also be a bowler.

My companion Vyas had also warned me that Hazare stayed scrupulously clear of controversy. Unheeding, I asked Hazare to compare men of different generations. He answered politely and indirectly, praising his contemporary: When I set the names of Merchant and Gavaskar side by side, he spoke of Merchant's exemplary technique, of how he would never loft the ball yet contrive to place it betwen the fielders. When I asked him to compare Bishan Bedi and Vinoo Mankad, he told the story of the Chepauk Test of February 1952. Vinoo got eight wickets in the first innings but was bowling ordinary stuff in the second. After the off-spinner Ghulam Ahmed got two wickets in succession Hazare, who was captain, went over to Vinoo and said in Marathi: 'I have never seen such a strange cricket wicket before. It turns only at one end.' Thus provoked, Mankad began turning them like a top, and with Ghulam bowled India to its first victory in Test cricket.

About the only cricketer Hazare did criticize, very gently of course, was the senior Nawab of Pataudi. On the 1946 tour of England, Pataudi, much against Hazare's will, commanded him to open the innings against Surrey. I got a *blob*, he recalled to us, the word accompanied by a lovely, low chuckle, the figure carved for good measure with the help of thumb and forefinger. Thereafter his skipper put him down to bat at six or seven, too low for him to make an impact. Then, against the county champions Yorkshire, India had to bat for half-an-hour late on the first day. Two wickets fell early, so Pataudi sent Hazare in more or less as a nightwatchman, to protect him and the other 'established' batsmen. The next day he scored 244 not out.

Vijay Hazare is, of all the cricketers I have met, the most courteous and transparently decent. Yet he takes just pride in his skills and his achievements. When I asked him about his strokes, he said that when he was set he played them all, adding that the wicket-keeper could not anticipate his leg-glance, so late was it executed. He told us of how he mastered Sunny Ramadhin when the Trinidadian slow bowler came with the Commonwealth team of the early fifties. The first time they met Hazare was bowled by Ram's leg-break, released slower and tossed higher than the stock ball, the off-break. He was never fooled again, scoring three hundreds in the later matches.

As player and captain Hazare was quietly assertive, a gentleman well aware of his own genius. In the late glow of his retirement he retains this distinctive combination of dignity and pride. When we left I asked his daughter-in-law for their postal address. She brought me the master's visiting card, but as I made to put it in my wallet he said, with authority, *I* will sign it. A pen was fetched, and the paper duly autographed. It is the only autograph in my possession, and it will retain that singular status till the end of my days.

Sunil Gavaskar: India's Cricketer of the Twentieth Century

IN the stereotypes so beloved of Western writers, Indian cricketers are said to play by instinct rather than by reason. The first of our greats, the Nawanagar prince K.S. Ranjitsinhji, is alleged never to have played a Christian stroke in his life. He batted in silk shirts with gold cuff-links, innovating the leg-glance, a shot that defied tradition by pushing the ball further in its own direction. Ranji inaugurated a line of distinctively Eastern batsmanship whose later exemplars included his nephew K.S. Duleepsinhji, Gundappa Viswanath, and Mohammed Azharuddin. These little men favoured the cut, the glide and the glance, delicate strokes that contrast so sharply with those muscular Anglo-Australian favourites, the pull and the drive.

Even better known as carriers of the mystique of the East are our spin bowlers. Consider Bishan Bedi, bearded, head covered in colourful *patka*, in appearance the most exotic sportsman to have stalked the turf of Lord's—and also a bowler who dared toss the ball into the sky. Or Bhagwat Chandrasekhar, of whom it was said that since he did not know what he was bowling—leg-break, googly, or top-spinner—how would the batsman? Or Anil Kumble, whose contribution to the art of cricket was summed up to me by a British visa officer at Heathrow in the summer of 1995. Playing for Northamptonshire in the County Championship, the Bangalore boy had been the first to reach a hundred wickets. 'And he doesn't even spin the ball', remarked the visa officer, in his opinion a device as peculiarly Indian as turning the ball a foot-and-a-half.

One of the first men to spin these stereotypes was George Robert Canning, the fourth Baron Harris (1851–1932). Harris had been cricket captain of England, president of the Marylebone Cricket Club and, between 1890 and 1895, governor of the Bombay Presidency. In his autobiography, published in 1921, Harris wrote that 'it is in the matter of patience that the Indian cricketer will *never* be equal to the Englishman.' This was a remark almost calculated to produce Sunil Manohar Gavaskar.

In truth, there had been Indian batsmen in the past who batted for long hours and by the rule book. Not by coincidence, these men all came from Maharashtra, though only fate can explain their common first name, 'Vijay'. These were Manjrekar, Hazare and Merchant, masters of the straight bat and the dead defensive, each possessing an armoury of strokes they were forbidden to exhibit. While they played for India, their side could scarcely win a Test match although it could possibly draw them—but only if one or two of the Vijays batted for ten hours at a stretch. Theirs was the tradition that Sunil Gavaskar inherited and deepened.

Gavaskar possessed a classical technique and all the strokes in the M.C.C. manual. He had a mind to match, with astonishing powers of concentration. To the purist, it was equally a pleasure to see him leave six outswingers in a row and see him play the cover drive. The best place to watch him bat was from over the sightscreen, to marvel thus at his precise foot movements and shot selection. On a hot winter's day at Chepauk I sat illegally in the Board President's Box while the captain of India ground down the Pakistanis for five-and-a-half hours, making 92 not out. In the morning he faced Imran Khan, hair flying as he ran in from the Walajah Road end. From eighty yards away I trembled, but not Gavaskar. He played about one ball in five, angering the Pathan into bouncers still higher and more futile. After lunch, as Imran sulked at fine leg, Gavaskar calmly took apart the other bowlers. Mudassar Nassar, honest medium pace, was driven repeatedly wide of mid on; Iqbal Qasim, slow left arm, was plundered through the off side. Next morning I had to catch the Coromandel Express to Calcutta; when the train stopped somewhere in Andhra Pradesh, a stray radio informed me that Gavaskar had just got out for 166. His side went on to win by 10 wickets.

Gavaskar was not named Vijay, but as it happened India won far more Test matches in his time than Merchant's or Hazare's. And not just at home either. In the West Indies and England in 1971—Indian cricket's *annus mirabilis*—in New Zealand in 1976, and in Australia in 1978 his side won handsomely with major contributions from his bat. To be sure, in those years we won at home as well, but then this lesser achievement is shared by the lesser men who now play for India. These fitful and unprecedented successes overseas—our victories in 1971 came after forty years of trying—coupled with the expansion of television, placed new burdens on Indian cricketers. Before one Test match, his former Somerset opening partner Peter Roebuck wished Gavaskar best of luck. He expressed the desire to see his friend score a hundred, then guiltily added that he did not intend to place extra pressure on him. Gavaskar replied that since eight hundred million others had the same expectations, his own hopes would not make a difference.

For the most part, Sunil Gavaskar bore these burdens stoically and with honour. There were also rewards, for the Australian magnate Kerry Packer had grossly improved the earning powers of Indian cricketers. In the past, some *desi* cricketers—paid, in their pomp, Rs 50 per Test—died destitute. Now they made plenty of money on the field, the fee rising, *circa* 1980, at one stroke from Rs 1000 to Rs 10,000 per match. It has since multiplied a further ten-fold. But unlike some others, as for example his brother-in-law Viswanath, Gavaskar understood there was money to be made outside the field too. He lent his name to shirts and socks, to ghosted columns and books, to company balance sheets. He was even reputed to have charged for attending a private dinner.

In the latter half of his career Gavaskar found himself matched as cricketer, popular icon and commercial success by Kapil Dev Nikhanj. Both were possessed of a self-belief that was communicated in their actions—these were Indians who would not bend before anyone else. Together they redefined India's position in world cricket. For the first time, their side expected to win matches and tournaments. For the first time, Western writers pencilled in the name of an Indian, and often two, in imaginary World Elevens to play Mars.

Bank balances and records brought Kapil and Sunil together, but little else. One epitomised flair and instinct, the other thought and reason. Simplifying slightly, I would say that Kapil Dev was born to play cricket while Gavaskar willed himself to the task. One was tall and slight and superbly athletic; the other short, squat, and naturally ponderous in his movements. The spontaneity of Kapil's lofted drive or his late outswinger could only be opposed to the studied care with which SMG played his forward defensive. Their leadership styles were also quite dissimilar. In the 1983 World Cup, Kapil Dev led by example. There were, I suspect, no extended team meetings or strategy sessions before the match. But watching their captain walk in at 9 for 4 to score 175 against Zimbabwe, or take a staggering catch running back from midwicket to dismiss Vivian Richards in the final, the Binnys and Madan Lals were inspired to play above their potential. A year later, under Gavaskar's captaincy, India won an equally creditable victory in the World Championship of Cricket. The skipper did not score many runs, his contribution coming rather in the tactics applied. Precise field placings for each batsman, experiments in batting order (notably, making Shastri open with Srikkanth), and the innovative use of a double spin attack mark this one as a triumph of reason.

We all know of Gavaskar's 34 Test hundreds. But he is as proud of his presence on that most select of cricket lists, of those who have taken more than a hundred Test catches. Truly is this testimony to his application. In his early years Gavaskar fielded often at mid on, which a long forgotten cricket writer described as 'the last refuge of mankind'. He knew that his build prohibited further advance in the outfield, but other options were available, certainly after he became captain. With strenuous effort he made himself into a first-class first slip. After he retired, the same effort and will have helped make him a highly readable columnist. The man who hired a ghost for his first two books now writes every word that appears under his name.

This is a man who chooses his words as carefully as he once chose his strokes, a man who thinks always of the long term. He is self-interested, as almost all of us are, but so singular and single-minded has been his pursuit of success that he has occasionally been accused of selfishness. Cricket lovers cannot easily forget his failure to condemn the vandalism by the Shiv Sena of holy cricket pitches and cherished cricket trophies. With fine timing, he was in New Zealand when the goons broke into the Board office, but one expected nonetheless that he would condemn the act on his return.

One can forgive him that lapse in view of his unsurpassed contributions to Indian cricket. And perhaps these contributions haven't ended. As a cricketer of prodigious achievement, high intellect, and ice-cool temper, Sunil Gavaskar would surely make an outstanding coach of the Indian team. His great rival Kapil Dev has the job now. Gavaskar once followed Kapil, with distinction, as cricket captain of India, and when the time comes he might—despite the dictates of caution and reason that have made him what he is—take his place as coach as well.

Sachin Tendulkar and History

I am interested in greatness, not in damn dots.
—John Arlott, writing on W.G. Grace

CRICKET chauvinism runs across two axes, those of nation and generation. When Steve Waugh came to the crease in the first Test of the 1998–9 Ashes series, Bill Lawry welcomed him on television thus: 'Here is the *best* batsman in the world.' It was a title Waugh himself would have quickly disavowed. In the space of a few weeks, earlier that year, he had fielded out to four centuries hit by a rival, two scored in Test matches played in India, two in one-day internationals played in Sharjah. At the end of it all he shook his head in wonder and remarked: 'There is no one who bats like this guy—but then I did not see Don Bradman.'

National pride promotes excess, while generational loyalty favours caution. In an article published in March 1996, and timed to coincide with the first floodlit match played at the Wankhede Stadium, I allowed that our man of the moment was the finest Bombay cricketer ever, but not yet the finest Bombay batsman. For I treated with deliberate respect the claims of Sunil Gavaskar, the hero of my youth, and Vijay Merchant, the hero of my uncle's. Ask me again in five years' time, I said, and I'll reconsider the question.

In less than four years I have an answer to report. Sachin Tendulkar is the greatest batsman produced by the city of Mumbai, and by logical extension the country of India. The chauvinism of Australian commentators notwithstanding, he is also by some distance the best batsman in the world. But what is the precise place commanded by the Bombay Blaster in the history of cricket? As Steve Waugh implies and millions of Indians confidently assert, is Tendulkar already in the Bradman class? Would he walk into an all-time World Eleven chosen to play against the Monsters of Mars?

If we follow John Arlott and do not go strictly by the numbers, we must judge cricketing greatness across three broad criteria: versatility, character, and peer review. Versatility is in part a gift of Dame Luck, a function of being in the right place at the right time. Sachin Tendulkar, in the nineties, had a far wider range of cricketing opportunities than did batsmen of previous generations. Don Bradman had a dazzling array of strokes all around the wicket, yet he was allowed only to unfold them in the Test match arena, and only in two countries. In his generation Australia did not tour the West Indies, India or New Zealand, while Sri Lanka, Pakistan and Zimbabwe did not then exist as cricketing entities.

But consider how swiftly and compellingly Tendulkar has seized the chances that fate has given him. Even that old reactionary racist P.W. Botha would, one thinks, have welcomed the end of apartheid for the two cricket tours by India it has allowed, in each of which Tendulkar hit rapid hundreds against the finest bowling and fielding side in the world. His skill and command of varying conditions is brought into relief when Sachin's record is placed alongside that of Mohammed Azharuddin. Azhar is an acknowledged master of slow to medium bowling on slow to medium wickets—but no *satta walla* would put his money on him scoring more than twenty against Curtly Ambrose in Kingston or Glenn McGrath in Perth.

The accident of birth has also permitted Tendulkar to excel in both versions of the game. At the time of writing he has twenty-two Test hundreds to his name, and twenty-five one-day hundreds too. The statistically-minded will add that Sachin's first limited-overs century was made in his 79th innings. Since then the tons have come at the rate of one in six innings. Considering the intensity and abbreviated time-span of the shorter game—the demands it makes on body and mind and how unforgiving it is of the slighest mistake—this is a feat comparable to Bradman's rate of one Test hundred in three innings. More than the mere numbers is the manner of their achievement. At different times and in various locations Tendulkar has made Allan Donald, Courtney Walsh, Wasim Akram and Shane Warne look like net bowlers.

In living memory only Vivian Richards and Graeme Pollock have so dominated the best bowlers in the world. While they batted, Richards answered to the few million black men of the Caribbean, Pollock to the equally numerous white rulers of South Africa. But Tendulkar now has placed on him the burdens of one-sixth of humanity; what's more, he has often to carry it alone. Richards and Pollock each embellished batting sides of staggering depth and consistency. One had Gordon Greenidge to bat before him and the likes of Clive Lloyd and Alvin Kallicharan to follow. If the other got a duck, he returned to the pavilion in the assurance that Barry Richards or Eddie Barlow would get the runs needed by his side. However, while Indian batsmen excel at home they are notoriously fragile overseas; given a bouncy wicket, they fall quicker than you can spell 'coalition government'. When Tendulkar opens in a crunch match nowadays, he knows that if he fails his side generally fails too.

The Mumbai columnist C.P. Surendran has written evocatively of what Tendulkar means to this nation of losers. Every time he walks to the wicket, 'a whole nation, tatters and all, marches with him to the battle arena. A pauper people pleading for relief, remission from the lifelong anxiety of being Indian . . . seeking a moment's liberation from their India-bondage through the exhilarating grace of one accidental bat.' No other cricketer has so fully represented the hopes of so many cricket-obsessed junkies.

Tendulkar knows not where he will play his next innings. He knows not whether his team-mates will bat more than a few balls each with him. He knows only that his bat has, willy-nilly, to make up for the fact that the United Nations authoritatively asserts that India is the one-hundred-and-forty-sixth most developed nation in the world. That he is so marvellously cool about this is perhaps the most remarkable thing about him. His gifts of character, if anything, exceed his cricketing gifts. Examine afresh how you reach to a child who wails at night; to a hard disk that crashes when you are finishing a book; to an examination paper that is to be answered at eight o'clock the next morning: we routinely respond with anger or disbelief to the most trivial tests of character. Yet Tendulkar meets with complete equanimity the intensely magnified and completely unfair expectations of a billion countrymen.

His adversaries know not of these burdens. They see only the cricketing genius, and rise to honour it. Some do it openly, as when Shane Warne walked around to the Indian dressing-room after the final of the Sharjah tournament in April 1998, to ask his tormentor to sign (left-handed) on his T shirt. Others do it indirectly, as when Brian Lara batted against Tendulkar in the 'mini-World Cup' in Dhaka in October of that year, batted, that is, with paranoid care against a part-time bowler. That night Lara displayed a fear not of his opponent's innocuous off-breaks but of his own declining reputation. How would it look if, having had the crown so abruptly and comprehensively seized from him, Lara the batsman got out to Tendulkar the *bowler*?

Even Englishmen, who are otherwise so parsimonious in praise of their opponents, have bent to Tendulkar. After the Princess Diana charity match in September 1998, Mike Atherton suggested that the authorities at Lord's be prepared to rename the W.G. Grace Gates. Eight years earlier, an infinitely greater England opener had borne testimony to the genius of Tendulkar. When Sachin batted at Headingley in the Test match of 1990, Sir Leonard Hutton told Freddie Trueman that he could not remember when he had last seen such quick and sure footwork. Trueman told the story on the BBC, adding his own recommendation. This is the only known occasion on which either of those Yorkshiremen is known to have paid a compliment to an Indian. The next year the Bombay cricketer became the first overseas professional to be contracted to Yorkshire. A little brown boy had found his way into the hearts and cheque-books of the most insular and tight-fisted community in the universe.

Sachin Tendulkar is a batsman of wide-ranging skills and matchless temperament, a cricketer who commands generous respect among his peers. That much is evident, today, but how do we judge him in the broad sweep of history? Would he, for instance, figure in a World Eleven against Mars? Now if the match was being played over a hundred overs, fifty overs for each side, and with the off-shore venue in Jupiter suitably lit up by meteorites, then Tendulkar's would be almost the first name this selector would pencil in. The eleven chosen by me would read, in batting order:

1. S.R. Tendulkar (India)
2. D.L. Haynes (West Indies)
3. I.V.A. Richards (West Indies)
4. Javed Miandad (Pakistan)
5. C.H. Lloyd (West Indies—captain)
6. S.R. Waugh (Australia—vice-captain)
7. A.P.E. Knott (England—wicket-keeper)
8. Wasim Akram (Pakistan)
9. S.R. Warne (Australia)
10. C.L. Ambrose (West Indies)
11. J. Garner (West Indies)

12th man: J.N. Rhodes (South Africa)

If this mythical match were played in pajamas and under lights Tendulkar will walk into the side. He shall take first strike, and later in the night chip in (aided by Waugh and Richards) as the 'fifth' bowler. What if this was a more conventional five-day Test? In 1988, when Sachin had not yet played for India, the Jamaican politician and cricket buff Michael Manley chose an all-time XI to play Mars. His side read:

1. J.B. Hobbs (England)
2. S.M. Gavaskar (India)
3. D.G. Bradman (Australia—captain)
4. G.A. Headley (West Indies)
5. I.V.A. Richards (West Indies)
6. G. St A. Sobers (West Indies)
7. W.A. Oldfield (Australia—wicket-keeper)
8. M.A. Holding (West Indies)
9. R.R. Lindwall (Australia)
10. D.K. Lillee (Australia)
11. W.J. O'Reilly (Australia)

Think, if you will, of the batsmen left out in this selection. They include Walter Hammond, Graeme Pollock, Miandad, Border, Neil Harvey, and the three W's. Indeed, in a display of the partisanship that is inescapable in this kind of exercise, Manley substituted Richards for Hammond in the proofs of his book. An indefensible substitution, in my opinion, for Hammond was as good as Richards with the bat or in the field, and a much better bowler besides.

Still, if we are to update this eleven in 1998, where does Tendulkar fit in? The first four in the order are impregnable. But the case can be made, and not with the *tiranga jhanda* alone, that Tendulkar is a better all-round batsman than Viv Richards was. But I would have chosen Hammond in the first instance. If push comes to shove, I might alternate between the two. Tendulkar could come in if the wicket was slow and dusty, like the ones at home, but he would yield to the Englishman if it was a green top, in conditions calling out for Hammond's defensive skills with the bat and his control of swing and seam with the ball.

That, in a capsule, is how history judges Tendulkar. Let me end with a more fallible but equally meaningful guide to greatness, namely individual memory. Indians who follow cricket at millennium's cusp will always remember the times they saw Sachin bat 'live'. Now I once watched Sunil Gavaskar bat all day against Pakistan in Chepauk. At stumps he was 92 not out, and next morning I had to catch a train to Calcutta. I never saw a Gavaskar hundred, and for a while it seemed that the jinx carried over to his successor. In 1990 I went to the Ferozeshah Kotla to see a Wills Trophy match, but Mumbai got the runs before their sixteen-year-old number four, fresh from his debut Test series in Pakistan, got to the wicket. Three years later I watched him, at the same venue, score 70-odd against Zimbabwe. Through a short winter afternoon Tendulkar took on John Traicos, a lawyer of Greek extraction who had taken Test wickets before he was born. He played the off-spinner with masterly precision, scoring mostly through cuts and sweeps. He looked set for a hundred, but then played an unknown fellow named Ujjesh Ranchod into the hands of extra cover. This was Ranchod's first (and as far as I know) last Test wicket—he is bragging about it in Bulawayo still.

Then, in February 1994, I timed a trip to Bangalore to catch a Test, and Sachin at bat. On this occasion a controlled innings exploded in the dying overs of the first day, when he plundered Pramodya Wickremesinghe for eighteen in an over, to reach 80 by the close. The next morning he proceeded carefully to 96, when he lost his off-stump trying to cut the left-arm spinner Don Anurasiri.

The last time I saw Tendulkar in the flesh was in the Bangalore Test of March 1998. I had arrived that morning from across the *kala paani*, and by the time I shrugged off Customs and jet-lag to get to the Chinnaswamy Stadium it was lunch. Four hours of cricket was all I would get, for next morning other business called. Sidhu got out after the interval, and Sachin came in. He started confidently enough, but I was not confident my jinx would be broken. I remembered Gavaskar at Chepauk, and saw too that Shane Warne was no Ranchod or Arunasiri. However, in three hours of almost chanceless batsmanship Tendulkar had got to his hundred. Of his strokes that day I remember most clearly two rifle-shot straight drives off Michael Kasprowicsz, and some lovely late cuts off Warne. He made one error though. Greg Blewett threw in a bouncer, and Tendulkar was struck momentarily by indecision, for it was the last over before tea. He was a little late on the shot, but the top-edge fell harmlessly between fine leg and the wicket-keeper. The normally phlegmatic Australian captain, at slip, violently stamped on the ground, a gesture that was, in its own way, as sincere a tribute as any spelt out in this essay.

My nine-year-old son has watched Sachin bat once, in a one-day against New Zealand that I was myself compelled to miss. He scored a hundred, at better than a run-a-ball. I tell my son about the innings I saw, about the mastery of Warne and Wickremesinghe and Traicos, and he tells me about the straight sixes hit off Dipak Patel. The conversations will, we hope, continue about yet-to-be hit centuries. Do we need to remind ourselves that the man is not yet thirty? And that Bradman and Richards both retired at forty, or Gavaskar and Border at thirty-eight? Is Sachin Tendulkar one of the three best batsmen ever known to the game of cricket? Ask me in ten, no, in five years' time.

The Socialism of Soccer

WHY do Bengalis love soccer so? Because American hate it so. A poll conducted during the 1994 World Cup revealed soccer to be the 84th favourite sport in the United States of America, ranking well below log rolling, chicken ringing, and passing the parcel. Although the tournament was being played in their own country, 99 out of a hundred Americans did not even know of it.

The sporting headlines in New York that summer were being made by the Yankees, then making a strong run for baseball's World Series, and the Knicks, who were doing unexpectedly well in the National Basketball Association championship. What the rest of the world regarded as the sporting event of 1994 was being shown in the US only on the Spanish channels. Meanwhile, the mass audience networks were bidding against each other for rights to telecast basketball, baseball and football (their kind of football, that is).

Years ago, the German sociologist Werner Sombart wrote a book called *Why is there no socialism in the United States*? Sombart searched for an explanation in all sorts of places—in the structure of the American trade union movement, in the influence of ecstatic Christianity, in the seduction of the frontier. Being a sociologist, he looked at economics, theology and geography, but not sport. However, the correct answer to Sombart's seriously important question is this—there is no socialism in the US because there is no soccer in the US.

Simply put, the game of soccer is too collective, too participatory, and too democratic for the achievement and profit-oriented Americans. They like golf and tennis because these individual sports are governed by the capitalist ethic of 'winner take all'. They like basketball because the numbers satisfy their immodest appetites—if the Chicago Bulls win a match, it is because Michael Jordan has scored no less than 38 points.

They like baseball because in this team game the result is decided by a home run hit by a single batter or a series of no strikes thrown, again, by an individual pitcher; whereas in soccer the goal that decides the game can never be attributed solely to the striker. Credit has to be shared around, some accruing to the midfielders who set it up, some to the defenders and goalkeeper who kept the opponents from equalising.

It might be claimed that the love of American football invalidates this argument. True, this is a team sport, but with a level of physical contact and intimidation that more readily satisfies a warlike people, preparing them for real combat in the sands of Iraq or the forests of Vietnam (soccer, by comparison, seems almost a sport for sissies). Moreover, in this version of football there is a clear hierarchy. The quarterback is the boss with the brains, the running forwards the followers with brawn or speed of foot. Only one man gives the orders. We can recognise (and respect) the managing director of this firm. That the quarterback is almost always a white male only binds the game more firmly to American ideals of the successful and all-conquering society.

Indeed, the evidence all around tells us that the love of soccer is most abundantly manifest among socialists and anti-imperialists. It has long been the favourite sport of the British working class, as it was of the East Berlin working class, before History ended for them in November 1989. The great Ernesto 'Che' Guevara was a passionate follower of the game. It is believed that Vladimir Lenin once played it too. Above all, there are the Bengalis.

'Had the British been thrown out of India in the violent, revolutionary way proposed by the Indian nationalist Subhas Bose', remarks one knowledgeable historian, 'rather than agreed to withdraw peacefully, football rather than cricket would have become the major game.' Unfortunately, in the 'twenties, control of the freedom struggle passed into the hands of Mohandas Gandhi, who had close links with the Parsi and Gujarati capitalists of western India, the Merchants and the Modis who both played cricket and promoted it. Gandhi's belief in the 'beauty of compromise' also helped the compradors of Bombay dominate the sporting culture of the country.

This meant, says our historian, 'that after independence there was no contradiction in accepting cricket—it could very simply be seen as one of the British goodies which ought to be retained.' However, 'had the Bengalis, who initiated the freedom struggle, retained their control then football—which is very strong in Bengal—might have become the national game.'*

In fact, the damage had begun before Gandhi. In 1911, Mohun Bagan defeated the East Yorkshire regiment in the final of the Indian Football Association Shield. Now there were three notable features of that victory. First, ten of the native footballers played in bare feet. (The exception, a man at left back named S.K. Chatterjee, has always intrigued me. What message did his boots carry? That Indians were not necessarily averse to Western technology?) Second, the result was acclaimed by Hindu and Muslim alike. Third, the partition of Bengal was annulled the same year.

Oddly enough, it was in the same year, 1911, that the British shifted the capital of the *raj* from Calcutta to Delhi. Recent memorialists of Mohun Bagan's victory have, alas, failed to notice *this* coincidence. *If* it is a coincidence—for it is highly likely that one was the cause of the other and that to preempt further humiliation the British adroitly and deliberately moved the seat of power from Bengal, away from its skilful footballers and its bomb wielding nationalists. The link between sporting prowess and militant anti-imperialism was thus undermined, to be finally rent asunder by Gandhi and the Bombay capitalists.

*Mihir Bose, *A Maidan View* (London, 1968), pp. 35–6.

The continuing obsession with football in Bengal is a psychosocial substitute for this twin loss, of the capital of India and of control over the Indian freedom movement. After World War II, as the US replaced Britain as the great imperial power, the passion for soccer gained an added legitimacy. To play and follow the game was to cock a snook at the imperialists who disdained it. Culturally and politically, it was of a piece with Bhupen Hazarika's song *Amar Comrade, Paul Robeson*!—with the first United Front government's renaming of Harrington Street as Ho Chi Minh Sarani so that the American consulate would be located on a road named after the greatest living anti-American.

To this day, the cadres of the world's most successful communist party are recruited by Alimuddin Street straight off the *maidan*. But the Americans, for their part, have remained resolutely indifferent to soccer. When the US played Germany in the 1998 World Cup, Bengali viewers worldwide would have outnumbered American viewers by a thousand to one. Germany won the match by two goals to nil, but I like to believe that there were at least some people in Calcutta who cheered the losing side.

For the eleven American players on the field, like their eleven hundred supporters who travelled to France or the eleven thousand following the game in Spanish back home, are political dissidents in their own society. It takes some courage to play, support, or watch a game that is so completely ignored by one's compatriots. These men deserve our support. They may be the vanguard of a socialist movement in a country that has not yet seen one.